The Underground Guide to
WORD FOR
WINDOWS™

Slightly
Askew
Advice
from a
WinWord
Wizard

Woody Leonhard

ADDISON-WESLEY PUBLISHING COMPANY

Reading, Massachusetts • Menlo Park, California • New York • Don Mills, Ontario
Wokingham, England • Amsterdam • Bonn • Paris • Milan • Madrid
Sydney • Singapore • Tokyo • Seoul • Taipei • Mexico City • San Juan

Library of Congress Cataloging-in-Publication Data

Leonhard, Woody.
     The underground guide to Word for Windows : slightly askew advice
   from a WinWord wizard / Woody Leonhard.
       p. cm.
   Includes index.
   ISBN 0-201-40650-0
    1. Microsoft Word for Windows.   2. Word processing   I. Title.
Z52.5.M523L46   1994
652.5'536--dc20   94-8463
                                                 CIP

Information Superhighway cartoon used courtesy of Mike Keefe and The Denver Post.

Sponsoring Editor: Kathleen Tibbetts
Project Editor: Claire Horne
Production Coordinator: Lora L. Ryan
Technical Editor: Eileen Wharmby
Cover design: Jean Seal
Text Design: Kenneth L. Wilson, Wilson Graphics & Design
Set in 10 point Palatino by Rob Mauhar, CIP of Coronado

1 2 3 4 5 6 7 8 9 -MA- 9897969594
First printing, May 1994

Addison-Wesley books are available for bulk purchases by corporations, institutions, and other organizations. For more information please contact the Corporate, Government and Special Sales Department at (800) 238-9682.

*D*edicated

to the people who've made WinWord what it is:
Its designers, developers, testers, tech supporters.
Its hackers, crackers, bug catchers.
Its users, abusers, fans, accusers.

The Original Gadflies:
Robert Enns, Guy Gallo, James Gleick, Barry Simon.

The WOPRFolk, natch:
Vince, Kateee, Lee, Scott, Jim, Ken, Ellen, Sal, Eileen.

And the *millions* of WinWord users all over the world. Who woulda thought, eh?

Who woulda thought…

The Underground Guide, particularly the Bugfest 6.0 chapter, owes much to the entomological experiences of:

Tracy Benton, Martin Blackwell, L. E. Brown, David Carson, Vince Chen, Steven Chien, Michael D'Amato, Scott Deboy, Peter Deegan, Ken Deifik, Paul DeRocco, Helen Feddema, Bill Fisher, Paul Friedman, David Fullerton, Guy Gallo, Michael Gat, Michael Gordon, Tom Griffiths, Steven Halford, Jim Hargrove, Lee Hudspeth, Nat Hummel, Durant Imboden, Roger Jennings, Laurence Johansen, Jim Kauffman, Scott Krueger, Don Lammers, Jim Lee, George Mair, Javier Mancera, Richard Mansfield, Hilary Miller, Vic Moon, John Navas, Bob Nelson, Paul Neshamkin, Chris Nettleton, Sally Neuman, John Notor, Keith Pleas B.C.E. (Bug Catcher Extraordinaire), Adam Rodman, Keith Rouda, Jonathan Sachs, Maurice Silberstein, Douglas Smith, Romke Soldaat, M. David Stone, Herb Tyson, Jim Vaughan, Brett Weiss, Eileen Wharmby, Raymond Wiseman, Robert Yriart, and several others—including Mary!—who must (regrettably) remain nameless.

Part of the proceeds from this book will be used to help Tibetan refugees and their families, most of whom live in relocation camps in India.

If you're curious about the plight of these horribly oppressed people and their rapidly vanishing way of life—or if you can find it in your heart to help their children—please contact:

Dawa-la Dorjee, Director

Tibetan Children's Fund
637 S. Broadway #B125
Boulder, Colorado 80303

Voice: 303-499-4168
Fax: 303-499-2125

Do *You* Need This Book?

You've been working with WinWord* for a month or two, maybe more. You took the tutorial but don't remember a lot of it. You've banged your head against the wall so many times it hurts, and you've driven yourself (and co-workers, neighbors, spouse, erstwhile friends, and even family pets) nuts with your inventive invective, blood-curdling screams and vociferous vituperations.

No, the user's manual doesn't do jack. There *are* demons in WinWord — things that don't quite work right, things that go bump in the night — and the manual doesn't warn you about them. The books and magazine articles gloss over the problems, too. Nobody, it seems, wants to point out the troublesome parts or give you an idea of what to *avoid* as well as what to use.

That's not all. You get the sinking feeling that you're behind the wheel of a Lamborghini, but don't quite know how to shift out of first gear. Worse, you're convinced that if you try some of those fancy gizmos, you're gonna break something. And, dammit, that's embarrassing.

You probably went out and bought an introductory WinWord book. If you're lucky, you got a good one, like *Word for Windows Companion* by Stone, Poor and Crane (Microsoft Press, 1993). If you weren't so lucky, you picked up a book that has more airy pabulum than down-and-dirty advice. (It's amazing how many times they've rewritten the user's manual, eh?) You aren't a dummy, nor an idiot. You're looking for some advice and help, and maybe a few new ideas, not a put-down.

If you're like most folks, you'll only use a tiny part of WinWord's capabilities —say, 20–30% of all the functions—and you don't want to waste your time on the rest of it. But you do want to set WinWord up so that the part that you use works well and so that WinWord helps and doesn't get in the way.

You know from bitter first-hand experience that WinWord isn't "easy" or "simple." It doesn't work like a typewriter with training wheels, can't be mastered in ten minutes by watching a video or listening to a tape... and you know, deep down inside, that anybody who says otherwise obviously doesn't know what they're talking about.

If you think it's easy, you haven't been trying.

Most of all, you have a stack of work in front of you, and you think WinWord can help, but you don't know how—or even where to start. Great. You're ready for this book.

* Okay, okay. Microsoft® Word 6.0 for Windows™. There. I'm official now.

I'm not going to try to cover all of WinWord's bases. The program has spread out so much it would take a book ten times this size to hit the high points, much less the details. Rather, I'm going to give you a broad overview of how WinWord really works — not how the manuals say it *should* work — with nitty gritty examples and tons of friendly advice.

I'll show you what works for me, and how you can mold WinWord so it works for you, too. No technobabble. No pulled punches. No glossing over the warts. I'm not a shill for Microsoft. My primary interest is in keeping you sane. I'll concentrate on the 20–30% of WinWord that you'll use day in and day out, and then I'll point you in the right direction to find out about the other stuff.

We'll start out by customizing WinWord, molding it to do things the way *you* work. Customizing is the easiest, fastest way to make WinWord work better for you, even though the user's manual pretty much ignores the topic until Chapter 31, on page 709. No joke.

Then, having dipped our toes into the WinWord morass, we'll step back and look at how WinWord hangs together; the concepts are crucial. I'll take a stab at giving you straight answers to the most frequently asked questions. Then we'll see how WinWord *doesn't* hang together — I'll clue you in on bugs and the things that go bump in the night.

Finally, I'll take you on a whirlwind, hands-on tour through templates, macros, forms, fields, and other power user goodies. I'll show you what works and warn you about what doesn't. Oh. And we'll have a lot of fun along the way. You'll see.

If all goes well, you'll learn how to *think like WinWord* — how to look at a problem from the document's point of view, how to find solutions that translate easily into WinWord's frame of reference, WinWord's way of looking at things. It's the **document-centric approach**.

Doc-centricity   You'll hear that "document-centric" term frequently in the next few years — indeed, it's well on its way to becoming another meaningless buzzword, like "object," destroyed by folks trying to sell you something — but right here, right now, you have an extraordinary opportunity to put "document-centric" ideas into action and make them work for you. I'll show you how. It ain't that tough.

*In cauda venenum.**

Woody Leonhard
Coal Creek Canyon, Colorado

---

*Beware the part you can't see. Literally, "in the (scorpion's) tail is the poison."

Contents

The Very First Step

All things in their beginnings are good for something.

George Herbert
Outlandish Proverbs, 1640

Before you dive in, the first thing you *must* do is ensure that you are running the most recent version of WinWord. Microsoft has a habit of releasing updates (read: bug fixes) without notifying all WinWord users.

Get the latest version.

Although WinWord's approach isn't as bad as it could be—some companies release "slipstream" updates without so much as a version number change, and I won't mention WordPerfect or the Visual Basic 3.0 runtime by name—it still leaves much to be desired. The onus is on you to find the latest version of WinWord. Microsoft won't tell you unless you ask.

Crank up WinWord. Click Help, then About Microsoft Word. The top line of the dialog box that you'll see includes the version number. The original version of WinWord 6.0 reads "Microsoft Word Version 6.0"; yours might have "6.0a" or "6.0.1" or some such notation. Jot down the version number and the serial number precisely as they appear in the dialog box.

Next, call Microsoft. In the U.S., call 800-426-9400; outside the U.S., call your country's Microsoft office. Tell the person answering the phone that you want to make sure your copy is registered properly, and you want to know if a more recent version of WinWord is available. Give the 'Softie your registration number and WinWord version number.

Who you gonna call?

If your copy hasn't been registered in your name, you'll be able to get the records updated right then and there. It's important that you get on the registered user database ("reg base" in Microsoft parlance) for upgrade notices and suchlike.

If a more recent version of WinWord is available, have Microsoft send it to you immediately. Typically there is no charge for the minor releases—which is just as well because the minor releases usually contain bug fixes more than anything else. It would be unconscionable (though not unheard of) to charge for bug fixes.

Got the latest version? Good. You're loaded and ready to go varmint huntin'.

The rest of this book is based on WinWord 6.0, the original version. It's possible that some of the problems mentioned in this book will be eliminated in later versions of WinWord 6.0, so don't be overly mystified if something that's badly broke in version 6.0 suddenly works in 6.0d or 6.013. You see, the 'Softies will read this book, too. Yes indeedy. *Heh, heh, heh.*

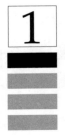

1 Power Toolbars

Microsoft's Word for Windows is the
best PC application I've ever used, period.
Its depth and intelligence are simply amazing.

Jim Seymour
PC Week, 12/13/93

Let's pay for this book right off the bat. The tricks I'm going to show you here at the get-go will save you ten or fifteen minutes a day, every day. By the end of a week or two you should've saved enough time to more than cover the cost of this book. Everything beyond Chapter 1 is just gravy.

We'll get into the esoteric stuff a little later. Let's concentrate now on fine-tuning WinWord's pretty face, cutting out the marketing crap, and turning WinWord into a more useful tool, more in keeping with the way you work.

If you ever hit the point that you've modified WinWord in some way that you don't like—maybe you really *do* prefer the original Insert Microsoft Graph Chart button!—not to worry. The very last section of this chapter is called UnInstall, and it tells you how to do precisely that, remove any or all of the changes discussed here in Chapter 1.

UnInstall

WHAT'S WRONG WITH THIS PICTURE?

Pictures are the books of the ignorant.

English Proverb
17th century

When you install WinWord, your desktop comes up looking, more or less, like the screen in Figure 1.1.

1

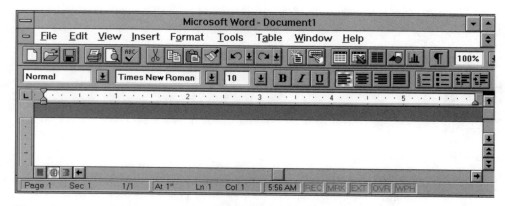

Figure 1.1 Demo Version at 800 × 600 Resolution, Large Buttons

**Pointer/
Question Mark**

Borders

Depending on how your particular video adapter works, there may also be a Pointer/Question Mark button on the right-hand side of the top Toolbar (or, in WordSpeak, the **standard Toolbar**).

There might also be a Borders button — which looks suspiciously like a window, eh? — on the right-hand side of the second Toolbar (the **formatting Toolbar**).

Take a while to grok your environs. This is home. This is where you'll be spending (depending on your predilections) two, four, or maybe even six, eight, ten, or twelve hours a day, every working day for the next year or two. If you take a few minutes right now to fine-tune your working home, the effort will repay itself many, many times over.

Here's one of those terrible True Facts of Windows Life your mother always warned about: *The bone-stock WinWord configuration is made to sell WinWord, not to make your life easier.*

Those Toolbars have been carefully crafted so that Uncle Bill and his Marketing Minions can pop up a plain-vanilla version of WinWord and immediately launch into a hard sell. What you see is the *demo* version of WinWord, not the working version.

The bone-stock Toolbars have all sorts of junk that you might use once a week — or once a month, or once a century. At the same time, buried knee-deep in some obscure menu somewhere are certain WinWord capabilities that you'll use a dozen times a day. We're going to change that. (You thought otherwise?) Changing the Toolbars so that they work right (Figure 1.2) is probably the easiest, most important productivity improvement you can make.

Figure 1.2 The Lean, Mean Anti-Demo Toolbar

A NONSTANDARD TOOLBAR

Let's take a look at the buttons on the standard Toolbar—the one up at the top of your screen—one group at a time, and see what can be done to improve them.

File Stuff

> To every action there is always opposed an equal reaction:
> or, the mutual actions of two bodies upon each other are always
> equal, and directed to contrary parts.
>
> Sir Isaac Newton
> *Philosophiae Naturalis Principia Mathematica*, 1687

The first three buttons on the standard Toolbar are grouped together because, logically, they do similar work. (See Figure 1.3.) They run three of the more common file operations.

Create a new file  Save the current file

Open an existing file

Figure 1.3 The File Buttons

The file buttons have a couple of problems. The first button is attached to the wrong command, and one very common file operation is missing entirely. Let's fix them.

The first button always creates a new file (or a new *document*, if you prefer WordSpeak) based on the "normal" template. Typically the normal template produces a stark-naked sheet of paper. That may be good enough for novices— and it's great for running demos—but more advanced users tend to use lots and lots of templates, each tailored to a specific job: one for memos, one for letters, another for faxes, a handful for various reports, and so on. (An entire chapter of this book, Chapter 8, is devoted to templates and their capabilities.)

Creating files

A Toolbar button that always creates a stark-naked file is kinda like an ice cream parlor that always serves vanilla. Hey, I ain't knockin' vanilla, but there's a whole lot more to life! Click on File, then New. See how the built-in WinWord FileNew capability gives you so many more options? That's what you need—a choice, not an echo.

I recommend that you switch around the first button so that it runs a standard WinWord FileNew—the same action you'd get if you clicked on File, then New. Changing the button in this case is a piece o' cake:

1. Crank up WinWord.

2. Click on Tools, then Customize.

3. Make sure that the Toolbar filecard is showing and that the Save Changes In list box shows NORMAL.DOT.

FileNew

4. Get rid of that old FileNew button by clicking on it and dragging it off the Toolbar.

There. Poof! It's gone.

Next, scroll down the Categories list, choose All Commands, and scroll down the Commands list to FileNew. Your screen should look something like Figure 1.4.

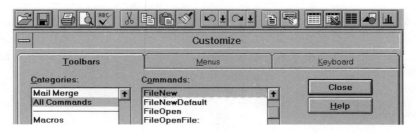

Figure 1.4 Out With the Old, In With the New FileNew

Click on FileNew there in the Commands list, and drag it up to the very left edge of the standard Toolbar, to the same place where the old button used to be. Choose a picture for the new button (or just use text), click Close, and *voilà!* you're set.

Your new FileNew button will be sitting pretty up at the very beginning of the standard Toolbar. Clicking on your new FileNew button lets you choose precisely what kind of new file you want. Congratulations. You've just taken control of your destiny, overridden a lousy WinWord design decision, and made things work the way they should. Feels good, yes? Now let's fix that missing button.

Closing files
The WordGods gave us Mortals a one-click means of creating a new file or opening an existing file. That's great. But somehow, in apparent defiance of Newton's principle of action and reaction, WinWord's designers neglected to give us an easy way to *close* those same files.

Since you're going to close at least as many files as you're going to open, the oversight is rather stunning. But that's how it's now done in all of Microsoft's applications: Uniformity reigns over usefulness in the Office.

I don't consider double-clicking on the hyphen-thingy in the upper left corner an easy way to close files. The location of the hyphen-thingy can flip-flop all over the place, and it will disappear entirely if more than one file is visible. It isn't located where all the other buttons live, so I have to think about it before I can locate it. When I'm writing, I hate to *think*. Sheesh. Besides, if I wanted to click twice, I'd stick to the menu!

Fortunately, Prometheus awaits. If you click on Tools, then Customize, make sure you're on the Toolbar filecard, check to see that the Save Changes In list refers to `NORMAL.DOT`, and click once on the little puke-yellow file folder with an arrow pointing up, you'll find that FileClose is readily available. Look at Figure 1.5, particularly the box labeled Description.

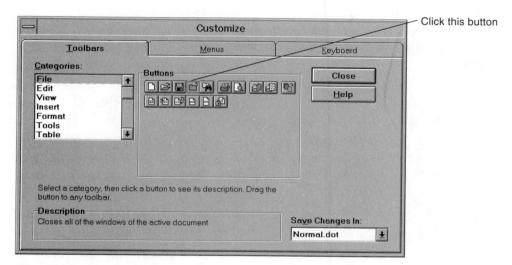

Figure 1.5 Close, Sesame!

Drag that yellow file folder up to the standard Toolbar, immediately to the right of the File Save diskette, click Close on the filecard, and you'll complete the transformation of your standard Toolbar file button array from pretty face to working stiff. Your files buttons are now in order. (See Figure 1.6.)

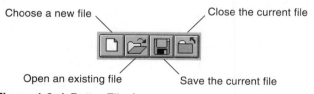

Figure 1.6 A Better File Array

At some point in the future, you may decide that you need a File Delete on your standard Toolbar, too—many WinWord add-ons have delete and a number of other file-manipulation routines available—but we'll leave that at your discretion: you won't delete nearly as many files as you create, open, save, or close.

Print Stuff

> A good many young writers make the mistake of enclosing a stamped, self-addressed envelope, big enough for the manuscript to come back in. This is too much of a temptation to the editor.
>
> Ring Lardner
> *How to Write Short Stories*, 1924

Standard printing   The next group of three buttons is more or less related to printing. Sorta. (See Figure 1.7.)

Print one copy of the current file   Check spelling

Flip into the Print Preview mode

Figure 1.7 The Original Printing Buttons

The one-click button for printing a single copy is neat. I use it all the time and can't think of any good reason to change it.

The Spell-check button works right, too. If you've selected something and then click the button, WinWord only checks the spelling of the stuff you've selected. If you haven't selected anything, WinWord starts a full spell check, beginning at the current cursor location. Bravo! Personally, I don't think of spell check as being in the same category as printing, so I move the button down, next to the AutoFormat button. You'll see where momentarily. No biggie.

The Print Preview button is another story altogether. Once again, a very important capability is missing from this group of buttons—two of them, actually.

Once upon a time, Print Preview was pretty useful—in fact, it was the only way you could see an accurate on-screen portrayal of the final printed documented. Nowadays, however, Page View (in WordSpeak it's called "Page Layout View") does almost everything Print Preview can do, and it does it better. Click on View, then Page Layout, and play with it a bit. You'll see.

Scale   While in Page View, the standard Toolbar's Scale button lets you quickly switch to show one or two full pages—what amounts to Print Preview mode, to my way of thinking. If you ever need Print Preview, perhaps to show more than two full pages on the screen at a time, it's easy to find: Click on File, then Print Preview.

Print Preview   Personally, I give Print Preview two thumbs down and remove it from my standard Toolbar. You can, too. Click Tools, Customize. Make sure that you're looking at the Toolbar filecard and that Save Changes In shows NORMAL.DOT. Click and drag the Print Preview button off the Toolbar. It's gone, outta here, bye-bye. Click Close, and you've struck yet another small blow for your individuality.

Along with the Print Preview button's being about as useless as high heels at a hog-tyin', two very important printing capabilities are missing completely from the standard Toolbar: envelopes and labels. I print a *lot* of envelopes and labels, and I'll bet you do, too. Why they aren't up there on the standard Toolbar is anybody's guess.

It's particularly perplexing when you consider that the envelope printing button came standard on the old WinWord 2 Toolbar. Back then envelope printing was something new, a revolutionary capability worthy of product demos by Bill and the Boys. Nowadays, I guess some muckety-muck decided it isn't as useful, so it doesn't go on the standard Toolbar. Go figger.

It gets stranger. The way WinWord gets around to printing envelopes and labels is … circuitous. (There. I can be diplomatic when I try real hard.) If you click on Tools and then the line that says Envelopes and Labels…, WinWord has to guess whether you want to print an envelope or print a label. Reasonably, WinWord keeps track of whatever you did last—that is, print an envelope or print a label—and sets you up to do the same thing again. You would think that the WinGods would give you a simple way to put two buttons up on the Toolbar, one for envelopes, the other for labels. *Not!*

The only built-in Toolbar button that WinWord provides behaves precisely the same way as clicking on Tools, then Envelopes and Labels…. You can't tell WinWord, simply, "Print an envelope" or "Print a label," but must settle for "Yo, WinWord! Print an envelope or a label … I know which one I want, but … uh … jeeeeez … there's no way for me to tell you which one, is there? … oh, I dunno, just go ahead and use whichever one I printed last." Bummer.

To get two separate buttons up there on the standard Toolbar, one for envelopes, the other for labels, you'll have to roll your own. Click on Tools, then Customize. Make sure that the Toolbars filecard is showing and that Save Changes In points to **NORMAL.DOT**. On the left side, scroll down to All Commands; on the right side, scroll down to ToolsCreateEnvelope. (See Figure 1.8.)

Envelopes and labels

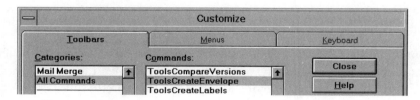

Figure 1.8 Print an Envelope

Now click on ToolsCreateEnvelope and drag it over to the right of the Printer button. See how WinWord is smart enough to give you a button that looks like an envelope? Good deal. Now click on ToolsCreateLabels and drag it immediately to the right of the Envelope button. (You'll have to draw your own picture for the Labels button.)

Your printing buttons might now look like Figure 1.9, with your most common printing tasks now a click away. (I'll show you where I stick the Spell-check button shortly.)

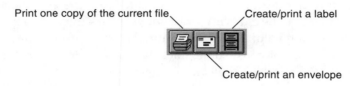

Print one copy of the current file   Create/print a label

Create/print an envelope

Figure 1.9 A Better Print Array

Moving Stuff

The next block of four icons covers three common functions for moving things around, plus one oddball that seems to have been thrown in as an iconic demonstration of the Peter Principle.

Cut, copy, paste   The first three icons are just great. They're Cut, Copy, and Paste, respectively, and they work as cut, copy, and paste in all Windows apps should work. (See Figure 1.10.) You'll probably find yourself using these buttons frequently, even if you do tend to prefer drag-and-drop copies and moves (which have the added advantage of not dirtying your clipboard) or the standard Windows keyboard shortcuts—which I can never remember—for cut (CTRL+X), copy (CTRL+C), and paste (CTRL+V).

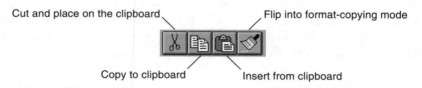

Cut and place on the clipboard   Flip into format-copying mode

Copy to clipboard   Insert from clipboard

Figure 1.10 Moving Buttons

The politics of painting   But what the hell is the format-copying mode button doing up there? Funny you should ask. Back in the days when WinWord 2.0 ruled the roost, Lotus' Amí Pro 3.0 introduced a format-copying ability. The idea is pretty simple. Click on the stuff that's formatted the way you like, click a button, and "paint" the formatting by selecting some other text, which would dutifully acquire the new formatting. You could laboriously change all the headings in a document to 17-point bold italic Renfrew, for example, by "painting" that formatting onto each heading.

For reasons I never understood, the computer press picked up on this format-copying "feature" and touted it as a significant advantage for Amí Pro 3.0, over WinWord 2.0. The WinWord team flew into paroxysms of format envy. WinWord 2.0 had a similar capability, but it was buried in a macro command somewhere. The folks in Redmond just hated to see all that good press for the competition, illusory as it may have been. My guess is that this button appeared in WinWord 6.0 to prove to the world that WinWord is just as good as Amí Pro, which, from the user's point of view, may be the silliest possible reason for putting a button on a Toolbar.

Format "painting" has all the advantages of a 40-kilo croquet mallet: it's laborious, error prone, and obfuscating. (*Which* formatting are you painting? fonts? paragraph stuff? What happens if you "paint" more than one font? more than one format?) Worse, by its very nature, "painting" encourages folks to ignore styles, by applying ad-hoc formatting to chunks of text that should be given uniform styles.

This button deserves to go into the circular file, relegated to the bit bucket. I don't care what the magazine reviewers say. Give it the heave-ho. Click on Tools, Customize. Make sure the Toolbar filecard is on top and that Save Changes In shows NORMAL.DOT, and then drag the button off the Toolbar, into oblivion. Good riddance to bad rubbish.

My final collection of moving/copying icons is just the first three buttons in Figure 1.10, without that stupid paint brush.

Navigation

> Go to, good man, go to.
>
> William Shakespeare

I still can't believe Microsoft left the Find functions off of the WinWord 6.0 standard Toolbar. Not one of the common navigational functions made the cut: no Find, no Replace, no GoTo. Yet the WordGods *did* make space for, oh, changing the number of snaking newspaper-like columns on the fly. I don't know about you, but I need to use Find dozens of times every day, but I adjust the number of slithering columns on the fly about twice a year, tops. Another triumph of marketing over usefulness: snaking columns are sexy; Find is merely … crucial.

As they say on-line: *<sigh>* The folks who make the final decision as to which buttons go on the Toolbar obviously don't use the product — or, at best, they're more interested in dazzling you with mindless technoflash than in making your working day go faster. It shows.

Adding Find and Goto

Personally, I stick Find and GoTo after the clipboard functions Cut, Copy, Paste. You can, too, if you like. Click on Tools, then Customize. Make sure that the Toolbar filecard is showing and that Save Changes In shows NORMAL.DOT. On the left, scroll down to Edit and then click on the pair of binoculars, as in Figure 1.11. Now drag the binoculars over to the right of the Paste button. Click Close. There. WinWord's Find function is now one click away—where it should be.

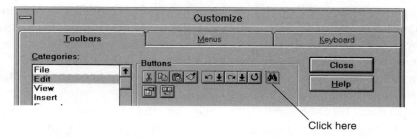

Click here

Figure 1.11 But Soft! What Light Through Yon Window Breaks?

If you want to stick GoTo next to Find, it's easy. (GoTo lets you hop immediately to any page or section, or to a bookmark. If you're good at memorizing key combinations—and I'm not—GoTo is what you'll get if you hit F5.) Click Tools, then Customize. Make sure that the Toolbar filecard is showing and that Save Changes In shows NORMAL.DOT. On the left, scroll down to All Commands. Then, on the right, pick up EditGoTo. Drag it onto the standard Toolbar, to the right of the binoculars. Pick a picture and click OK and Close to get out. My two navigational buttons are shown in Figure 1.12.

Find button   GoTo button

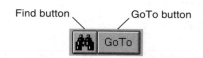

Figure 1.12 Ursus Major—My Navigation Buttons

Since WinWord's Replace function can be triggered with one click from the Find dialog box, I don't put Replace up on the standard Toolbar. If you do a lot of replacing, though, you might want to consider sticking it some place handy, right around here.

Undo, Undo, Damned Spot

Undo/Redo

WinWord's Undo implementation is top notch, what with the multiple levels and the option to choose any subset of the most recent actions for "undoing." I like the Undo and Redo Toolbar buttons just the way they are; wouldn't change 'em for the world. Except …

Occasionally I wonder if it wouldn't be smarter to take the Redo button off there—I use it so infrequently. Redo is one of those strange functions that's hard to find in the menus, perhaps because it isn't *in* the menus. It's buried down in the Word command EditRedo, which you can only find by clicking on Tools, then Macro! It'd be better to keep it where I can find it than to go scrambling for an obscure command at an inopportune time.

Auto This and That

What I tell you three times is true.

C. L. Dodgson
The Hunting of the Snark, 1876

WinWord has three Auto functions, two of which are quite powerful and genuinely useful. AutoFormat makes a brave (and usually pretty good) attempt at applying formatting to a dull document. AutoCorrect snoops over your shoulder, changing text as you type. They're both important, revolutionary (if not entirely original) improvements in Windows word processing. AutoText, the third auto, isn't nearly as spectacular.

AutoText forces you to type in some sort of shorthand and then hit an "expand" key or button. For example, you would type in "asap," and hit F3 to get "as soon as possible." Borland's Sidekick was doing this sort of thing a decade ago. AutoText has a few obscure uses (for example, putting a graphic on an envelope or adding text in a print merge), but by and large AutoText isn't very useful, and I recommend that you avoid it. Almost anything you might want to do with AutoText can be done better, faster, and easier with AutoCorrect.

> **Just between you and me, there's a reason why AutoCorrect works so much like AutoText, only better. AutoCorrect really *is* AutoText, with one small change: the spacebar and a few punctuation marks are treated as the expand key. That's it. That's the whole secret.**
>
> **Microsoft says it's IntelliSense™ — they even trademarked the term! I say it's IntelliNONsense, more marketing technocrap. Some smart programmer in Redmond somewhere figured out how Microsoft could reuse the AutoText programs, making them much more useful by simply getting rid of the expand key.**
>
> **Brilliant. A real time saver. We'll talk more about AutoCorrect later, but suffice it to say that it will improve your productivity substantially and reliably. That smart programmer deserves a medal.**

But I'm left scratching my head as to why Microsoft would put an AutoText button on the standard Toolbar! Even if you use AutoText, it makes no sense to put the expand key up on the Toolbar. AutoText is supposed to be a time saver; you subvert its entire purpose if you don't use the F3 expand key, opting instead to dive for the mouse every time you want to expand. (See Figure 1.13.)

AutoText nixed

Apply AutoFormat   Expand AutoText entry

Figure 1.13 The Standard AutoButtons

So I get rid of the AutoText button. The procedure should be second-nature by now. Click on Tools, then Customize. Make sure that the Toolbars filecard is on top and that Save Changes In shows NORMAL.DOT. Click and drag the AutoText button off the Toolbar, click Close, and AutoText is history.

ShrinkToFit Another important Auto feature is missing from the standard Toolbar. It's called ShrinkToFit. (Microsoft calls it "Tools" ShrinkToFit, but it sure feels like an "Auto" to me.) ShrinkToFit comes in handy when you have just a couple of lines on the last page of a letter or memo and would like an easy way to scrunch things down just a bit. It reduces the size of all the fonts in the whole document by a smidgen and looks to see if that's enough to reduce the page count by one. Quite a paper saver, when it works. You have to treat it with some respect — it can change the size of *every* character — but if you watch what you're doing and don't hesitate to Undo, you shouldn't have much trouble.

For some reason Microsoft puts ShrinkToFit on the Print Preview Toolbar, but leaves it off the Standard Toolbar. For folks like me who avoid Print Preview like the plague, it's totally wasted there. Sticking it next to AutoFormat is easy as pie, though. Click on Tools, then Customize. Toolbars filecard should be on top and NORMAL.DOT in Save Changes In. File is highlighted on the left. (What "Tools" ShrinkToFit is doing in "File" boggles my imagination, but that's where Microsoft stuck it.) Click on the ShrinkToFit button (see Figure 1.14) and drag it to the right of the AutoFormat button. Click Close and you can shrink whenever you like, without flipping into Print Preview mode.

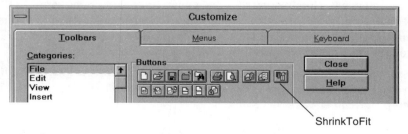

Figure 1.14 Levi's 501 — The ShrinkToFit Button

Finally, I stick the Spell-check button over here, simply to remind me to check spelling (and possibly hyphenate) before trying to ShrinkToFit. That's not a very good reason for putting Spell-check here, but it makes more sense to my twisted brain than putting Spell-check with the printing buttons. My buttons look like Figure 1.15. They are basic finishing tools, things you'll use only after the bulk of the work on a document is done, typically just before printing.

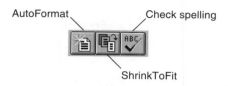

Figure 1.15 Finishing Tools

Miscellaneous

The final collection of standard Toolbar buttons refers to five miscellaneous functions, oddball things that WinWord can do when properly coerced. (See Figure 1.16.)

Two of the buttons crank up other applications, automatically establishing a link back to WinWord. Some of them might be useful to folks with very specific WinWord needs—if you are constantly inserting EXCEL spreadsheets into your WinWord documents, for example, you might want one of the buttons—but by and large I think they're more marketing fog than useful shortcuts. Let's take 'em one at a time.

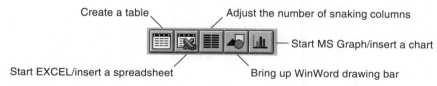

Figure 1.16 Standard Miscellaneous Buttons

The Create Table button is flashy because, immediately upon clicking the button, you can drag your mouse around to specify the number of rows and columns you want for your new table, as in Figure 1.17. That's moderately cool, and very visual, but it doesn't compare to the workhorse that's available if you click on Table, then Insert Table, as shown in Figure 1.18.

Inserting Tables

Clicking on Table, then Insert Table, lets you get straight at the Table Wizard and the Table AutoFormat options, both of which I find very valuable—formatting a table is about as much fun as a prostate probe. The standard Toolbar button bypasses the formatting shortcuts entirely, and that alone is good enough reason to axe it.

Figure 1.17 A Flashy Table

Figure 1.18 A Working Table

To get rid of the standard Create Table button, click on Tools, Customize, Toolbars. Make sure that Save Changes In shows NORMAL.DOT, click on the button on the standard Toolbar, and drag the button off the Toolbar. Click Close and the button's gone.

Insert EXCEL Spreadsheet

The Insert EXCEL Spreadsheet button, like the Insert Microsoft Graph Chart button farther to the right, cranks up a different Windows application (EXCEL or the Microsoft Graph applet, respectively) and lets you play around in that application.

Insert MS Graph Chart

Microsoft Graph is a rather underwhelming graphing applet that Microsoft ships with WinWord. It's free, and at that rate arguably not overpriced. (Seriously, the ability to highlight a table in WinWord, and then having that data automatically import itself into MS Graph *is* impressive. But I digress.) Using old-fashioned Object Linking and Embedding (OLE 1.0) technology, you can pop into Graph, construct a simple graph, and then File/Exit back to WinWord. Your graph comes back with you. Double-click on it at any time and you'll find yourself transported back to Microsoft Graph, ready to do battle with the DataDemons. Ho-hum.

EXCEL 5 is a horse ... er ... cockroach of a different color. Click on the Insert EXCEL Spreadsheet button and you'll find that you're still in WinWord, sorta—your document is still up on the screen, but all the ancillary stuff, including the Toolbar and the menus and the window title, is pure EXCEL. It's a great demo of "in-place editing," part of the newer, greater OLE 2.0 technology.

If you have EXCEL 5 installed, you should try clicking on the Insert EXCEL spreadsheet button at least once, just to get the hang of it—before you nuke it, that is. It's a waste. Unless you're one of the three people in the world who are constantly inserting EXCEL spreadsheets into their WinWord documents, you don't need it.

Both Insert EXCEL Spreadsheet and Insert Microsoft Graph Chart are special **Insert Object** instances of an umbrella WinWord command called Insert Object. Insert Object is the magical entry way to many, many other Windows applications, including the Equation Editor, WordArt, Multimedia player (for sound and video clips), and Microsoft Draw packages that ship with WinWord, and every other Windows app that supports OLE (or, more correctly, every Windows app that supports OLE and has been installed properly).

You can see Insert Object in action by clicking on Insert, then Object (rocket science, eh?). You'll get a dialog box that looks something like the one in Figure 1.19.

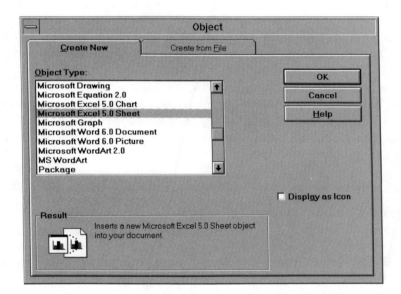

Figure 1.19 Pick an Object, Any Object

I don't understand why Microsoft decided to put two of those applications up on the standard Toolbar, to the exclusion of the others. It's particularly vexing that they would put MS Graph on the Toolbar for bringing in charts, when EXCEL (which is also on the bar) has its own charting functions and "objects" — and EXCEL's are vastly more capable than MS Graph's.

Oh, well. Two thumbs down, I say. Let's get rid of the teensy-weensy specialized buttons and bring in the mother lode, Insert Object herself.

Removing the XL and MS Graph buttons

Click on Tools, then Customize. Make sure that the Toolbars filecard is on top and that Save Changes In shows NORMAL.DOT. Then click and drag the Insert EXCEL Spreadsheet button—the first of this gang of five—off the Toolbar. Repeat the procedure with the Insert MS Graph Chart button, the last of this group.

On the left, under Categories, scroll down to All Commands. Then, on the right, click and drag Insert Object onto the standard Toolbar. Give it an appropriate picture (pretty tough since this command can do so much!) and click Close. *Pax vobiscum.*

Sssssssnaking Columns

Now let's snip that stupid snaking columns button. Pardon my alliteration. Yeah, yeah, yeah. There probably *is* one WinWord user who changes the number of columns in their documents, day in and day out. I bet they live in Bothell and commute on I-90. For the other 2,999,999 WinWord users, though, this serpent button is about as welcome as taste at a Howard Stern party—good, bad, or otherwise. Nuke it. You know the tune: Tools. Customize. Toolbars. NORMAL.DOT in Save Changes In. Click and drag the button off the standard Toolbar. Close. *Finis.*

Finally, some folks really do use the WinWord drawing layer. I used it extensively to do the "callouts" (the little lines and text attached to the figures) in this book.

Show Drawing Toolbar

If you don't do much drawing, go right ahead and zap out the Show Drawing Toolbar button. You can always get at the drawing Toolbar—or anything else to do with Toolbars, for that matter—by sticking your cursor in any Toolbar and clicking the right mouse button, or by clicking View, then Toolbars. It's quick and it's easy.

Final Flourish

My standard Toolbar

I keep the final three standard Toolbar buttons intact. The "show all" paragraph mark, the zoom drop-down list, and the Help question mark work fine for me. My standard Toolbar looks like the one in Figure 1.20. That leaves lots of room for additional buttons, which I add and delete with wild abandon as the situation —or my mood—warrants.

Figure 1.20 Oh Toolbar, My Toolbar

Show All

Oh. There's one last trick for the standard Toolbar. I change the function of the Show All button so that it shows all of what *I* want to see, not what the WinWord Thought Police believe I should see. More about that later in this chapter.

FORMATTING TOOLBAR

If the beard were all, goats could preach.

Danish Proverb

In direct contrast to the standard Toolbar, WinWord's formatting Toolbar is all business, its utility not compromised by a tendency to show off. (Perhaps the folks doing the WinWord demos never get beyond the standard Toolbar?)

Indent/Undent

I, personally, don't increase or decrease indenting all that often, so I wiped out the Increase Indent and Decrease Indent buttons. You might call them "indent and undent." Whatever. They're on the Toolbar bass-ackwards anyway. Since increase indent is much more frequently used than decrease, its button, to my mind anyway, should be on the left. Oh, well.

Increase/ Decrease Indent

The method for exorcising them is just as before: Tools. Customize. Toolbars. NORMAL.DOT. Drag the buttons off the Toolbar, one at a time. Close.

Character Styles on the Bar

Character is that which reveals moral purpose,
exposing the class of things a man chooses or avoids.

Aristotle
Rhetoric, ca. 322 BC

The Formatting Toolbar is the most logical place to put other formatting buttons. For example, it seems that I'm always fishing around for an easy way to set off text, typically by switching fonts. Throughout this book I put file names like NORMAL.DOT in a different font, for example. I must do that a couple dozen times a day. You probably do the same thing, albeit in a somewhat different context—perhaps you set off your company name in different type or sign your name with a script font.

The easiest, fastest way to set off text is with a combination of a character style **Fast fonts** and a formatting Toolbar button. (All right, all right. It's probably faster to use a custom key combination like CTRL+ALT+W, instead of a Toolbar button, but I always forget custom key combinations!)

If you get the character style and the button working together, changing fonts couldn't be simpler. You select the stuff you want to change and then click the Toolbar button. Poof! The character style you've set up is applied to the selected text, and it instantly changes to the new font.

Character style
raison d'être

Even better, by establishing and consistently using character styles (described in Chapter 4), you'll be able to change your mind at a later date—or have your boss change your mind *for* you—with the changes rippling effortlessly through your documents. It's infinitely better than "painting" a character format or hand-applying formatting.

Trust me on this. The first time your boss says, "Oh, by the way, I don't like *Wexler's Widgets* in italics. Make it bold, and a little bigger, all through the report, OK? And have it on my desk in fifteen minutes," you'll thank me. I guarantee.

Putting the character style/Toolbar button combination together is very simple. Start by clicking on Format, then Style, then New. Over in the Style Type box, choose Character. Then in the Name box, type in a name. I call my oddball font "Code" because it reminds me of programming code. (See Figure 1.21.)

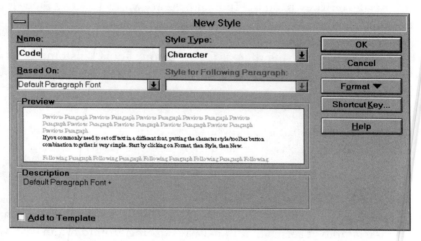

Figure 1.21 A Style Is Born

**First the style,
then the button**

To define the style, click on Format, then Font, and pick whatever character formatting you like: a different font, weird size, bold, italic, whatever. Click OK twice, then Close. Good. That defines the character style. You can see the style if you click on the first down-arrow on the formatting Toolbar.

To put a button for that character style on the formatting Toolbar, click on Tools, then Customize. Make sure that the Toolbars filecard is on top and that NORMAL.DOT is in Save Changes In. The usual stuff. Over in the Categories box, scroll all the way down to Styles. Then pick your style from the Styles box, and drag it to the formatting Toolbar. Choose a picture (or use text), click Close, and you're done. My formatting Toolbar looks like Figure 1.22.

Figure 1.22 Belly Up to the Formatting Bar

Simple, eh? Congratulations. By making all these nips and tucks and learning how to use them consistently, you just saved yourself many hours of work.

TOOLBAR REDUX

> An ill workman quarrels with his tools.
>
> John Ray
> *English Proverbs*, 1670

So there you have it, pilgrim—my own personal rendition of a WinWord workin' stiff's Toolbars and desktop. I'm not about to claim it's the best for you— far from it! But I *will* claim that it's a hell of a lot better than the version that ships with WinWord. If you use it as a starting point, you won't be far off.

Why Bother?

Adjusting your Toolbar to the way you work can give you an enormous productivity boost. I'm talking day-in and day-out, hard core speed-ups, not shaving a tenth of a second off a productivity lab's benchmark. Getting those buttons just right, and using them religiously, can make your final documents look better, help you organize your life, and get you home earlier at night. Hard to beat.

Some folks don't like the Toolbar. They tend to be mouse-o-phobes; they think of the mouse as a weapon of last resort. As my granddaddy used to say, *de gustibus non est disputandum,* eh wot? If you're smart enough to memorize all those F-key and CTRL+ combinations, more power to ya—I can't, and I gave up trying years ago.

If you can't hack the mouse and stubbornly stick to the keyboard, keep one thing in mind: every time you look up the keyboard "shortcut" on a cheat sheet, you're losing more time than you think. It may behoove you to give mice a chance.

Once More, Unto the Breach

> Men of few words are the best men.
>
> William Shakespeare
> *King Henry V*

If you haven't played around with WinWord's innards before, I hope you've learned a couple of things that may not be immediately obvious.

First, the program is magnificently malleable. If you don't like the way a certain part of WinWord works — and the Toolbars are a great example — all it takes is a little gumption and a bit of reading, and you can probably change things around so they work the way *you* want 'em to. WinWord is one of the most complex, most sophisticated, and most useful pieces of software ever created. It's there for you to mold to your way of working. You don't have to settle for the built-in stuff.

Second, you aren't gonna break it! Yeah, some parts are screwy, and some things behave strangely, but you should feel mighty confident now that you can dive in and change anything you like, any way you like. WinWord can take it.

2 Custom Settings

Veni, vidi, vici.

Julius Cæsar
dispatch to the Roman Senate, 47 BC

Adjusting the Toolbar was only the first step along the road to becoming a power user. WinWord offers hundreds of additional options that you can—and should!—change to suit your predilections. Chapter 2 digs deeper into customizing WinWord, setting things up so WinWord's innards (if not its information!) are at your fingertips.

The primary problem with the bone-stock Toolbar, as you've seen, is that it embodies the "demo" version of WinWord. The Toolbar was constructed more for the hard sell than for the workin' stiff.

The primary problem with the bone-stock View settings — scrollbars, rulers, invisible paragraph marks, and on and on — is that they were constructed with the novice in mind. What you see is the stripped-down "intro" version of WinWord. Let's take off the training wheels.

THE GENERAL VIEW

All living creatures are led astray as soon as they are born,
by the delusion that this relative world is real.

Sri Krishna
Bhagavad-Gita, ca. 500 BC

WinWord's View settings control what you see on the screen and, therefore, how you interact with your documents.

View à la Mode

Page View   I always run in Page View, as opposed to Normal View, and recommend that you do, too, providing your computer has the horsepower to do it. Well, yes, there *are* some rare exceptions, but by and large Page View (in WordSpeak, "Page Layout View") is where I live. (See Figure 2.1.)

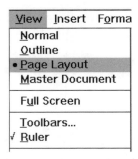

Figure 2.1 The View Menu

When you're in Page View, you can see everything—drawings, frames and the way text flows around them, drop caps, headers and footers, footnotes, and much more. There's almost no need for Print Preview. You can see the results of ShrinkToFit immediately. You'll probably use Rulers less often, freeing up more room on the screen. (Funny how the WordGods let you use a horizontal ruler with no vertical ruler, but not vice versa, eh?) Page View is reality, the straight scoop, *cinéma vérité.*

Normal View   Not so Normal View. In **Normal View** you're forever guessing how the page will look, wondering what lines up where and how. In Sanskrit they would call Normal View *maya*—an illusion, a convenient fiction. I rarely drop into Normal View, just as I try to look beyond *maya.*

The exceptions? Well, when I'm running on anything less than a hefty 80386 (say, a 386/33) with a lot of memory (4 MB will do, but 8 MB is much better), I find Page View as slow as winter slop. WinWord 6.0 eats every cycle an 80386 can muster. It's no slouch at the 80486 trough, either. If the machine can't handle it, I won't push it. Lousy performance is the best reason for staying in Normal View.

Sometimes I flip into Normal View so I can see manual page breaks and section breaks. Maybe someday WinWord will be smart enough to show manual page breaks and section breaks in Page View, as a Tools/Options/View option. (Are you listening, Redmond?)

On very rare occasions I want to see the names of all the paragraph styles alongside the paragraphs, so I go into Normal View with a half-inch setting in the

Tools/Options/View Style Area Width. That, too, could be easily covered with a Tools/Options/View option someday, if the WordGods ever get around to it.

I also switch to Normal View whenever I'm looking at Field Codes, those largely hidden { brackets } lurking behind the scenes that lie at the heart of so much of WinWord's power. It's hard to imagine any time it would make sense to have Field Codes visible and yet remain in Page View.

The only disadvantage to working in Page View is its relative sluggishness when scrolling. I've found that WinWord running in Page View can keep up with very, very quick typists—in excess of 100 words/minute—on just about any 486 computer made. So that isn't a worry. But if you're stuck with a 286/12 and 2 MB of memory, you'll probably want to run in Normal View, with the Tools/Options/ View Draft Font box checked.

Many people find that boosting their RAM memory to 8 MB or more takes care of the slow scrolling blues of Page View.

The other views can come in handy, but they're intended to be special-purpose views. **Outline View** is a great way to create a To-Do list as well as a useful way to organize and reorganize long documents. Master Document View helps with huge documents. | **Outline View**

Full Screen View on an 800 × 600 or larger monitor is a joke, another reaction to good press accorded one of WinWord 2.0's competitors. In one fell swoop it eliminates nearly all the advantages of Windows word processing, rocketing you back to the 1950s in an excellent IBM 1620 emulation (except for that pesky ruler, which seems to persist no matter how hard you try to kill it). | **Full Screen View**

WinWord even has a **Doogie Howser View**, named in honor of the TV series that subliminally advertised a WinWord competitor at the end of each show. Click on Tools, Options, General, and check the Blue Background, White Text box. (Bet you wondered what that box was for, eh?) Click on View and Full Screen. Type away. For the full effect, jack the font up to about 20 points. You can almost hear Doogie's "outtro" music. | **Doogie View**

Scroll, Scroll, Scroll Yer Boat

> Human status ought not to depend upon the changing
> demands of the economic process.
>
> Archbishop of Canterbury
> *Malvern Manifesto*, 1941

WinWord has a handful of additional settings that can make a big difference in how you work. If you click on Tools, then Options, and make sure that the View filecard is on top, you'll see some of them. My personal preferences for general working settings are shown in Figure 2.2.

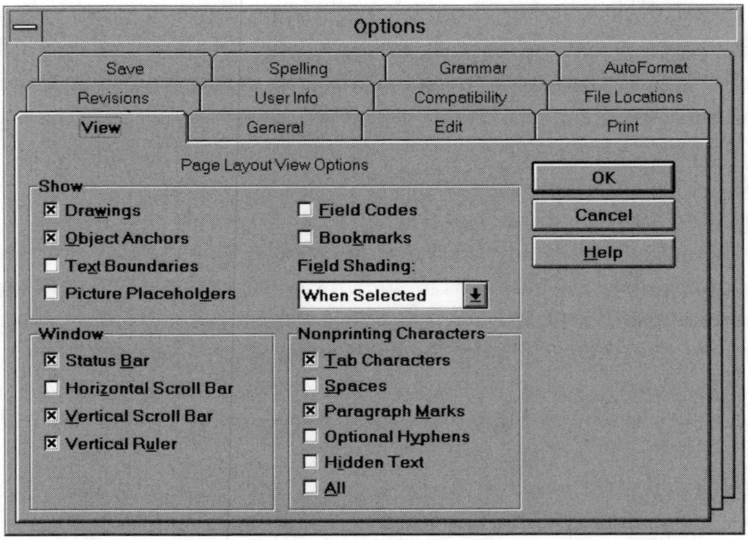

Figure 2.2 The View, As I See It

Drawings

I like to see the stuff I draw, and I'll bet you do, too. That's why I check the Show Drawings box. If you have a lot of drawings in a document, you don't particularly care if you get them confused, and scrolling has slowed down to tortoise levels, you might consider unchecking the box.

⚓

Anchors

Object Anchors look like anchors and show you where your drawings and frames are **anchored**—where they're attached to the document itself. When you work with drawings and frames, anchors are important. They're your only fighting chance at understanding why and how callouts flip-flop around, for example, and they let you quickly specify how frames should travel with body text. I keep the Show Object Anchors box checked.

Boundaries

Text boundaries don't mean much to me. I tend to set boundaries in the Format dialog boxes, where precise measurements are possible. I leave this box unchecked.

**Placeholders,
Field Codes,
Bookmarks**

Picture placeholders—where pictures are replaced with empty boxes—are nice to speed up scrolling in huge documents, but they can be confusing when you're trying to sling pictures around. We'll talk about Field Codes and Bookmarks in the next part of this chapter (The Great Wordini), where you get to write your first macro. Start sweating now; it's excruciating. Believe me. *Heh, heh, heh.*

Field shading

Fields are simply the results of {field} codes. Many people find them baffling. As a power user, you'll come to work with {field} codes and soon realize that by and large they aren't as confusing as you probably thought.

By setting off the results of {field} codes, you keep a constant visual reminder that something lurks beneath what appears on the screen and what prints on the printer. If you screw up a {field} while field shading is on, it's your fault, not WinWord's.

For most power users, shading should be either Always (in which case, {field} results always show up against a light gray background), or When Selected (in which case, {field} results show gray when they're selected or when the cursor is inside a {field}). I prefer the latter just because I use a lot of {field}s, and I get distracted when the background color flip-flops. It's no biggie either way.

If you've attained WinWord enlightenment, don't make many mistakes, are accustomed to working with {field}s, and won't be mystified when WinWord starts behaving strangely—as it is wont to do in the presence of {field}s—you may want to set shading at Never, particularly if screen contrast tends to obscure your cursor while you're in a shaded {field}.

I use the **status bar** (see Figure 2.3) constantly. Sometimes it's the only way to tell what's going on. I *do* wish Microsoft would give me the option of making the OVR overstrike box flash a nuclear red, to warn me that I have switched to Overstrike mode (where typed characters replace what's on the screen). I wouldn't mind if they could hook it up to deliver an electric shock to the keyboard, for that matter, to send pulses of stunning pain through my fingertips. But I digress. Besides, we'll disable the OVR/Insert key in a few minutes. Keep the Status Bar box checked.

Status Bar

Figure 2.3 Status Bar

You need a **horizontal scroll bar**—the one that goes left to right, down at the bottom of the screen—like Bill needs cash. If you have to run for your mouse to move the page left to right, you'll spend most of your life mousing around. (The horizontal scroll bar's little Normal/Page/Outline View buttons are nice, but hardly crucial.) With very rare exceptions, you should adjust the Zoom setting so you that can see across the entire width of the page, and so that you don't need the horizontal scroll bar.

Scroll bars

Contrariwise, unless you're a dyed-in-the-wool mouse-o-phobe, it's hard to imagine a situation where you *wouldn't* want the **vertical scroll bar**—it's the one that goes up and down, on the right side of the screen. I keep the Horizontal Scroll Bar box cleared and the Vertical Scroll Bar box checked, and I strongly recommend that you do, too.

The **vertical ruler**—the one that measures distances down the page, over on the left side of the screen—only shows up when you're in Page View, and then

Vertical ruler

only when the **horizontal ruler** is showing. (Turn the horizontal ruler on and off by clicking on View and setting or clearing the check mark on Ruler.) I usually don't use any rulers, but when I do, I want them out in force, so I keep the Vertical Ruler box checked.

Providing you run in Page View, the current vertical location of the cursor, that is, the distance down the current page, is shown in the Status Bar. Thus you generally won't need a vertical ruler just to check how much room is left at the bottom of a page. (It would sure be nice if Microsoft gave us the option to show Distance To End of Page on the Status Bar, eh? Isn't that what you *really* want about 90% of the time?)

This lopsided treatment of horizontal and vertical rulers bugs me. Don't let it confuse you. The horizontal ruler, up at the top of the screen, is controlled by the setting on the View menu. The vertical ruler, over on the left side of the screen, is controlled by the setting on the Tools/Options/View filecard. You can see the horizontal ruler without the vertical ruler, but not vice versa. The horizontal ruler must be showing for the vertical ruler to appear. Bleccch.

Nonprinting Characters

> The evening papers print what they do and get away with it
> because by afternoon the human mind is ruined anyhow.
>
> Christopher Morley
> *Kitty Foyle*, 1939

The View filecard has a final block of settings marked Nonprinting Characters. That's a cryptic way of saying, "If you check the corresponding box, this particular kind of character will show up on the screen, just to help you; the character will not appear when you print."

It's a little tough coming from the world of typewriters and such to adapt to the idea of a **nonprinting character**—one that only exists to provide some structure to your document. If the concept is new to you, don't worry, you'll get used to it pretty quickly. When you push the spacebar on a Selectric, you don't "get" anything. The paper just moves forward one space. Push the Tab key, and the platen moves up to the next tab stop. And so on.

In the computer world, those actions have to be kept somehow. Since there's no sheet of paper to move forward one space, no heavy bar with protruding metal tabs to stop the movement of the platen, your instructions have to be stored away in a somewhat different guise. That's why computers have characters that represent spaces, tabbing, and carriage returns. The characters don't print on your printer, but they're in the document, adding structure and—at least occasionally—doing your bidding. The question is whether you want to see these nonprinting characters on the screen. That's all.

When WinWord installs itself, it clears out all these Show Nonprinting Characters boxes, and that's a big mistake.

Tab characters are crucial to lining up text when you're working with a **proportional font** (that is, one in which the "i" and "m" have different widths). I don't care what Microsoft recommends, you should always, always, always show tabs on the screen. You don't stand a snowball's chance of figuring out how text lines up otherwise. Keep the Show Tab Characters box checked.

Tab characters

Spaces, on the other hand, may be better left unseen. WinWord can set the screen up so each space shows as a little dot (see Figure 2.4). Presumably you would want to see the little dots just in case you put an extra space between words. The presence of two little dots next to each other would alert you to an errant space, one you surely want to delete.

Spaces

Horsepucky.·All·those·little·dots·drive·me·nuts.·I·can't·tell·when·there's·two·little·dots·cuddling·up·next·to·each·other---they're·too·small.·Besides,·an·extra·space·here·or·there·ain't·gonna·hurt·anything.·My·eyes·see·enough·spots·already.¶

Figure 2.4 Dots All, Folks—Too Many Dots

Personally I can't hack those dots! I've finally trained my fingers so they only put one space after a period—the politically correct method for spacing sentences—so I rarely stick two spaces back to back. Thus, I have very little reason to show the dots; I keep the Show Spaces box unchecked.

Paragraph marks (¶) are another story altogether. If there is one setting crucial to your understanding of WinWord and the way it works, this is it, right here, buried in the middle of an obscure backwater dialog box.

Here's the most important quick tip in this book. You *must* show paragraph marks while working on a document. Why? Because *the paragraph mark holds the key to most WinWord formatting*.

More time has been lost, more tears have been shed, over the intransigence of paragraph marks than over any other facet of WinWord. Paragraph marks control fonts, formatting, lines, boxes, tabs, shading, languages, styles, and on and on and on. The single greatest conceptual jump you have to make to master WinWord is the conquest of paragraph marks. Bizarre, but true. And you can't work with paragraph marks unless you can see them!

As you've probably guessed, I leave the Show Paragraph Marks box checked. Always. More than that, I think it's criminal that WinWord doesn't show paragraph marks automatically, at the very least as an installation default. Hundreds of thousands of would-be WinWord users have given up on the program

—thrown up their hands in disgust and anger—because they didn't "get" paragraph marks. *Millions* of hours lost over a stupid little character.

We'll give the paragraph mark its due in Chapter 3. Meanwhile, don't even touch a WinWord screen unless paragraph marks are showing.

Optional hyphens

Optional hyphens are hyphens you insert with the key combination* CTRL+– to tell WinWord that it's okay to hyphenate a word at the indicated location. These hyphens are applied manually and normally can't be seen. In the odd event that you actually want to see where you've told WinWord it's okay to hyphenate, you can check the Show Optional Hyphens box. If you do, there's no reason to stay in Page View—all those weird ¬ hyphens screw up line and page breaks anyway. I keep the box cleared.

Hidden text

Hidden is a type of text formatting, like bold or italic. It's a great way to keep secret notes to yourself, notes that are visible on the screen (if the Hidden Text box is checked) but never print, unless you go to great lengths to do so. Several WinWord add-ons use hidden text, to great effect.

Whether or not you check the Hidden Text box often depends on the type of document you're using. Since I don't usually have hidden text in my files, I keep this box cleared. Your situation may be different. Regardless, if you have the Hidden Text box checked, there is rarely any reason to run in Page View—the hidden text affects line and page breaks, knocking Page View out of whack.

The Show All box

Checking the Show All box is the same as checking all five of the preceding boxes. WinWord shows the five nonprinting characters: tabs, spaces, paragraph marks, optional hyphens, and hidden text. Clearing the All box reverts to the status of each individual check box. Pretty straightforward.

Show All

In essence, the Show All button on the standard Toolbar checks and unchecks this Show All box, alternately showing and then hiding the five nonprinting characters (more correctly, reverting to the five individual show settings). That would be great if I wanted to flick those five on and off, but I don't: I *always* want to see tabs and paragraph marks; I just about *never* want to see spaces, optional hyphens, or hidden text; *sometimes* I want to see {field} codes, other times their results; *sometimes* I'm curious about bookmarks, other times not. In the best of all possible worlds, I'd be able to click this Show All button and have it show me what I want, no muss, no fuss.

The WinWord Thought Police aren't so accommodating. I can have it their way—all five nonprinting characters appear or disappear—or I can have nothing. That's all she wrote. *Heh, heh, heh.*

---

*Alas, the PC keyboard has no separate hyphen key, so I usually call it the "minus" key. The CTRL+– convention I've used here is terrible, but don't be confused: hold down the CTRL key, then push the minus key.

THE GREAT WORDINI KNOWS ALL, SEES ALL

The magician is an infidel, but his magic is truth.

Hindu Proverb

WinWord's macro language, WordBasic (and the WinWord version of Visual Basic for Applications, VBA, when it's available*) gives you the power to create macros that can make changes to WinWord, deep down inside, to make it work the way *you* want it to work.

Your first macro

I detest the buzzword "seamless," but this is one place where it applies. If you take some care, you can weave a macro into the very fabric of WinWord, in such a way that you'll never know where the bone-stock product leaves off and your extensions begin. It's like changing the Toolbars, only a bit more ... visceral.

I'm going to start building a macro here in Chapter 2, and then pick it back up again and improve on it in Chapter 6, where we can go through all the nitty-gritty details. Think of this first installment as lip-sync programming. For now it's enough that you type along, lip-syncing to the tune. If the details go over your head, don't worry about it. What's important at this point is that you get a feel for macros — feel the beat, move your feet — and while we're at it we'll add an important capability to your Toolbar.

The Underground ShowAll

Every time you click on the Show All button, WinWord runs a command called ShowAll. (Rocket science again, eh?) In effect, this built-in ShowAll command looks to see if the All box is checked in the Tools/Options/View filecard. If it is checked, ShowAll clears it out; if it isn't checked, ShowAll turns it on. Easy.

Show All

This book's version of ShowAll, though, goes much deeper. In hinges on {field} codes. If you've never come across {field} codes face to face, consider yourself lucky. In my experience they're one of the most confusing, yet one of the most useful, aspects of WinWord. Ya cain't live with them and ya cain't live without them.

{field} codes lurk inside your WinWord documents. They go out and find information to stick in the document. For example, today's date shows up where the {date} field appears in a document. The {author} field grabs the author's name (from the file's Summary Info) and puts it in the doc. The {filename} field finds the name of the file and slaps it in the doc. Print Merge is built on various kinds of

Intro to {field} codes

---

*As of this week anyway, Microsoft calls VBA the "Visual Basic programming system, Applications Edition." That's a crock, really — VBA doesn't look much like Visual Basic and doesn't come close to VB's power — but they own the names and can call them anything they like. Vince Chen and I discuss the VB vs. VBA conundrum in our columns in the February and March, 1994, issues of *PC/Computing*. The WinWord version of VBA is promised for WinWord 7.0.

{field}s. You can edit graphs and spreadsheets inside your WinWord docs because of {field}s. Index entries. Table of contents. And on and on. If you've ever used Insert on WinWord's menu, you've probably used a {field}. They can get mighty complex, mighty tricky, mighty quick.

Most of the time you can let the {field} codes remain hidden. They do their thing, you do yours, and all's right with the world. Sometimes, though, weird things start happening—characters change mysteriously in a document, a merge doesn't work right, a table of contents gets screwed up—and the only way to figure out what's really happening is to go behind the mask and look directly at the {field} codes. It ain't pretty, but that's how life is out here on the bleeding edge.

Reveal codes

By the way, if you were raised on older versions of WordPerfect, WinWord's {field} codes are completely different from WordPerfect's reveal codes. {field} codes go out in the WinOoze and bring information back to the document. Contrariwise, **reveal codes** turn these oddball formatting codes on and off—a sequential kludge* in an objectified world. Completely different breed of cat. Don't get confused.

Makin' Macros

> Nine times out of ten, in the arts as in life,
> there is actually no truth to be discovered;
> there is only error to be exposed.
>
> H. L. Mencken
> *Prejudices III*, 1922

Believe it or not, you can replace the built-in ShowAll command with a program of your own devising, a **macro**. I don't like the way ShowAll works. I want to make it do things my way, thank you very much, so I'm going to write a macro that takes over. (Ever wonder what the difference is between a program and a macro? Me, too. I've written a few books that touch on the topic, and I *still* dunno. Got any good ideas?)

Yeah, yeah, yeah. This is programming. If you break out in hives when you see that word, well, hold onto your seat, bucko. This is so easy Beavis and Butt-head could do it, unassisted, with the power off.

Creating a new macro

Okay. Click on Tools, then Macro. Make sure that the box labeled Macros Available In shows NORMAL.DOT. Then type ShowAll (all one word: WordBasic doesn't let you put spaces in the names of macros) and click Create. (See Figure 2.5.) You're about to create your own version of ShowAll. By putting it in NORMAL.DOT, WordBasic will automatically run *your* version of the program

---

*kludge /klooj/ n. A clever programming trick used to solve a particularly nasty problem in an expedient, if not clear, manner. *New Hacker's Dictionary* (MIT Press, 1992).

instead of the built-in version of ShowAll that comes with WinWord. You'll see why when we look at the concept of context in Chapter 4.

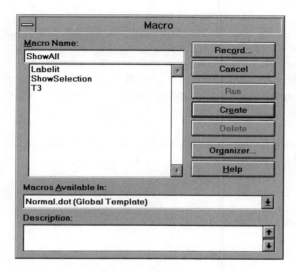

Figure 2.5 The Start of a New ShowAll

WordBasic automatically kick-starts your macro writing adventure by opening an area for you to type in (a **macro window**), bringing up the macro editing Toolbar, and even supplying a perfectly valid three-line macro (Figure 2.6). Start by selecting the line that says ShowAll and deleting it. We're going to take things into our own hands.

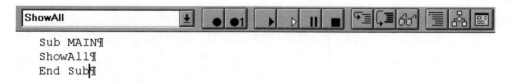

```
Sub MAIN¶
ShowAll¶
End Sub¶
```

Figure 2.6 ShowAll As It Was in the Beginning

My idea of a good ShowAll isn't something that flips back and forth between showing and hiding nonprinting characters. I'm very opinionated about which nonprinting characters I want to see, and—even if your choice of nonprinting characters doesn't agree with mine!—I'll bet you know which ones you want to see, too.

To my way of thinking, ShowAll should alternate between showing reality and showing what lies *behind* the reality. Kind of a gestalt-on/gestalt-off switch, if

The ShowAll "program spec"

you know what I mean. ShowAll should flip-flop between showing {field} codes and the results of {field} codes; it should jump between showing what's going to print and what's going on behind the scenes.

Showing the reality behind the document is an important capability that, somehow, has eluded WinWord's designers since the dawning of WinTime. The built-in version of ShowAll is a half-hearted attempt at showing what's going on behind the scenes. Some of what it shows is vital; some of it is utterly trivial. And it misses the most important behind-the-scenes player of all: {field} codes! I say let's stomp this sucker and do it right.

As a first cut, I'd like the Underground ShowAll to flip-flop between showing {field} codes and showing their results. That's a good starting point, and it's easy to write a program to do the flip-flop:

```
If ViewFieldCodes() Then
   ToolsOptionsView .FieldCodes=0
Else
   ToolsOptionsView .FieldCodes=1
End If
```

In English that says, "If ViewFieldCodes() is ON—that is, if you see {field} codes in the current document, not the results of {field} codes—then turn them OFF, otherwise turn them ON." (No, you aren't supposed to know all this stuff off the top of your head, pilgrim. You're lip-syncing, remember?)

Type in those lines and push the right-wedgie button on the macro Toolbar. It's the solid blue button, the one that's supposed to look like the "**Play**" button on a VCR. (See Figure 2.7.)

Figure 2.7 Our First Macro Bombs

Oops. In Figure 2.7, WordBasic's Error 509 is trying to tell you that there can't be any {field} codes in a macro, so you can't do anything to {field} codes while you're looking at a macro.

This programming quandary has many possible solutions. The easiest (that is, easiest to program, for the time being at least), and the one we'll take for now, is to just tell WordBasic to bypass everything if an error appears. That's done with the On Error statement:

```
Sub MAIN
On Error Goto HeyYoureInAMacroTurkey
If ViewFieldCodes() Then
  ToolsOptionsView .FieldCodes=0
Else
  ToolsOptionsView .FieldCodes=1
End If
HeyYoureInAMacroTurkey:
End Sub
```

The next-to-last statement there just sets up a label, a place for WordBasic to go if it encounters an error—it's the "destination" of the On Error statement.

If you open up a WinWord document, or create a new one, and click the "Play" button over and over, you'll see how this macro of yours works. The results are a little more dramatic if you open a document with a {field} in it. If you don't know whether you have a doc with a {field} lying around, just click Insert, then Date and Time…, pick a date format you like, and make sure that the Insert as Field box is checked. Now click the "Play" button. See how you flip back and forth, between the date and the {field} that creates the date? (See Figure 2.8.)

April 11, 1994 { TIME\@"MMMM d,yyyy"}

Figure 2.8 Date and Its {field}

Perhaps a little more surprisingly, your new ShowAll macro is already hooked up to the Show All button on the standard Toolbar. Try clicking on the Show All button. See how it runs your macro the same as clicking on the "Play" button on the macro Toolbar?

Refinement and Kultcha

> Culture is what your butcher would have
> if he were a surgeon.
>
> Mary Poole
> *A Glass Eye at the Keyhole*, 1938

So far the Underground ShowAll is pretty cool. It lets you accomplish in one click what otherwise would take some hunting and pecking in the Toolbar/Options/View menu. Now let's make it better.

First, let's look at the settings that let you see behind the scenes. Every time you flip over to see {field} codes, you may as well put WinWord in Normal View. Since the codes screw up page formatting and whatnot, there's no sense making WinWord go to all the trouble of repaginating the whole document. And while we're at it, we may as well show Hidden Text and Optional Hyphens. But I'll be hanged if I want to see Spaces—no reason to toss the baby *in* with the bathwater!

Ends up all of that is pretty easy. Down underneath the Else line you need to add one line and change another:

```
Else
   ViewNormal
   ToolsOptionsView .FieldCodes=1, .Hyphens=1, .Hidden=1
```

By switching into Normal View first, you keep WinWord from repaginating, a process that can take forever.

Contrariwise, every time I flip over to see the results of {field} codes, I'd like to see a bit of reality, a good indication of how the document will print. I want to make sure WinWord hops back to Page View. The Optional Hyphens go away; Hidden Text, too (though you may want to keep Hidden Text).

I want WinWord to reset all of my View settings: Show Drawings and Anchors, Field Shading When Selected, Show Status Bar and Vertical Scroll Bar and Ruler, and Show Tabs and Paragraph Marks. I want all the others turned off. It ends up that it's all pretty easy, although it takes a bit of typing.

```
Sub MAIN
On Error Goto HeyYoureInAMacroTurkey
If ViewFieldCodes() Then
   ToolsOptionsView .FieldCodes=0, .Drawings=1, .Anchors=1, \
      .TextBoundaries = 0, .PicturePlaceHolders = 0, \
      .BookMarks = 0, .FieldShading = 2, .StatusBar = 1, \
      .HScroll = 0, .VScroll = 1, .VRuler = 1, .Tabs = 1, \
      .Spaces=0, .Paras=1, .Hyphens=0, .Hidden=0, .ShowAll=0
   ViewPage
Else
   ViewNormal
   ToolsOptionsView .FieldCodes=1, .Hyphens = 1, .Hidden = 1
End If
HeyYoureInAMacroTurkey:
End Sub
```

Continuation characters (\)   Those little backslashes (\) on the end of long lines just tell WordBasic to keep on going, that the next line is really part of the current line. (If you're a programmer, you're no doubt familiar with such **continuation characters**.)

So what can you do if you don't like my preferences? Easy. Roll your own! Stick your cursor on the line that says ToolsOptionsView and hit F1. You'll be transported into WordBasic's Help system, with all the ToolsOptionsView settings right in front of you. Want to Always see Field Code Shading? No sweat. Change .FieldShading = 2 in the macro to say .FieldShading = 1. All the settings are explained right there in the F1-Help file.

I don't know about you, but I learn best by playing around with something that works, seeing how it can be changed, how it breaks. This is an ideal time to do precisely that! Click File, then Save, so you don't clobber the macro terminally (or if you do zap WinWord, you'll be able to come back to where you were), and then change things around.

Don't worry about breaking anything. The worst you could possibly do is crash WinWord with a **General Protection Fault** (**GPF**) or some such. WordBasic isn't supposed to GPF with these kinds of commands, but you never know… and if you can reliably trigger a GPF at this point, you should contact Microsoft immediately and claim your rightful place as an ace bug catcher!

If the worst happens—if somehow WinWord *does* lock up—recovery is easy. Restart Windows, restart WinWord, click on Tools, then Macro, click once on ShowAll, and click Edit. There. You're right back where you started. Nothing broken. Nothing lost. So go ahead and give it a good shot. Bang it around a bit. Make WinWord work the way *you* think it should.

Your Underground ShowAll should be working pretty well. Click on the **Saving** Show All button a couple times to convince yourself that it's what you want. When you're satisfied—satisfied for now, anyway—click File, then Close. Yes, you want to save changes. There. That's it. You now have a completely customized ShowAll, ready to work for you, the way you want it to.

MI CASA ES SU CASA

> Be bright and jovial among your guests.
>
> William Shakespeare
> *Macbeth*, 1605

When I'm feeling quite contrary, which is the most common state of affairs, I grab the standard Toolbar by the corner and drag it around so it sits on the left side of my screen. That's a rather unnatural position at first, but I've come to like it. The buttons change around a bit—for example, the Zoom button changes from a number with a down-arrow to a magnifying glass and the multilevel Undo reverts to one at a time (I consider both to be bugs)—and the text buttons read sideways, but I tend to look at the world a bit cockeyed anyway.

Placing the standard Toolbar on the left side of the screen frees up one or two more lines for text at the bottom of the page, at the expense of a little bit of white space on the left that I rarely use anyway. Most often, my WinWord home looks like Figure 2.9.

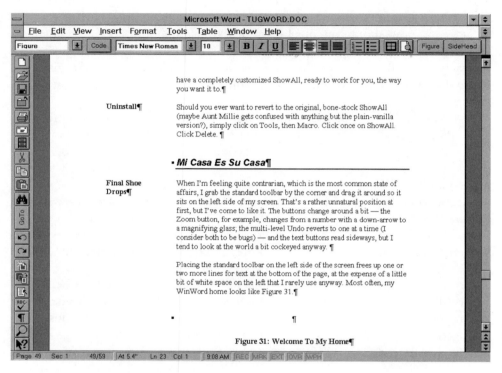

Figure 2.9 Welcome To My Home

Did you notice the last three buttons on my formatting Toolbar? Huh? Sharp eyes, pilgrim. That's where I stick all the handy, quickie macros that I knock out to keep my documents rolling. As you become more adept at macros, you'll be doing much the same thing.

You've seen how macros can make WinWord work better, work faster. The Underground ShowAll, for example, condenses eight or ten common mouse clicks into one pop at the Toolbar. Every time I use the new Show All button, I save at least 15 or 20 seconds—a total of 10 or 15 minutes for me on an average day.

This is a sidehead. I wrote three macros to make producing this book (and the other *Underground Guide*s) easier and faster. The first one, with the magnifying glass on the button, retrieves the {field} code behind anything I've selected, not unlike clicking the new Underground Show All button twice and looking real quick in between clicks to see what's there. The Figure button inserts a figure and prompts for a caption. The SideHead button inserts a sidehead. We'll look at all three of those macros in Chapter 6.

TOOLS OPTIONS SETTINGS

> He who has a choice has trouble.
>
> Dutch Proverb

We've turned around the Toolbar. Why stop there?

WinWord ships with a handful of other "defaults" that drive me nuts. You may agree, you may disagree, but I urge you to spend a few minutes thinking about each of them.

Tools/Options/General

Click on Tools, then Options, and bring the General filecard up to the top. (See Figure 2.10.)

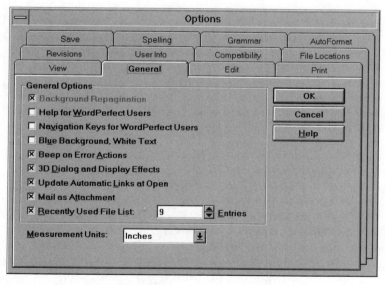

Figure 2.10 PFC Options Reporting for Duty, *Suh!*

I keep the Background Repagination box checked (and it's always checked if you're in Page View) because I like to keep close tabs on how my documents are bloating. If you usually run in Normal View, commonly work with long documents,

Background Repagination

and/or find yourself twiddling your thumbs waiting for WinWord to "come back," you might want to consider turning this box off.

Recently Used File List   I also crank the Recently Used File List—the number of files that appear at the bottom of the File menu—up as high as it goes. There's nothing to lose, no performance hit that I'm aware of, and everything to gain by putting as many file names there on the menu as you can.

Tools/Options/Edit

> Give a sop to Cerberus.
>
> Ancient Greek saying

Far as I'm concerned, Microsoft really screwed up the standard Tools/Options/Edit settings. (See Figure 2.11.)

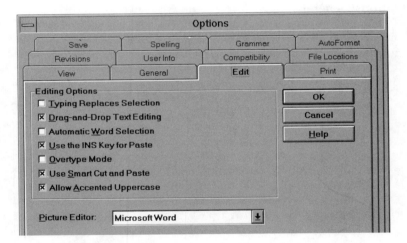

Figure 2.11 Edit Options

Typing Replaces Selection   One of my pet peeves, going way back to WinWord 1.0, is its slavish adherence to a select subset of Windows conventions. Such is the Typing Replaces Selection box you see here in Figure 2.11.

When you highlight some text with the mouse and then type on the keyboard, one of two things can happen: either WinWord can immediately wipe out the highlighted item, and replace it with the character you typed, or WinWord can hop to the beginning of the highlighted item and put the typed character there. If this Typing Replaces Selection box is checked, WinWord wipes out the highlighted item; if it is not checked, WinWord leaves the highlighted item alone.

When WinWord installs itself, it checks this box. That makes it behave like Windows Write: the first character you type replaces whatever is selected. I don't like the way Windows Write works. I hate to see my carefully constructed sentences disappear in a puff of smoke just because I got sloppy with the mouse. So I uncheck this box and recommend that you do, too. In fact, immediately after I install WinWord for other folks, the very first thing I do is uncheck this box. It bugs me that much.

Drag 'n Drop text editing is wonderful. You can highlight text and either drag it to a new location or, by holding down the Control key, copy it to wherever you like. It's a real time saver.

Drag 'n Drop

The only problem I have with Drag 'n Drop is getting WinWord to slow down as it scrolls. (I'll bet you never expected me to say WinWord is too fast! Don't tell the folks in Redmond; it'd ruin my reputation.)

This Automatic Word Selection setting drives me bananas. Let me show you why. Crank up WinWord, make sure that the Automatic Word Selection box is checked, and type this sentence:

Automatic Word Selection

"Yes, we have no bananas!"

Now, using the mouse, make *bananas!* italic. Guess what? With this box checked, you can't do it! WinWord won't let you select *bananas!* without picking up the final double quote. No way, no how. Bizarre. This is just one manifestation of Automatic Word Selection stupidity. Play with it a bit, and you'll find many other frustrating permutations.

Yeah, yeah, yeah. The reviewers loved it. If you read some of the major reviews, you probably expected Automatic Word Selection to be a major step forward. Well, all I can conclude is that the reviewers didn't use it for more than a day, or try to select *bananas!* I hate it when computer programs think they're smarter than I am. Whoever made this Automatic Word Selection the default choice obviously didn't work with it—although I'm sure it makes for a great demo. I say two thumbs down to this bit of IntelliNONsense, and uncheck the box.

The Use INS Key for Paste check box, to me, is a great way to overcome one of my most common typing mistakes. Day after day I reach for the Home, Delete, or End key and accidentally push the Insert key. When I start typing, WinWord goes into Overtype mode, with new characters replacing existing ones one by one by one. If I type fast and don't pay attention (an all too frequent combination), I can wipe out entire paragraphs, figures, all sorts of things, in nothing flat. Bleccch.

Use INS Key for Paste

Since I can never remember the Windows key combinations for copy, cut, and paste, this is a neat alternative. Having "INSERT" in big letters on top of a key is a somewhat … subtle … reminder of what the key actually does. So I check this box, not only for what it enables (that is, it lets me use the Insert key to insert), but also for what it disables—that bloody Overtype mode.

Overtype mode   Speaking of which, you probably guessed that I don't put WinWord into permanent Overtype mode, eh? Checking this box would send me directly to the Seventh Ring of Writer's Hell and no doubt would provide the sop as I entered the Gates.

Smart Cut and Paste   Smart Cut and Paste is, to my mind, a matter of taste. The concept is great: click this box and WinWord will take care of extra spaces and missing spaces when you cut, paste, move, or copy text.

A friend of mine calls this setting "Dumb Cut and Paste." He has a point. If you select the last word in a sentence and hit the Delete key to delete it, WinWord closes in the space that came just before the selected word, even though that space wasn't selected. It's a bit eerie. Personally, I've gotten used to it and leave the Smart Cut and Paste box turned on.

I've only heard of the Allow Accented Uppercase setting in action on paragraphs that are formatted with a Language setting of French. If this box is checked and you hit SHIFT+F3 to change the case of words, WinWord supposedly asks if you want to put accents on the initial uppercase letter where WinWord figures is appropriate. I've heard that "standard" French doesn't permit accents on initial caps, but I don't like to have the accents zapped as I cycle through. So I check the box. Sacré bleu!

Tools/Options/User Info

> Know thyself.
>
> Inscription
> Apollo Temple, Delphi, ca. 600 BC

The Tools/Options/User Info box keeps track of your name. (See Figure 2.12.)

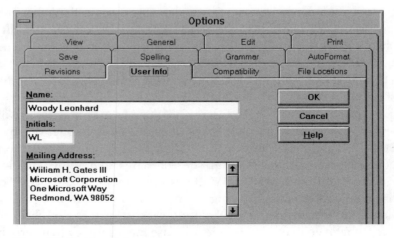

Figure 2.12 User Info

It's important that you take a quick look at the User Info tab to make sure WinWord got your name right. WinWord uses the Name here to automatically fill in the Author's Name field in the document info part of each file you create.

Initials are used for annotations. If you've played with annotations (click on Insert, then Annotation), you've seen how the initials here get stuck in the document to identify who made what annotations.

Initials for annotations

The mailing address is used as a return address when you create an envelope. You may as well get it right, even if you use an add-on envelope printer.

Mailing address

Tools/Options/File Locations

> So the Path and its mystery waits
> In the world of material things:
> The good man's treasure,
> The bad man's refuge.
>
> Lao-tzu
> *Tao Te Ching,* ca. 250 BC

These file locations are established when you install WinWord. With one exception, you'll probably rarely play with them. That one exception is the location of AutoSave files. (See Figure 2.13.)

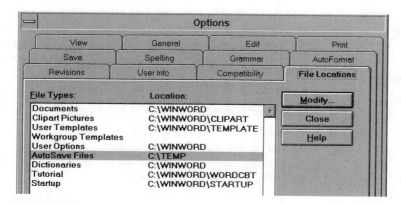

Figure 2.13 File Locations

Unless you do something to change it, WinWord automatically saves a backup copy of your files every ten minutes. The backup copy, a file with an extension of `.ASD`, can really come in handy if WinWord crashes—an all-to-frequent occurrence, in my experience. WinWord has to stick those AutoSave files somewhere, and this is where you pick the location of your safety net.

AutoSave

Bone-stock WinWord doesn't put a file name in this entry. When no specific file name is listed here on the File Locations card, WinWord sticks your `.ASD` AutoSave files in the Windows temporary directory.

What's the **Windows temporary directory**? Good question. It's the location specified by the `TEMP=` variable in your DOS environment string. Translating to plain English, if you look through your `AUTOEXEC.BAT`, you'll probably find a line that looks like this:

```
set temp=e:\somethin
```

That's the location I'm talking about, the directory on the right side of the equals sign. Every time WinWord starts, it checks to see if that directory contains any `.ASD` files. If it does, WinWord sets in motion an intricate recovery procedure.

Unfortunately the Windows temporary directory is a lousy place to put AutoSave files. Many folks point the TEMP= variable to a RAM disk, hoping to speed processing. (In fact, it doesn't; see Chapter 8 of *The Mother of All Windows Books* for a discussion of what's going on, but that's another story.) A RAM disk can be very fragile, particularly if your machine freezes so badly that you have to reboot to get WinWord going again. The entire contents of the RAM disk will be wiped out, taking your AutoSave backup along with it.

I strongly recommend that you take a few seconds right now and change this AutoSave Files location to point to a hard disk. You don't want your AutoSave files on anything but a hard disk, the faster the better. To change the location, just double-click on AutoSave Files and navigate WinWord to any valid subdirectory.

Other Tools/ Options

I leave the Print, Revisions, Compatibility, Spelling, Grammar, and AutoFormat tabs under Tools/Options as they come standard when WinWord installs itself.

I also leave the Save tab under Tools/Options as it stands, but you may want to take a hard look at those settings. In particular, Fast Saves are nice. WinWord only saves changes made to a document, which speeds up processing times. However, Fast Saves, since they contain a "base" document and any changes made to that document, can lead to very large files.

I leave the AutoSave time at ten minutes, but there are very good reasons to disable AutoSave entirely. Among other things, WinWord performs AutoSaves even when it's turned into an icon. Since AutoSaves tend to take hold of the machine and not let go, the sporadic, drastic decrease in processing speed—particularly when you aren't working with WinWord—can be a real pain.

TOOLS AUTOCORRECT

How much easier it is to be critical than to be correct.
Benjamin Disraeli

No discussion of WinWord's options could be complete without a close examination of the AutoCorrect settings. Click on Tools and then AutoCorrect and you'll see something like Figure 2.14. I leave the settings as they are, but then I hack at them in different ways to make them work the way I want them to. Let me explain.

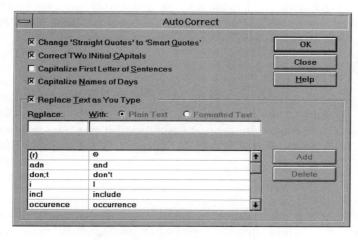

Figure 2.14 Da Brains of da AutoCorrect Operation

Straight and Curly Quotes

I really like WinWord's ability to change "straight quotes" into "curly" or "publisher's quotes." It adds immensely to the legibility of documents, gives them a kind of polish that's almost subliminal. Curly quotes have two downsides, though.

First, WinWord insists upon changing my apostrophes (') into open single curly quotes ('). Apostrophes are great; I use 'em all the time. But I almost never use open single curly quotes ('), and I'll bet you don't either, unless you're a novelist who specializes in convoluted dialog. **Apostrophes rule**

Well, there's a little trick that lets you have your curlies and apostrophes, too. It involves a tiny macro <*shudder*>, and it's discussed later in this chapter in the section titled Apoplectic Apostrophes.

Second, when WinWord converts a document to straight text—what computer jocks call ASCII—it forgets to convert the curly quotes back to straight **ASCII drools** quotes. Once in a blue moon you might actually want your curly quotes to make their way into an ASCII text file, but most of the time those oddball characters only get in the way.

Alas, I'm not aware of any simple workaround to this problem. Somebody *could* write a macro to do it, but to do things right, the macro would have to convert bullets and dashes and all sorts of odd characters, then hook into the ASCII Text save options ... and I don't know of anyone who's tackled it yet.

If you've avoided Smart Quotes in the past because you need your apostrophes, you no longer have reason to fear. I'll show you how to reclaim your apostrophes in a minute. On the other hand, if you commonly write documents in WinWord that dumb ASCII text editors must read, you may want to leave the Smart Quotes box unchecked.

Correct TWo INitial CApitals

> Books are fatal; they are the curse of the human race. Nine-tenths of existing books are nonsense, and the clever books are the refutation of that nonsense. The greatest misfortune that ever befell man was the invention of printing.
>
> Benjamin Disraeli
> *Lothair*, 1870

Why can't I type XTree? I often type two initial caps. It's a bad habit that stems, I believe, from my misspent youth, when I learned to type by banging on an old manual typewriter. I double them up often enough that this setting saves me a lot of work.

I leave the Tools/AutoCorrect setting to Correct TWo INitial CApitals turned on, as in Figure 2.14. It's very handy, except ... some words are *supposed* to have their first two letters capitalized. There's PCuser and XTree and CDs and XWindows and PCjr and all sorts of PC-things. I hit this problem when trying to write about the Hacker's UNguided Tour of Asia and WOPR's TBedit. You can probably think of a few valid pairs of initial caps right off the top of your head; if you're in the PC biz, the list could be quite long.

Unfortunately there's no built-in way to tell WinWord to ignore words that should have two initial caps. Fortunately there's a trick. Like many other cool WinWord tricks, it involves IntelliNONsense and selectively disabling—or, more correctly, hacking around—its limitations.

I was tempted to turn off the Correct TWo INitial CApitals setting just because it was so dadblamed infuriating to have to go back and change the correct double caps to what they should be. That really bothered me, though, because I often type doubled-up caps, and the setting really could come in handy if it would just ignore the words that *I* want it to.

The INitial CAp trick uses AutoCorrect entries to bypass WinWord's TWo INitial CAps scanning. Take XTree, for example. Click on Tools, then AutoCorrect. Type in xtree (no caps), hit Tab, and type in XTree (two initial caps). Click Add. Click OK.

That's the whole trick, right there. Now, no matter what your Correct TWo INitial CApitals setting, WinWord will leave XTree alone. As a little lagniappe, it'll also correct xtree and Xtree to XTree.

You can do the same thing for any word that should have two initial caps. Just put the lowercase-only version on the left and the initial caps version on the right. I have no idea *why* this works, but it does. Neat, huh?

Capitalize First Letter of Sentences

> A sentence is a word or set of words followed by a pause and revealing an intelligible purpose.
>
> A. H. Gardiner
> *Theory of Speech and Language,* 1933

The Captialize First Letter of Sentences setting is a joke. It's only in here for the demo version of WinWord; it's only present to impress the reviewers. People who write real documents will tear their hair out if they leave this setting on for more than an hour. Why? Because WinWord couldn't tell the first letter of a sentence if MSFT's stock depended on it! Consider:

Earlier today Microsoft Corp. Officials denied any wrongdoing.

See how the "O" in "Officials" is capitalized?

If you have the Capitalize First Letter of Sentences box checked, WinWord looks to see if you've typed a period or exclamation point, followed by a space. If so, the WinGods light up: this must be the beginning of a sentence! The next letter is automatically capitalized. Something this squirrelly should not be an option.

(Actually, this incarnation of IntelliNONsense is a little more sophisticated than first appears. You can have a period, followed by a quotation mark, followed by a space, and WinWord picks that up as the end of a sentence, too. Same for paragraph marks. All together now: Oooooooh. Aaaaaaaaah.)

As the preceding cap "O" in "Officials" so amply demonstrates, a period followed by a space is not synonymous with "end of sentence" in many situations. This bogus setting will only cause you grief. Keep the box unchecked.

AutoCorrect Entries

> An expert is a man who has made all the mistakes which can be made, in a given field.
>
> Niels Bohr

WinWord comes with a handful of excellent AutoCorrect entries, a few dozen glaring omissions, and at least one entry that doesn't belong there at all. Follow along and we'll straighten things up.

First, get rid of the one that doesn't belong there. In many situations you'll want to type "incl" or "incl." presumably meaning "inclusive." WinWord's abject insistence on changing those to "include" defies logic. Click on the line that says

incl   include

then click Delete. Another blow for your freedom.

Your abbreviations   Second, though, you can and should add entries to this list with wild abandon. I haven't detected any performance penalty, at least nothing worse than the usual WinWord 6.0 speed blues, even with a list several hundred items long. See Table 2.1 (on the following page) for a list of some of my favorites.

Ken Deifik, L.E. Brown, and Tom Griffiths created a gigantic collection of hundreds of AutoCorrect entries and posted them on CompuServe (see Chapter 10); they install with a single mouse click. That list alone will pay for your CompuServe membership, several times over. Look in the GO MSWORD forum for TYPOS.ZIP.

For each entry, type the left-hand text in the Tools/AutoCorrect's left Replace box, then tab over and type the right-hand text in the right With box, and click Add.

Perhaps surprisingly, the widnows/Windows entry corrects both "widnows" and "Widnows" to "Windows." Capitalization replacement rules in these entries are a bit complex.

Symbol shortcuts   Perhaps most importantly, you should stick a whole bunch of symbol shortcuts into the list. Symbol shortcuts are those character combinations that don't appear on the keyboard and require a hunt-and-peck through Insert Symbol land to put in a document. WinWord already comes with (r) hooked up to turn into a Registered ® symbol. That's great, but there are many more to consider.

Start by making sure NumLock is on—with most keyboards, a little light marked NumLock glows whenever NumLock is turned on. You may have to push the NumLock key, which is often on the number pad, way over on the right. Every keyboard is different, so you may have to hunt around a bit.

Then, for each of these entries, type the left-hand text (marked Shortcut in Table 2.2 on the following page) in the left Replace box and tab over to the Replace

Table 2.1 A Few Suggested AutoCorrect Entries

Incorrect	Correct	Incorrect	Correct	Incorrect	Correct
adn	and	jsut	just	thta	that
ahd	had	liek	like	ti	it
ahve	have	mena	mean	tihs	this
amd	and	mkae	make	tje	the
becasue	because	nad	and	tjhe	the
becuase	because	nwo	now	toi	to
cds	CDs	ot	to	tp	to
coudl	could	pcs	PCs	tyhe	the
eb	be	rae	are	tyo	to
eh	he	sa	as	tyr	try
ehr	her	ta	at	waht	what
fi	if	tahn	than	watn	want
fo	of	taht	that	wehn	when
fro	for	tath	that	whta	what
godo	good	teh	the	wiht	with
haev	have	tehy	they	widnows	Windows
hda	had	theri	their	wnat	want
hre	her	thge	the	woh	who
hsa	has	thier	their	wsa	was
hsi	his	thna	than	wtih	with
hte	the	thne	then	ww6	WinWord 6.0
ihs	his	thsi	this	yuo	you

Table 2.2 My Favorite Symbol Shortcuts

Symbol	Shortcut	ALT +
©	(c)	0169
™	(tm)	0153
¢	c/	0162
£	L=	0163
¥	Y=	0165
§	(ss)	0167
$1/4$	1/4	0188
$1/2$	1/2	0189
$3/4$	3/4	0190
÷	./.	0247
«	<<	0171
»	>>	0187

box. Make sure that the NumLock light is on, hold down the Alternate key (which may be marked Alt on your keyboard), type the numbers you'll find in the right-hand column using the numbers on the number pad, release the Alternate key, and click Add.

For example, to tell WinWord that it should turn any (c) you type into the © copyright symbol, type (c) in the dialog's Replace box, tab over to the With box, hold down the Alternate key, type 0169 on the number pad, release the Alternate key, and click Add. It ain't as tough as it sounds.

If you'd like to use a different shortcut key combination, by all means help yourself!

The number in the final column here, the ALT+ character number, may be a bit confusing, but don't let it worry you. Every character has a number. The letter "a" for example is character number 97; "b" is number 98; "¹/₄" is 188; and so on. By going through these NumLock ALT+ shenanigans, you're just telling WinWord very explicitly which character you want to go into your documents.

WinWord vs. WordPerfect

As far as I'm concerned, judicious use of the AutoCorrect feature in this way, to create your own Symbol Shortcuts, makes WinWord's touch-typist symbol feature every bit as useful as WordPerfect's. Better, in some respects.

More AutoCorrect

Personally, I put a few formatted entries into AutoCorrect: a.m. becomes AM; p.m. becomes PM; a.d. becomes AD and b.c. becomes BC. (The latter are all formatted with a Small Caps font.) My company and product names go in there.

Here's the fast way to insert formatted entries. First, do the formatting in a document somewhere. Then select the formatted text—the "result" text—and only then click on Tools, then AutoCorrect…. Make sure that the Formatted Text button is checked, and you're off.

You must remain ever vigilant in your pursuit of AutoCorrect entries. I screw them up all the time. For a few minutes I had a plain "am" hooked up to become AM. I AM embarrassed to say that it took as long as it did to discover.

Finally, you'll probably want to add the em-dash to your AutoCorrect collection, and therein lies a story.

WHERE'S THE EM-DASH?

> Who'er writ it writes a hand like a foot.
>
> Jonathan Swift
> *Polite Conversation*, 1738

This is where I start splitting hairs. If you aren't overly concerned about the appearance of your documents, these suggestions won't make much sense to you, and you can safely ignore them. If you don't know a hyphen (-) from an em-dash (—), couldn't care less about the direction your apostrophes (') and curly quotes

(") break, and don't really want to spend time worrying about the difference, you can skip on down to the Styles and Class section. I won't mind. Really. On the other hand, if you're picky—and I think you should be!—these little touches can be implemented easily, and you can use them with minimal fuss.

A little hidden agenda is floating around here. Pursuit of the perfect em-dash and curly quote actually involves quite a few nooks and crannies of WinWord that can be mighty important, little things that just might save your tail-end some dark and stormy night. You might want to follow along here just to see some of the strange contortions you have to go through to customize WinWord. Although you may not want to make these precise changes, you might find the general exposure useful sometime in the future.

The Many Faces of Em

> Even where the sense is perfectly clear, a sentence may be deprived of half its force—its spirit—its point—by improper punctuation.
>
> Edgar Allen Poe
> *Marginalia*, 1845

I use the em-dash—the extra-wide dash—all the time. Taking away my em-dash would mute my writing style as surely as cutting off my arms would change the way I talk. WinWord has several built-in ways to insert an em-dash quickly and easily, but I don't like any of them.

Part of the problem lies in how you (or your editor!) want to handle the spaces before and after the em-dash itself. I've seen three different approaches. (See Figure 2.15.)

The em-dash—with no intervening space.¶
The em-dash — with full intervening space.¶
The em-dash—with teensy-tiny intervening space.¶

Figure 2.15 Three Em-Dash Treatments

I don't like the first approach—the one with no space before or after the dash itself—because it squishes the text together too much. Besides, without a space tucked in there, WinWord refuses to break a line before or after the em-dash.

The second approach — where a full, normal space precedes and follows the dash — confuses me, visually, especially when lines are fully justified and the width of the space expands to fill the available room. Given a choice, I'd pick this full-space method over the earlier, no-space method — at least lines can break before or after the dash. (See how I did that? Heh, heh, heh. The fingers never leave the hands.) — but it still doesn't look as good as the teensy-tiny space.

The teensy-tiny space approach puts a regular space before and after the em-dash, but those spaces are squished down to, oh, say, 6 points, instead of the usual 11 (or 10 or 12). To my mind, this is the best of possible worlds—there's some breathing room around the dash, WinWord can break on the dash, but when WinWord sticks extra room around the dash to right-justify a line, the amount of room is minimized.

The No Space Em-Dash

If the first "no space em-dash" approach is good enough for you, WinWord is already set up to treat the key combination of CTRL + ALT + the minus key on the number pad as an em-dash. (The minus key on the number pad is probably wayyyyyyy over on the right side of your keyboard.)

Quick key combination for the no space em-dash

If you don't want to press three keys to get a single em-dash, you can click on Tools, then Customize, and bring up the Keyboard filecard (see Figure 2.16), making sure that NORMAL.DOT shows in the Save Changes In box. Then scroll down to Common Symbols on the left and highlight Em-Dash on the right.

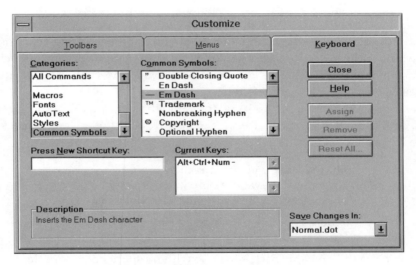

Figure 2.16 Em-Dashiel Hammett on Keyboard

Now here's the really screwy thing. As far as I'm concerned it's a bug. Since the Press New Shortcut Key: label is sitting there ready for action—it isn't grayed or anything—you might expect that you could simply press a new shortcut key or key combination for the em-dash. But, *nooooooooooooo....* The WordGods have determined that you must first click somewhere in that Press New Shortcut Key: box before pressing the new shortcut key. Very strange.

Anyway, once you see how it works, it isn't too bad, as long as you remember not to do what this dialog tells you to do. Say you want to turn CTRL + the hyphen key into an em-dash. (The hyphen key is the minus sign up on the top of the keyboard, right next to the zero. CTRL + hyphen is preordained to be the Optional Hyphen, which I use about once every other decade, so, for me anyway, it's a good candidate for an em-dash.) Here's how you do it, starting at the beginning:

Em-Dash as CTRL+hyphen

1. Click on Tools, then Customize, bring the Keyboard filecard to the top, and make sure that NORMAL.DOT is listed under Save Changes In.

2. On the left, scroll down to Common Symbols. On the right, click Em-Dash. Then click inside the Press New Shortcut Key: box.

3. Press the key combination that you want to establish as the em-dash. In this case, hold down CTRL, and press the hyphen key, which is the minus sign next to the zero on the top of your keyboard.

4. WinWord warns you that this key combination is already assigned to the Optional Hyphen. If you couldn't care less about a quick key combination for the Optional Hyphen, click Assign, then Close.

That's it. From that point on, you will always be able to put an em-dash in your documents by holding down CTRL and hitting the hyphen. It's not a great improvement over CTRL + ALT + the minus key on the number pad, but it's a step in the right direction.

The Full Space Em-Dash

If you like the second style of em-dash, the one with a regular space before the em-dash and another one after the em-dash, there's a much quicker way to go. You're probably already accustomed to typing two hyphens for an em-dash. Certainly if you started your typing career with a real bang-on-the-keys type-writer, you've used the two-hyphen substitute for an em-dash countless times.

Using WinWord's AutoCorrect, you can continue to use two hyphens for the em-dash, providing you don't mind having a space before and another space after the em-dash. It's easy, with AutoCorrect:

Quick key combination for the full space Em-Dash

1. Click on Tools, then AutoCorrect. Your cursor should automatically pop up in the Replace: box. (See Figure 2.17)

2. Type two hyphens (that is, push the minus key, the key next to the zero at the top of your keyboard, twice). Then hit the Tab to jump over to the With: box.

3. Make sure that you have NumLock turned on; usually there's a light on your keyboard marked NumLock. You may need to push the NumLock key.

4. Hold down the Alternate key, then, *using the numbers on the number pad*, type 0151 (that's zero, one, five, one), and let go of the Alternate key. You should see an em-dash in the With: box.

5. Click Add and you're done.

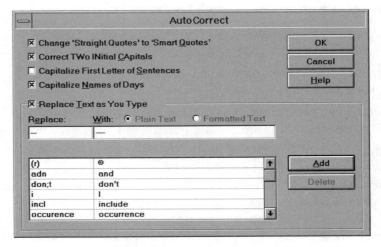

Figure 2.17 Two Hyphens Become an Em-Dash

Hyphens to 151   From this point on, every time you type a space, two hyphens, and another space, WinWord's AutoCorrect will jump in and change that into a space, an em-dash, and another space. Internally WinWord is using AutoCorrect to convert each pair of hyphens into character number 151, which just happens to be the em-dash. The spaces come along for the ride, as a fallout of how AutoCorrect works anyway. Magic.

Far as I'm concerned, the number-one benefit of AutoCorrect is changing "teh" to "the", and the number-two benefit is changing "- -" to "— ". Those may be the two most powerful reasons for using WinWord 6.0 on a daily basis. They're the two things I miss most when I have to forgo the use of my beloved WinWord for a dumb text editor. It's amazing how much time I save with those two simple AutoCorrect entries.

The Teensy-Tiny Space Em-Dash

> He who can take no interest in what is small
> will take false interest in what is great.
>
> John Ruskin
> *Modern Painters*, 1846

The very best em-dash, the one with teensy-tiny spaces before and after, involves writing another *<shudder!>* macro. But it's so easy you can do it in a couple of minutes.

Start by clicking on Tools, then Macro. Make sure that NORMAL.DOT is in the Macros Available In box. Type in an interesting name—I use InsertEmDash—and click Create. (See Figure 2.18)

Quick key combination for the teensy-tiny space Em-Dash

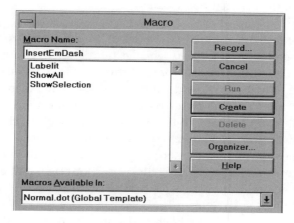

Figure 2.18 Insert Em-Dash Macro

WordBasic automatically provides the first and last lines of your new macro, Sub MAIN and End Sub. You need only fill in the guts, which look like this:

```
CurrPoints = FontSize()
FontSize 6
Insert " "
FontSize CurrPoints
Insert Chr$(151)
FontSize 6
Insert " "
FontSize CurrPoints
```

InsertEmDash macro

The macro is pretty simple, if you can put up with the funny language. Translating it line by line into English, we have:

1. Remember the current point size; put it in a variable called CurrPoints (I made up that name, it could've been almost anything).

2. Switch to 6 point.

3. Stick a space in the document.

4. Switch back to the original point size.

5. Stick an em-dash, character number 151, in the document.

6. Switch to 6 point.

7. Stick another space in the document.

8. Switch back to the original point size.

Sheeesh. Who says macros are hard to write? We'll pick back up on this macro in Chapter 6 and add a few bells and whistles (and maneuver our way around a couple more bugs in WinWord), but for now this is entirely usable.

Using InsertEmDash

You might want to start a new document (click on File, then New) and play with the macro a bit. Click the right-wedgie "Play" button (see Figure 2.7) and make sure that it's running right. When you're happy with it, click on File, then Close. Yes, you want to save changes to NORMAL.DOT.

Finally, you need to make the macro easy to get at. It wouldn't be much use if you had to click on Tools, then Macro, click InsertEmDash, and click Run every time you wanted an em-dash, would it?

Personally, I'd like to have InsertEmDash run every time I hit the minus key on my number pad. I rarely use my keyboard's number pad, and I'll bet you're the same way. I never use the number pad's minus key while I'm working with WinWord, so the number pad's minus key is a great choice for the em-dash. Besides, on my keyboard there's a big, fat, loooooong dash on that minus key, and it *looks* like an em-dash.

If life were easy and WinWord were flexible (and wishes were horses and beggars did ride), it would only take a couple of mouse clicks to "assign" the InsertEmDash macro to the number pad's minus key. Alas, life is not so simple out here on the bleeding edge. If you try the usual method of assigning keys to macros — click on Tools, then Customize, and bring the Keyboard filecard to the top (as we did earlier, in Figure 2.16) — and then you try pushing the number pad's minus key, you'll find that WinWord doesn't respond. It doesn't realize that you want to change the function of the num pad minus key. (Indeed, there are *thousands* of key combinations that WinWord won't let you change!)

Well, you can *force* WinWord to run InsertEmDash every time you push the number pad's minus key, but it ain't pretty. So grab your thirty-ought, pilgrim; we're gonna shoot some bar…

As is so often the case, the way to take your word processing destiny into your own hands, the way around WinWord's manifest shortcomings, is through

WordBasic. If WinWord won't do it, more often than not you can write a macro and do it yourself. I call it up-yours word processing.

> **If you bypass WinWord's built-in key-assigning capability and write your own macro, you can assign *any* key to do *anything*. Type the letter "z" and WinWord could, oh, open a file. Hit the Tab key and you could send a form letter to WinWord's creators, complaining about the bugs. The Page Up key could print the envelope. And on and on. Any key can do anything. That's a phenomenally powerful capability. It's inherent to WinWord, designed into it from day one. But WinWord's designers go to great lengths to make it hard for you to take advantage of the capability.**

In this case, we want to "assign" the macro InsertEmDash to the number pad's minus key. Ends up that's a one-liner in WordBasic, *even though it's impossible using WinWord's built-in menus*. Here's how:

1. Click on Tools, then Macro. (It doesn't matter what's showing in the Macros Available In box.)

2. Type something (I use temp because I won't be saving this macro anyway. I just want to run it once.)

3. Click Create.

4. Type in this one line:

```
ToolsCustomizeKeyboard 109, .Name = "InsertEmDash"
```

5. Click the right-wedgie button to run the macro.

6. That's it. You're done. Since you won't need this macro again, just click File, then Close. No, you don't want to save changes.

That one-liner says, "Yo! WinWord! Assign key number 109 to the InsertEmDash macro!" If you run the macro, it changes WinWord so that, from that point on, any time you push key number 109, it runs InsertEmDash.

Back when we looked at Symbol Shortcuts, I talked about character numbers: the character "a" is number 97, a "b" is 98, and so on. Well, this being the computer biz, keys on the keyboards have numbers, too, and the keyboard numbers are different from the character numbers. (Whaddya think this would be, logical?) For example, the "a" key on the keyboard is number 65.

Character numbers vs. keyboard numbers

It just so happens that key number 109 is the number pad's minus key. You can verify that by pushing F1 while your cursor is sitting on that line of the macro and scanning down the list of keys and their numbers.

Unless you tell WinWord otherwise, the key assignment is stored in NORMAL.DOT, so it's always in effect. That's precisely what you want.

Admittedly this is a bit convoluted. You just wrote a macro that inserts an em-dash. Then you had to run *another* macro—a throw-away macro that you used only once—to get the em-dash macro connected to the number pad's minus key. Unfortunately you're going to find that WinWord's limitations will force you to do equally convoluted things over and over again in many guises and many variations. The power is there, but it's buried deep. Very deep.

Which Em Is Best?

> Twa gudes seldome meet—
> what's gude for the plant is ill for the peat
>
> Scottish Proverb

Which of the three em-dash methods to use? Hey, that's easy. I use all three! On my machine CTRL + hyphen is the "no space" em-dash, space+hyphen+hyphen+space is the automagic "full space" em-dash, and the number pad's minus key is the "teensy-tiny space" em-dash. Why not?

APOPLECTIC APOSTROPHES

Apostrophes are another one of my pet peeves, right up there with intransigent em-dashes. I'll bet it bugs you, too.

Sorta-SmartQuote

Straight 'n curly   WinWord's Smart Quotes are mighty cool. I love being able to type a straight "double quote" on the keyboard and have WinWord automatically convert it to the correct gender, curling left or right as the occasion dictates. WinWord handles double quotes nicely, and when it comes to double quotes, WinWord's Smart Quotes are, indeed, Smart.

Not so for single quotes. Call them what you like—apostrophes, hash marks, publisher's quotes, or curly single quotes—I think WinWord botches 'em.

If you nest quotes—I said, "ChrisP said, 'You do not.'"—WinWord's Smart Quotes are just what you need. Surely ten of WinWord's 3 million users nest quotes all the time. Maybe twenty. But almost all the rest of us use apostrophes (Microsoft calls them Single Closing Quotes) much more often than the single open quote, whether it's for contractions or substandard use o' the mother tongue, or even dates such as '94. I mean, in WinWord 6.0, you can't even write Drag 'n' Drop without resorting to some high jinks. Strange.

How it works   With SmartQuotes turned on, WinWord watches while you type. If you hit the apostrophe key (next to the semicolon), WinWord looks to see if the immediately preceding character is a space or one of the special characters shown in Figure 2.19.

({ [> <

Figure 2.19 The Opening Curlers

If the immediately preceding character is a space or one of these opening curlers, a tab, or a paragraph mark, WinWord curls the apostrophe or quote so that it's "opening." If the preceding character is anything else, WinWord curls it so it closes.

Look closely at your monitor while you're typing; you may even see the hesitation as the quote curls. (Sounds like a soap opera, eh?)

WinWord has a built-in key combination for the apostrophe. Here's how you are supposed to get the apostrophe: hold down CTRL, hit the apostrophe, let go of CTRL, then hit the apostrophe again. That's a lot of effort for something so simple.

InsertApostrophe

The solution to the apostrophe catastrophe? A macro, of course! You had any doubt?

The InsertApostrophe macro puts a curly apostrophe—which just happens to be character number 146—in your document. It's a Henny Youngman.

1. Click Tools, then Macro. Make sure that Macros Available In shows NORMAL.DOT (Global template).

2. Type InsertApostrophe or something equally erudite.

3. Click Create. Note the Sub MAIN and End Sub in passing.

4. Type in one line, the middle one:

```
Sub MAIN
Insert Chr$(146)
End Sub
```

5. Click on File, then Close. Yes, you want to save changes to InsertApostrophe.

Now all you need to do is hook InsertApostrophe up so that it runs whenever you push the apostrophe key, bypassing WinWord's Sorta-SmartQuotes. This procedure does have one downside: once the apostrophe key is hooked up to run InsertApostrophe, you won't be able to type apostrophes directly into WinWord dialogs. To me, that's a minor annoyance, but you may well feel differently!

Unfortunately WinWord doesn't let you reassign the apostrophe key without jumping through some serious hoops. Just like the number pad's minus key, which we hijacked for the em-dash, WinWord's standard keyboard reassignment dialog won't let you get at the apostrophe key.

The solution? (Stop me if you've heard this one before.) All it takes is another Heny Youngman macro, a simple, throw-away, one-line macro that bypasses WinWord's built-in restrictions.

Click on Tools, then Macro. (Hey, you can do this in your sleep by now, huh?) Type in something, say, temp. Click Create. Between the Sub MAIN and End Sub type this:

```
ToolsCustomizeKeyboard 222, .Name = "InsertApostrophe"
```

The 222 there refers to the apostrophe key on the keyboard. If you put your cursor on this line and hit F1, you'll find number 222 down at the bottom of the list. This one command says, "Yo, WinWord! Every time I type an apostrophe— that is, every time I hit key number 222—I want you to run this here macro, called InsertApostrophe."

Got it? Good. Click the right-wedgie button to run the macro once, and you're done. From this time forward and forever more, whenever you hit the apostrophe key you'll get, *mirabile dictu*, an apostrophe! Yet all the other SmartQuotes functions will remain intact. To clean up after yourself, click File, then Close. No you don't want to save changes.

Manual open single quote On the very, very rare occasion that I really want an open single quote ('), I click on Insert, then Symbol. If my mind weren't so befuddled, I'd probably sit down and memorize the explicit key combination, which is ... hold on, I gotta look this up ... lessseeee ... CTRL + the accent grave (`) (which is under the tilde (~), next to the 1), let go of CTRL, then the accent grave again.

STYLES AND CLASS

I perform one last bunch of customizations on every WinWord installation I encounter. They all have to do with NORMAL.DOT, the template that holds many of your default (or "normal" or "customary" or "preset" or "what you get if you don't change anything") settings.

Your Defaults

You can change the default settings for fonts, styles, paragraphs, page sizes, printer paper sources, and whatnot in several ways. Most often the manuals advise that you use little built-in shortcut keys that tap into NORMAL.DOT (or whichever template is currently active) and change the settings there.

For example, if you click on Format and then Font, the Default... button in that dialog burrows into NORMAL.DOT (or the current template) and changes the default font there (see Figure 2.20).

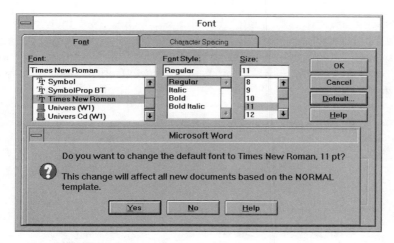

Figure 2.20 Setting Default Font from Format/Fonts

The button in the Style dialog that accomplishes the same thing is called something completely different: Add To Template. It isn't a button, it's a check box. And on and on.

I, for one, don't like all these different shortcut methods. Microsoft was forced to put all those shortcut buttons and check boxes in the dialogs because WinWord users were forever calling the tech support lines saying, "I want to change my default font from 10-point Times New Roman to 11-point bold italic Star Trek NextGen. How do I do that?"

The first 10,000 times people called and asked that question, the techies on the other end of the phone patiently stepped novice users through the steps. But the calls kept piling in. 20,000. 50,000. 100,000 or more callers, all asking the same question. It was just too much. Something had to be done.

Instead of putting a card in every box that explained the (very simple!) method for changing default fonts, styles, paragraphs, and whatnot, Microsoft decided to scatter shortcut buttons and boxes throughout many formatting dialogs. The buttons and boxes make explanations quick and easy, but — in my experience anyway — they tend to confuse folks, and for no good reason. The concept is pretty simple, if explained succinctly.

This is something that cries for a Wizard, but until one arrives on the scene, you'll have to take your destiny into your own hands.

Do It Directly

I strongly recommend that you open the template that you want to change and just bloody well change it. Forget the shortcut buttons, the futzing around. Go straight to the source. Eschew the sugar coating.

I'll talk at length about templates and context and all that techy stuff in Chapter 4, but for now let's get your defaults set so they'll work fer ya, not agin' ya.

Click on File, then Open. Hop down to the \TEMPLATE subdirectory and type NORMAL.DOT. Hit Enter. There. You have the *paterfamilias* staring at you, the *template di tutti templatti.* (See Figure 2.21.) Not very impressive, eh?

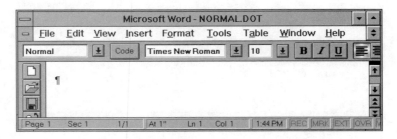

Figure 2.21 NORMAL.DOT au Naturel

Any changes you make at this point will affect new documents you create based on NORMAL.DOT. What you do now will *not* change any existing documents or templates. So don't fret.

Normal's Normal

Click on Format, then Style, then Modify. You want to change the Normal Style in NORMAL.DOT. (See Figure 2.22.)

New default font
If you want to change the default font—say, you're tired of 10-point Times New Roman (who isn't?) and you want to switch so new documents start out with your 11-point Coolatino—click on Format, then Font, and pick the font combination you like most, click OK. Personally, I go with 11-point Garamond, which happens to be one of the fonts my printer gobbles up fastest. So much for the default font.

I also recommend that you seriously consider setting up your standard paragraph formatting so you only have to hit the Enter key once at the end of each paragraph. Blasphemy, eh? Hear me out.

Ever since the dawn of the typewriter age, and well into the PC age, typists like you and me have learned to hit the Enter key twice to end each paragraph. It's more than automatic. It's ingrained, like exhaling once for every inhale, or taking the first stair step with your right foot.

New default paragraph formatting
You really *will* type faster—and, ultimately, formatting will be much more straightforward—if you force yourself to hit the Enter key just once at the end of each paragraph. Yeah, yeah, yeah. I, too, once balked at doing this. And Microsoft still won't put it in as the bone-stock installation default. But it really does work better, faster, more reliably.

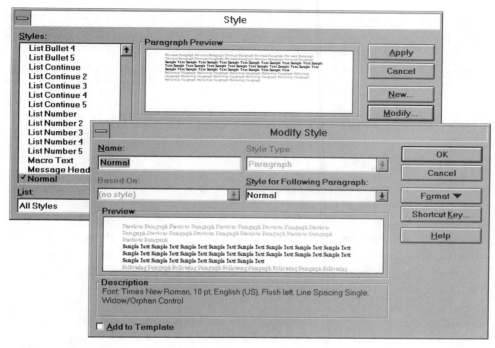

Figure 2.22 Change the Normal Style

I know you don't believe me. You got that look in your eye. So humor me, OK? Try it for a week. Switch things around right here and now so you end each paragraph with a single Enter. That's all I ask. If you try it for a week, I doubt that you'll ever go back. Single enter to end paragraphs really makes a difference.

So you're still in NORMAL.DOT, with the dialogs in Figure 2.22 showing, right? Good. Click Format, then Paragraph. You'll get the standard paragraph formatting rigmarole (see Figure 2.23).

Figure 2.23 12 Points After

In the Spacing box over there on the right, you want the After spacing to read 12 points. By doing so, you're telling WinWord that you want it to skip 12 points (one line) after each paragraph mark.

Click OK a couple of times, then Apply, then File Close to put `NORMAL.DOT` back to bed. There. Your `NORMAL` is now all souped up and ready for action.

BETTER WINWORD THAN WINWORD

Try your own tricks

That's my bag of tricks for converting the demo version of WinWord into the working version. These tricks, while exhausting, are by no means exhaustive, if you know what I mean. Every document you write, every click of the keyboard, offers new opportunities to tweak and fiddle, new avenues to explore.

Yes, you could spend your entire working day playing and twiddling, lavishing your attention on the tool, rather than on the work. Although that may strike some folks as fun—and I've wasted much more than my fair share of working time delving into WinWord's innards, so I'm hardly one to talk!—it can be mighty frustrating, too.

Diminishing returns

Sooner or later, you reach the point of diminishing returns. And that's what I wanted to warn you about. If you find yourself doing the same work day after day, or if you have a dozen people depending on you and they do the same work day after day, it's probably worth it to explore some of WinWord's far-flung capabilities to make that work run faster. You might want to create your own template, or define a new style, or write a macro to help you along.

It rarely pays to customize something you'll only do once or twice, or even once or twice a week. You'll probably spend more time creating a rarely used style, say, than simply formatting things as they come up. That's blasphemy for a "tips" book, but it's the truth.

UNINSTALL

Now that I've taken all these pages to tell you how to customize WinWord, I'm going to do something you've probably never seen before in a computer book. I'm going to show you how to *un*customize the program, how to reverse each of the changes you may have made—changes you may have encountered in this book, or changes you might have made on your own—and bring back the original bone-stock WinWord.

Back to Square One

Sometimes you get WinWord so hopelessly screwed up that you're tempted to throw everything away, and start all over again. Hey, I can relate to that. I've been there many times!

There's a smart way to revert to the bone-stock WinWord, a way that keeps some stuff hanging around, just in case you want to use those neat styles or Toolbars or macros again. Here's how:

1. File/Exit out of WinWord.

2. Go into WinWord's template directory, which is probably called `\WINWORD\TEMPLATE`**.**

3. Rename normal.dot to `NORMAL.OLD`**.**

4. Start WinWord.

There. You're ready to start all over again. WinWord rebuilds `NORMAL.DOT`**, thereby wiping the slate clean, driving out all your customizations, macros, defaults, styles, and on and on.**

Although WinWord settings are floating all over the place — mostly in `WINWORD6.INI`, which should be in your Windows directory, but also in `WIN.INI` and Windows' Registration Database—nearly all the customizations you're bound to worry about are located in `NORMAL.DOT`.

Once you've started out clean and forced WinWord to build a brand-new `NORMAL.DOT`, you can bring back your old styles, AutoText, Toolbars, and Macros. Click on File, then Open, and open `NORMAL.OLD`. Then click on File, then Template, and click the Organizer button. You should see something like Figure 2.24.

Bringing it back, one step at a time

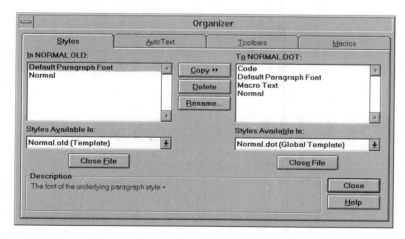

Figure 2.24 Moving `NORMAL.OLD`

Now you can pick and choose, one style, one AutoText entry, or one Toolbar or Macro at a time, selectively moving it in to the virgin `NORMAL.DOT`. Take it slowly and you should be back in good shape in no time.

WINWORD.OPT   If you really want to start afresh, with hardly a vestige of your old installation remaining, rename WINWORD.OPT in your WinWord directory, and that should wipe out just about everything, including all your View and Tools options. Be sure you save a copy of WINWORD.OPT. This draconian measure is only half a step away from deleting WinWord from you disk and starting all over again.

Toolbar Throwback

Resetting individual Toolbars so that they regain that unmistakable demo quality is also very easy. If you make a backup copy of your original Toolbars while you're at it, you even stand a fighting chance of successfully changing your mind in the future.

1. File/Exit out of WinWord.

2. Make a copy of NORMAL.DOT and store it in a safe place. Should you later decide that you really didn't want to revert to the demo version of a certain Toolbar, you can use the preceding Organizer steps to restore your customized version from this backup copy.

3. Start WinWord.

4. Click View, then Toolbar. Your screen should look like Figure 2.25.

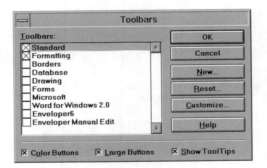

Figure 2.25 Toolbar Torture Rack

5. Highlight the Toolbar you want to revert to its original state, then click Reset. You'll get a box that looks like Figure 2.26.

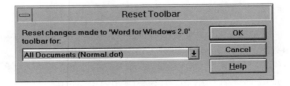

Figure 2.26 Which Toolbar Is Reset?

6. Pick the All Documents option and click OK. From that point onward, the original Toolbar will grace your screen.

Restoring View and Options Settings

The general method for restoring these settings is to simply go back into the appropriate menu or dialog box and click or unclick the setting. Again, if you're really serious about wiping out all your work, you can rename `WINWORD.OPT` (in your WinWord directory), and that should do the trick. But if you aren't quite so masochistic, here are the initial settings for a standard U.S. installation, should you ever wish to restore them:

View menu	View Normal
	Rulers
	Standard and Formatting Toolbars.
Options/View filecard	ON: Drawings
	Status Bar
	Horizontal Scroll Bar
	Vertical Scroll Bar
	Vertical Ruler
	OFF: Object Anchors
	Text Boundaries
	Picture Placeholders
	Field Codes
	Bookmarks
	All Nonprinting Characters
	Field Shading: When Selected.
Options/General filecard	ON: Background Repagination
	Been on Error Actions
	3D Dialog and Display Effects
	Update Automatic Links at Open
	Mail as Attachment
	Recently Used File List (4 Entries)
	OFF: Help for WordPerfect Users
	Navigation Keys for WordPerfect Users
	Blue Background, White Text
	Measurement Units: Inches.
Options/Edit filecard	ON: Typing Replaces Selection
	Drag 'n Drop Text Editing

Automatic Word Selection
Use Smart Cut and Paste
Allow Accented Uppercase

OFF: Use the INS Key for Paste
Overtype Mode

Picture Editor: Microsoft Word

AutoCorrect

ON: Change Straight Quotes to Smart Quotes
Correct TWo INitial CApitals
Capitalize Names of Days
Replace Text as You Type

OFF: Capitalize First Letter of Sentences

Removing ShowAll, InsertEmDash, InsertApostrophe

Icing a custom macro is usually a two-step process. First, you get rid of the macro itself. Second, you get rid of whatever shortcuts you may have installed to make it easy to use the macro.

Should you ever want to revert to the original, bone-stock ShowAll, simply click on Tools, then Macro. Click once on ShowAll. Click Delete. Similarly, to get rid of the other custom macros, click on Tools, then Macro, click InsertEmDash (or InsertApostrophe) once, and click Delete. It's that clean.

Toolbar, menu removal

We didn't put any custom buttons on the Toolbar or items in the menus to run any of the Underground macros, but if we had, removing them would be trivial. I'll mention them here just in case you're curious — or worried. To remove a custom Toolbar button, click Tools, Customize, and bring up the Toolbar filecard. Then click and drag the button that you don't like off of the Toolbar. To remove a custom menu item, click Tools, Customize, bring up the Menu filecard, click on the item that you don't like, and click Remove.

Keyboard removal

Recall that InsertApostrophe was hard-wired into the keyboard's apostrophe key and that we attached InsertEmDash to the number pad's minus key. Both were hard to do. We had to write custom, throw-away, one-line macros to convince WinWord that it should hook the macros up where we wanted them. That was a real pain because WinWord lets you assign many keys quite easily.

Perhaps not surprisingly, removing them isn't as simple as it should be, either. You'd think Microsoft would let you get rid of a keyboard assignment by clicking on Tools, Customize, and bringing up the Keyboard filecard, but noooooooooo. *In loco parentis* still applies, absurd as it may be.

The keyboard assignments for InsertEmDash and InsertApostrophe can be removed by running yet another macro. Click Tools, then Macro, type something like temp, click Create. You'll see a Sub MAIN and End Sub. To get rid of the number key pad's minus key assignment for InsertEmDash, type this line:

```
ToolsCustomizeKeyboard 109, .Remove
```

then click the right-wedgie VCR "Play" button to run the macro. If you want to get rid of the apostrophe key's assignment to InsertApostrophe, type this line:

```
ToolsCustomizeKeyboard 222, .Remove
```

and click the "Play" button again. There. The keys are back to normal. WinWord is back to its old, boring itself.

3 Basic Concepts— What's *Really* Going On

As the world is, an honest and wise man
should have a rough tongue.

George Gissing
Private Papers of Henry Ryecroft, 1903

Time now for a general overview of how WinWord hangs together, and how its various pieces affect the way you work. This chapter is highly condensed. If you try to absorb it all in one sitting, you'll miss most of it.

I suggest that you read a few pages of this chapter, and then put it aside. Work on what you've read about for a while, and then come back and bite off a few more pages of the chapter. Do that several times, over the course of a few days (or even a few weeks!), and you'll find that this stuff suddenly starts making some sense—that Aha! light will flash in your brain many, many times. Don't expect to breeze through this chapter in a few hours. Even the guri get confused on these points, all the time. So much for the warning. Off we go.

Caveat reador

THE WAY WE WAS

He who first shortened the labor of copyists
by device of movable types
was disbanding hired Armies,
and cashiering most Kings and Senates,
and creating a whole new Democratic world.

Thomas Carlyle
Sartor Resartus, 1833

In order to understand WinWord's in's and out's you need to understand a bit of the history. The technology of typography changed very little from the time of Gutenberg (who died in 1468) until the introduction of metal type around the

Movable type

beginning of the twentieth century. In many parts of the world, wood-cut blocks and brushed-on ink are still the norm for delivery of the word to the masses. For example, modern wood block Buddhist scripts, in Pali—a language that's been dead for a couple of centuries—can be found through much of Asia. Much of the confusing terminology you've been struggling with dates back to the era of metal type, an era that's fast drawing to a close. (You can find a thorough discussion of the terms and inanities of typo-terminology in Chapter 2 of *The Mother of All Windows Books.*)

If you're like me, you probably grew up with a typewriter. Fortunately our kids won't be so encumbered. The typewriter legacy brings with it much baggage, stuff you have to *un*learn before you can start using a computer to do your typesetting. It's confusing. It's the first conceptual jump in your road to mastering WinWord.

Alignment   No doubt by now you've discovered that you shouldn't hit the Enter key (Carriage Return) at the end of every line. That's a start. You've probably endured no end of frustration trying to line up indented paragraphs

- like
- these

by typing spaces, just as you did with a typewriter, only to discover that they flip-flop all over the page. I bet you've wasted at least an hour trying to get fill-in-the-blanks forms to line up on the right-hand side

like _____   this _____
and _____   this _____

and discovered that, no matter how hard you tried, no matter how many times you count underscore characters (_) or how many of them you type, WinWord just can't act like a typewriter.

I'll bet you're convinced that there are gremlins inside WinWord, little devils hopping around wreaking random havoc, changing your paragraphs when you aren't looking, rearranging text, shifting pages backward and forward, and doing everything conceivable (and much that's not conceivable) to drive you nuts.

Well, there's a reason for all that. WinWord *isn't* a typewriter. In many respects it acts more like a typesetting machine, like a "Lino," but it's much more power-ful. If you fall into the trap of thinking that WinWord should behave like a typewriter, you haven't a chance of reaching WinWord enlightenment.

We're going to look at this from a completely fresh point of view. One that's never appeared in print before. One that puts a kind of framework around WinWord's far-flung capabilities and describes the beast as she really is. Oh. The part about gremlins? That part's true.

FORMATTING

> That man is so bad
> he shouldn't be left alone in a room with a typewriter.
>
> Herman Makiewicz

Forget everything you know about typewriters. Good. Let's start with a plain sheet of paper. That's the primeval "document," the progenitor of all things "document-centric." It's just a regular ol' everyday sheet of paper. That's all. Onto that sheet of paper, we're gonna put ... things. Letters and words and phrases and sentences and lines and paragraphs and pictures and borders and colors and ... lots of things.

You want to control how those things appear on the page, right? It wouldn't make much sense to toss stuff on the paper willy-nilly. That's what formatting is all about: control over what the page looks like.

Here's how WinWord looks at documents:

The components

- A document contains one or more *sections*.
- A section contains one or more *paragraphs*.
- A paragraph contains one or more *characters*; the ¶ paragraph mark is considered to be a character.

In deference to this view of a document, WinWord has three types of formatting: section, paragraph, and character. I used Visio 2.0 to put together a rather simplistic diagram (Figure 3.1) of how a document hangs together and what kinds of formatting pertain. Perhaps surprisingly, there's no such thing as document formatting.

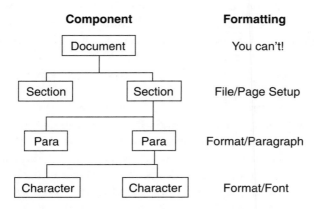

Figure 3.1 Formatting WinWord's Components

The formatting shtick   If you want to format a character, you select the character and click on Format, then Font. That makes some sense, although Microsoft's terminology is atrocious —you aren't formatting a font, you're formatting a character. If you want to format a paragraph, you stick your cursor in the paragraph you want to format (or select more than one paragraph), click Format, then Paragraph, and wreak your havoc.

However, if you want to format a section, you have to click on File, then Page Setup. The only way to format an entire document is to be careful to choose the correct Applies to Whole Document option while formatting a section!

Let's take a look at character and paragraph formatting. We'll dive into section formatting—truly a horse of a different color—a bit later in this chapter.

CHARACTERS

> To adorn our characters by the charm of an amiable nature
> shows at once a lover of beauty and a lover of man.
>
> Epictetus
> *Encheiridion,* ca. 100 AD

In WinWord documents, characters are elemental: they are the fundamental building blocks from which all else emerges.

Character Numbers

The character you see on your screen or printed on a sheet of paper is but an illusion, a pretty face pasted onto a raw, ugly number.

Ultimately everything in the computer biz is a number, and your fancy fonts are no exception. WinWord documents exist only as numbers—ones and zeros, by the thousands, by the millions—and everything else is interpretation.

So it shouldn't surprise you too much to learn that every character in your document is, at its heart, an ugly, boring number. Many a weird phenomena in the WinWord milieu can only be explained when you get down to those <*ugh!*> disgusting numbers.

Bracketing the wheel of dharma   Here's a simple example. Start with a new document—a clean sheet of paper —and type in a right bracket (]). You might think that you just put a right bracket onto your clean sheet of paper, but that's just an illusion. In reality, you stuck a number into your document. Don't believe it? Select that right bracket and change it to the Wingdings font. (See Figure 3.2.) See? The character itself didn't change, but its appearance sure did! It went from a right bracket to a ✸ wheel of dharma. What happened?

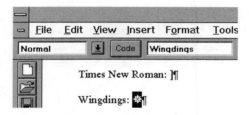

Figure 3.2 Right Bracket Transformed

The] character you saw on your screen is really character number 93. As character number 93, it doesn't have an appearance until a font is applied to it. Character number 93 in Times New Roman is a] right bracket, but character number 93 in Wingdings is a ✸ wheel of dharma. Did you ever see the TV series "The Prisoner?" Same problem. It isn't enough to simply be a number; the number must wear a mask, acquire a font, before it takes on meaning.

For example, in Times New Roman (and most fonts, for that matter), the letter "a" is character number 97; the "b" is number 98; the "A" is number 65; the "B" is number 66. An em-dash (—) is character number 151. And on and on. You'll find a list of characters and their numbers in Appendix A.

Be ever mindful that behind those characters lurk numbers, and those numbers can wear different masks, bear different appearances, depending on which font is in effect.

Character Formatting

> Non teneas aurum totum quod splendet ut aurum.*
>
> Alanus de Insulis
> *Parabolae,* 1270

Character formatting is pretty straightforward, although it offers many options. You select the text you want to change, then click the right mouse button or Format, then Font. See Figure 3.3.

In WinWord's world, characters (actually, in a very real sense, character *numbers*) have:

Character formatting choices

- A font—actually a typeface, but what the hay

- A point size

- A treatment like bold or italic, which the dialog box in Figure 3.3 calls a Font Style (no doubt to confuse the holy jeewillickers out of everybody), which has absolutely nothing to do with Styles in the WinWord sense of the term

*Do not take as gold everything that shines like gold.

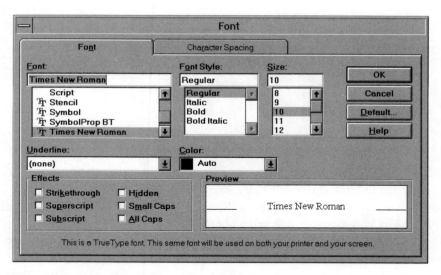

Figure 3.3 How to Format a Character

- <u>underlining</u> in four variations
- color, including a couple shades of gray (The Auto setting tells WinWord to use the text color you chose in the Desktop applet of Windows' Control Panel.)
- ~~strikethrough~~
- ^{superscript}, and $_{subscript,}$ both of which reduce the size of the font by about 4 points —at least that's what it looks like to me, Microsoft's docs don't say for sure— in addition to moving the selected characters about 3 points above (superscript) or 2 points below (subscript) the base line
- SMALL CAPS, which shows and prints lowercase letters as capital letters 2 points smaller than the indicated size (for example, a lowercase 10-point character appears as an uppercase 8-point character; uppercase characters are not affected)
- ALL CAPS, which shows and prints lowercase characters as capital characters of the same point size.

Hidden is another type of character formatting, like bold or the point size. Hidden makes the chosen characters invisible. They only appear on-screen if you check the Show Hidden checkbox in the Tools/Options/View dialog box. They only print if you choose the Hidden Text checkbox in the Tools/Options/Print dialog box.

Spacing

The pathos of distance

F. W. Nietzsche
Beyond Good and Evil, 1886

WinWord also permits you to move the characters themselves around, in relation to other characters on a line. Unlike standard formatting, these options are not the least bit straightforward. See Figure 3.4.

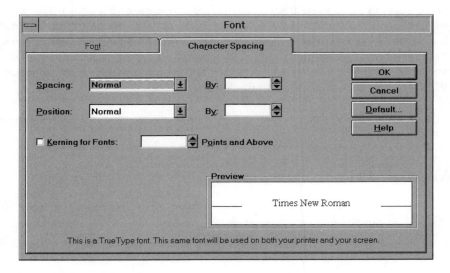

Figure 3.4 Font Spacing

The Position setting here moves the selected characters above or below the baseline by whatever distance you choose. It is *not* the same as formatting a character as superscript or subscript (see the Effects box in the lower left corner of Figure 3.3), because it does not change the apparent point size of the characters.

Vertical Position

The Spacing setting in Figure 3.4 is not the same as kerning. **Kerning** squishes together predefined pairs of letters—the distance between the A and the W in PAWN might be reduced, for example, to make it visually more appealing—whereas **spacing** can be adjusted for any single character.

Spacing vs. kerning

The Spacing box here really should say "Tracking" (which is the correct technical term), or at least something like "Space After," because it lets you manually adjust the white space that's automatically inserted after a character.

Kerning always works on predefined pairs of letters. It changes the distance between the two letters, squishing them together by an amount preordained by the folks who designed the font. Tracking, on the other hand, only applies to a single character. It only changes the width of the white space after that single character; and you can twiddle with it to your heart's content. See the difference?

As of this writing, WinWord will only kern TrueType fonts. That's a travesty: nobody's gonna convince me that it's any harder to kern Type 1 (PostScript) fonts than Microsoft's beloved TrueType. Although I use TrueType fonts exclusively—I only fall back on Type 1 fonts if forced to—a whole bunch of WinWord fans are still in the Type 1 stage of development.

Once again the kids in Redmond are playing favorites, and it stinks. This feud with Adobe is hurting WinWord's users; it doesn't help anybody. Microsoft did the same thing with the original Windows Printing System, which printed TrueType fonts like a-ringin' a bell, but croaked on Type 1. It isn't a bug, in the technical sense of the term. It's just a bit of parochialism that's beneath WinWord and should be beneath its designers.

Oh, well. Soapbox OFF. Anyway, that's what you can change at the character level.

PARAGRAPHS

> Just as the sentence contains one idea in all its fullness, so the paragraph should embrace a distinct episode; and as sentences should follow one another in harmonious sequence, so paragraphs must fit onto one another like the automatic couplings of railway carriages.
>
> Sir Winston Churchill
> *My Early Life*, 1930

The key to WinWord formatting, the foundation of how everything looks on your sheet of paper, is in paragraphs. Strange, eh, but it's true. In WinWord's world, paragraphs rule the roost. The paragraph is the tail that wags the document's dog—or something like that. Let's put this puppy through the hoops.

What Makes a Paragraph?

So, you ask, "*What* is a paragraph?" Very perceptive question, pilgrim. In the real world, a **paragraph** is usually described as a bunch of sentences. Webster says a paragraph is "a subdivision of a written composition that consists of one or more sentences, deals with one point or gives the words of one speaker, and begins on a new usu. indented line."*

*Webster's New Collegiate Dictionary, *Merriam-Webster*, 1979.

That's a rather mushy definition, wouldn't you say? Open to all sorts of interpretation. Given a handful of words, or sentences, it would be mighty difficult to say with all certainty whether you have a paragraph or not. That kind of ambiguity has a certain quaint charm to it—one that's led to hundreds of learned discourses, and more than a thesis or two—but computers tend to choke on quaint charm. It doesn't translate into bits.

In the WinWord Way, a paragraph is: (1) a ¶ paragraph mark, plus (2) all the stuff preceding the paragraph mark, up to but not including the previous paragraph mark.

In Figure 3.5, you'll see five paragraphs.

Count 'em¶   In Figure 51, you'll see five paragraphs.¶

 ¶

Figure 51: Look At All the Paragraphs¶
Let's count them, starting in the upper left corner.¶

Figure 3.5 Look At All the Paragraphs

Let's count them, starting in the upper left corner:

1. The words "Count 'em" followed by a ¶ paragraph mark.
2. The words "In Figure 51, you'll see five paragraphs.¶".
3. The Cool picture followed by a ¶ paragraph mark.
4. The caption, "Figure 51: Look at All the Paragraphs¶".
5. The words "Let's count them, starting in the upper left corner.¶".

That wasn't too hard, was it? See how a paragraph is just a funny ¶ paragraph mark, plus whatever goes before it? It doesn't have anything to do with sentences, words, or dealing with one point or one speaker. In the WinWord world, all that nuance gets swept away. *Sic transit gloria mundi.*

The Paragraph Mark

life's not a paragraph

e e cummings
Since feeling is first, 1926

The paragraph mark didn't exist in the world of typewriters. Well, yes, folks marking up manuscripts would add little backwards-P marks, but in the sense that we're talking about here—where a paragraph is *defined* by the ¶ mark—

there's no analog outside the computer realm. That's important. The ¶ mark stakes out a brave new world, indeed.

How to make little paragraph marks

You put a **paragraph mark** in a document by hitting the Enter key. Most important of all, you can *see* the paragraph mark when you put it in your document because you were smart enough to follow the admonitions in Chapter 1 and ensure that your paragraph marks are always visible. Right?

In many respects, the paragraph mark is a character just like any other character. It has a font, a point size, a color; you can select, move, copy, or delete it. You can have a document that contains nothing but paragraph marks—chances are good your NORMAL.DOT is one of those. When you hit the right arrow key, you have to "go over" the paragraph mark to move on to the next paragraph.

But in other respects, the paragraph mark is something different, something accorded special treatment. For example, if you flip into Overtype mode, WinWord overtypes almost any kind of character, but not a paragraph mark. Sometimes if you try to delete a paragraph mark by hitting the Delete key, WinWord beeps at you, keeping you from deleting the ¶ unless you explicitly select it and then delete it. Hit the End key and you go to the end of a line, unless the line ends in a paragraph mark, in which case the cursor ends up before the paragraph mark. There is always, always, always a paragraph mark at the end of every document.

Most of all, the rules for creating new paragraph marks are very different from the rules for creating new characters. New characters are easy. Unless you take a specific action to change matters (like clicking the Italic button), every new character you type takes on the characteristics of the character immediately before it. If you're typing along in 10-point Times New Roman bold, the next character comes out in 10-point Times New Roman bold. No surprises there.

However, new paragraphs aren't so simple. Not by a long shot. In their attempt to make WinWord easy to use, "intuitive" for lack of a better term, the folks at Microsoft created something that's very complex. As long as you're typing simple letters, memos, or Christmas lists, you won't encounter this weird stuff. But as soon as you start mucking around with tabs or borders, shading, styles, spacing, bullets, indents, or almost anything beyond very straightforward typing, this stuff will hit you right between the eyes. And it is *not* intuitive. No way.

I'll talk about creating new paragraph marks, how they inherit their characteristics from existing paragraph marks, after we look at Styles.

Whence Formatting?

> The power and the effect of a mantra depend on the spiritual attitude, the knowledge and the responsiveness of the individual. The *sabda* or sound of the mantra is not a physical sound, but a spiritual one.
>
> Anagarika Govinda
> *Foundations of Tibetan Mysticism*, 1960

I have a mantra for you, grasshopper, a little saying that you can keep as your guiding light. Repeat it slowly, a hundred times a day. Clear your mind of all else. Relax your body. Inhale deeply. *OMMMMMMM....*

The paragraph mark contains the formatting.

There. Tattoo it inside your eyelids. Because until you truly understand the WinWord mantra, you will forever be doomed to rebirth as a WinWord flunky, a thousand thousand thousand times broken on the karmic wheel. Your soul will rot in WordHell, Sisyphus nodding as he follows the WordPerfect path.

Nearly all of WinWord's formatting is stored in the paragraph mark. That fact may be the single largest source of WinWord frustration, pain and tears. I'll bet you've lost days of work because you didn't know that the squirrelly things WinWord does are tied inextricably to the paragraph mark.

Character formatting is in the paragraph mark. Unless you explicitly override it, the font, point size, color, "treatment" (bold, italic), whatever, of every single character in the paragraph takes on the formatting dictated by the paragraph mark.   **Character formatting**

Indents are in there, too. This paragraph has a first line indent of one-half   **Indents**
inch. That fact is stored in the paragraph mark.

> This paragraph has a left indent of one inch, and a right indent of one inch. It's also set up to be "justified," so WinWord stretches out all the lines to finish at the same point. All of that information is stored in the ¶ paragraph mark.

This line is formatted for double spacing. Yeah. You figured it out. The spacing   **Spacing**

information is stored in the paragraph mark, too.

But wait. There's more. All of what's been mentioned so far are what you might reasonably expect to be associated with paragraph formatting. WinWord sticks a whole bunch of other stuff — stuff you probably never thought of as paragraph formatting — in the paragraph mark, too.

Tabs

> E pur, si muove.
>
> Galileo*

Take tabs for instance. On older typewriters, a **tab stop** is a piece of metal that   **What *is* a tab?**
makes the platen go *clunk*. It stops the movement of the paper so that you can resume typing in a predetermined location. Hit the Tab key and the platen would

---

*On April 30, 1633, Galileo recanted his heretical belief that the earth moves about the sun. As he rose from kneeling to his inquisitors he mumbled, *"Even so, it moves."*

go into free-fall, coming to rest when it hit a tab stop. If you could reach around to the back of the typewriter, or if you had a fancy typewriter and the Tab Set/Clear button was well oiled and working properly, you could change tab stops any ol' time. The Selectrics and their ilk changed the process a bit, but not much. Instead of the platen going into free-fall, one of those funny type balls went *ziiing*! But the basics are the same.

In the computer age we aren't so lucky. There's no platen to go *clunk*—if there were, you'd have a hell of a time keeping your laser printer from rocking off the table. Instead, we have to settle for a cheap imitation, an ersatz tab stop that's enormously more confusing that the old-fashioned kind. You can't feel it. You can't hear it. Worst of all, the new-age tab isn't one thing, one place, one stopping point; it's a weird combination of two very different components.

Tab dichotomy   Whereas the typewriter's tab stop is a single piece of metal, **WinWord's tab stop** has two parts: a tab character (a real, live character, just like any other character) and a bunch of invisible stopping points buried inside the document. When WinWord is putting text on the screen or printing on your printer and it sees a tab character, it jumps forward to the location of the next invisible stopping point, the location of the next tab stop. The physical character and this bunch of invisible stopping points, taken together, are kinda, sorta, almost like a typewriter tab stop. As long as you don't think about it too hard.

Where are the invisible stopping points stored? Why, in the ¶ paragraph mark, of course. You were expecting somewhere else?

You might think that we could set up different tab stops on each line, right? I mean, that's what makes sense. On this line, I have tab stops set every inch, on the next line I want 'em every half inch, and on the line after that I want a tab set at 3 inches so I can type a table of numbers. But nooooooo….

In WinWord, you set up tab stops for a *paragraph*. Every line in a given paragraph has the same tab stops, same location, all in lockstep. You don't have any choice in the matter.

Lining Things Up

> Conformity gives comliness to things.
>
> Robert Herrick
> *Hesperides*, 1648

The most important, most frustrating aspect of paragraph formatting is using tab stops to line text up. If you're working with a **monospaced font**, a typewriter-like font, where the "i" and the the "M" have the same width, it's easy to line text up so that columns all start in the same location and underlines all end on the right margin. You simply type as you would on a typewriter, count the number of characters, and everything comes out hunky-dory.

Courier is a common monospaced font; you probably have it or its identical twin Courier New on your system right now. If you've been frustrated in your attempts to line text up the way I've shown in Figure 3.6 and Figure 3.7, switching to the Courier font is a quick, easy way to get yourself going. Simply select the paragraphs you want to line up, and pick Courier or Courier New in the font box on the formatting Toolbar, pretend you're using a typewriter by counting out the spaces and the underscores, and you're set.

Quick and dirty alignment

Last Name: _____ First: _____ M.I.: _

Address: _____

             _____

City: _____State: _____Zip: _____

Figure 3.6 Address Book Entry

Why do you prefer Homer's Squirrelburgers? _____

_____

_____

Figure 3.7 Q & A Fill-in-the-Blanks Form

But finking out and using a monospace font isn't the best way. No way. What's the downside? Well, monospace fonts look like a kid's scrawl compared to those glorious proportionally spaced fonts that you've grown accustomed to. And, believe it or not, counting and typing out underscore characters and spaces is much, much slower than doing all of this with tabs and tab stops. Once you learn the "correct" way, you'll find it not only looks better, it actually works faster. Trust me on this one, okay?

Tabbing to a better way

Here's a cookbook approach to creating an underscored form, like the one shown in Figure 3.6.

There's a trick to getting tabs to work the way you want. When you start monkeying around with tabs, *make sure that every line is a paragraph, and that every paragraph contains just one line.* The ¶ paragraph marks are already showing, so you shouldn't get too confused if you stick to the one line/one para rule.

One line = one paragraph

Start by hitting Enter enough times to cover every line in your form. The form in Figure 3.6 needs four lines, so you should put four paragraph marks in your document by hitting Enter four times.

I always stick a couple extra paragraph marks in the doc, just in case I need to grab a "clean" one quickly. You're going to be mucking up each paragraph— each line, each paragraph mark, however you want to say it—and you'll find it much easier if all the to-be-clobbered paragraph marks are sitting there staring at you.

Next it's time for some planning. Try laying out your form, figuring out where you want the underscores to begin and end. Measure everything in terms of "distance from the beginning of the line." In all four lines of Figure 3.6, the first underscore starts 0.7 inches in from the beginning of the line, and all of them end at 4 inches from the left. The first line, which looks like this:

Last Name: _____ First: _____ M.I.: _

has the word "First:" starting at 2¼ inches and "M.I.:" starting at 3½ inches. There. That's all the planning you'll need.

Stick your cursor in what will become the first line of your form and click on Format, then Tabs. You'll be greeted by the Tabs dialog box. (Figure 3.8 shows how the dialog box looks when it's completely filled out.)

Figure 3.8 Filled-in Tabs Dialog Box

Tab position   The Tab Stop Position box tells WinWord where to put a tab stop. Your first tab stop is at 0.7 inches, so type in 0.7. (With non-USA versions of WinWord, you'll probably want to translate that into centimeters, or points, or furlongs—whatever you like.)

Tab alignment   WinWord tab stops come in four flavors, left-aligned, right-aligned, centered, and decimal-point aligned. You're probably accustomed to each of the four: they control whether the tabbed stuff is butted up against the tab stop to the left or to the right, centered around all the text, or aligned on the first period in the text.

That **Bar** tab stop alignment is utterly crazy; it doesn't belong here. It isn't a tab stop. It doesn't control how tab characters are interpreted. It merely draws a line up and down inside the paragraph, at the indicated point, kind of like a **Borders** setting. Don't let it confuse you. And three loud Bronx cheers to the folks in Redmond who snuck it in here. Tab stops are confusing enough without this kind of extraneous crap floating around. But I digress.

All four of the tab stops in our example are left-aligned. We want WinWord to scoot up to the tab stop, and then, *stop!*

That leaves us with the box marked Leader and brings us to the reason for our being here in the first place. **Leader** (rhymes with "bleeder") **characters** for tab stops have nothing to do with leading (rhymes with "bedding"), the spacing between WinWord's lines. In fact, this box would probably be better called Fill In the Spaces With. It isn't complicated, doesn't come down to us from the last 100 years of printing history, and has nothing to do with hot lead. It's just a space filler. That's all.

Leader

When you pick a character in this box, you're telling WinWord, "Yo! If there is any empty space leading up to this tab stop, fill it in!" You can fill with any of the three indicated choices: dotted lines ...., hyphens ------, or underscores _____.

In our example, we want underscores for all the tab stops except the first, and the first one is set to None, or blank. If you want to follow along with the example, type in the location of each tab stop, select the correct leader, and click Set. When you're done, click Close. Now play around hitting the Tab key while the cursor is inside your newly tabbed paragraph. See how that works?

Putting it all together

Variations on a Theme

> Music is a higher revelation than philosophy.
>
> Ludwig van Beethoven
> 1810

The example you just stepped through is really a worst-case scenario. Most of the time you work with tabs, you won't be concerned with leaders at all; you just want to get your columns to line up.

If you're trying to line things up from top to bottom, *you have to use tabs*. In the brave new world of proportional fonts, you can't ever rely on hitting the spacebar to get things lined up right. It's a sad, but true, fact of modern life.

WinWord has a rather odd way of setting up tab stops, and the default behavior frequently mystifies people. Every paragraph starts out with tab stops set every half inch (non-US versions are slightly different). As you add tab stops manually, the preceding default stops disappear. For example, if you put a manual

Default tab stops

tab stop at 1.25 inches, the default stops at 0.5 and 1.0 go away. But the default stops to the right of the right-most manual tab stop—in this case, at 1.5 inches, 2.0, 2.5, and so on—stay in full effect. It's almost as if WinWord keeps those default tab stops hanging around, just in case it hits a tab character that falls outside the area you've established manually.

If you've ever wondered why things lined up just fine until you jumped in and manually set a tab stop—and then everything went to hell in a handbasket— well, now you know why.

There are other ways to draw fill-in-the-form style lines, and this seems as good a place as any to discuss them. Back in Figure 3.7 we had a line that looks like this:

Why do you prefer Homer's Squirrelburgers? _____

Setting up the underline on the right-hand side there is pretty easy, now that you know the trick. You set up a tab stop (in this case, at 4 inches), and specify an underline "leading" character, leading up to that tab stop. Type in the text and hit the Tab key, and the underline magically appears in that erstwhile "blank" space before the tab stop.

There are several other ways to skin this cat, and they're all pretty instructive; they show alternate methods of putting lines where *you* want them. One of these tricks may come in handy some day, so bear with me.

The tab character

First, that tab character is just like any other character. *You do have tab characters showing, don't you?* Since the tab character acts like almost any other character, it can have a point size, a color, and, most important to the task at hand, it can be underlined! That's a rather bizarre concept, if your mind is still stuck in the typewriter mold. But it's a fact: tab characters can be underlined, double-underlined, dotted-underlined, the works.

Double underscore

How does that help? Well, if you wanted to have a line that looks like this:

Why do you prefer Homer's Squirrelburgers? _____

with a double-underline over on the right, you can't do it with the tab stops' leading characters. WinWord doesn't support double-underline leading; with the standard leading shtick, you're up the ol' creek without a paddle. You *have* to format the tab character with a double-underline.

Along the same ... uh ... lines, if you wanted an underline like this:

Why do you prefer Homer's Squirrelburgers? _____

where the underline extends underneath the whole line, it's a lot easier to set up the tab stop without leading, select the whole line, click on Format, then Font, and pick Underline.

If you want to do some fancy stuff with underlines, one more observation pertains: the tab "leading" underline lies in a different location from the Format Font underline. You can mix and match and create all sorts of strange patterns. Play with it a bit and you'll see. **Line virtuosity**

Finally, you can use a paragraph "border" to draw horizontal lines like these. But that's a story unto itself…

Other Paragraph Formatting

> Oh, East is East, and West is West, and never the twain shall meet,
> Till Earth and Sky stand presently at God's great Judgment Seat.
> But there is neither East nor West, Border, nor Breed, nor Birth,
> When two strong men stand face to face,
> though they come from the ends of the earth!
>
> Rudyard Kipling
> *Ballad of East and West*, 1889

There are other types of formatting that you might think would be better applied to lines. Take borders. In WinWord, a **border** is a line or a box above or below or around a paragraph. A border doesn't go around a single line of text. It goes around a *paragraph*. Same for shading: you don't shade a block of text, or even a line. You shade a paragraph like Figure 3.9. **South o the border**

This is an indented paragraph with a three-point border and a 20% gray background shading.

Figure 3.9 Sample Shaded Paragraph

Not surprisingly, borders and shading are stored in the paragraph mark (¶). If you move or copy a paragraph mark from one part of your document to another, its borders and shading (and tabs and default fonts and spacing and indents and Gates-knows-what-all) come along for the ride.

There's even more. WinWord's automatic numbering and bulleting of lists

1. like
2. this

is accomplished with paragraph formatting. That's a rather strange concept—and some of Redmond's implementation leaves much to be desired—but it's a handy way to keep lists together. A "bulleted" paragraph is identified in much the same way as, oh, a "centered" paragraph; it's all right there in the paragraph mark. Paragraph formatting is a gnarly, complicated topic that lies at the heart of WinWord. I'll revisit it often.

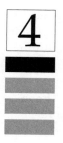

4 Advanced Concepts —Shortcuts

Listen with your ears to the best information;
behold with your sight, and with your mind;...
And may we be those
who shall make life progressive and purposeful.

Zoroastrian *Gathas*
ca. 600 BC

So much for the basics of formatting. Now let's pull the camera back for a wider angle shot, and take a look at how the formatted pieces hang together.

STYLES

Power users do it with style.

"Pensées Pinecliffius"

So many otherwise sane WinWord users break out in a cold sweat when they read about styles. They're convinced that styles are complicated, beyond the ken of mortal users. Nothing could be further from the truth!

Hell, I don't use styles all that often. They're a pain to set up, and they're of questionable benefit in many situations. I never use styles in one-of-a-kind documents, I only fall back on them when I figure I must. If you find yourself applying the same formatting over and over again or if there's the slightest chance you'll want to change the formatting of similar material scattered throughout a big document, you owe it to yourself to check styles out.

Styles are just a formatting shorthand, a quick way of applying or changing all sorts of formatting with a click or two. The term "style" doesn't quite capture the spirit of the beast: if I were in charge of the WinWord zoo, I'd call it QuickieFormat. No doubt somebody has already trademarked that name. Ah, well.

QuickieFormat

The concept is simplicity itself: you gather up a bunch of formatting settings and give the collection a name. That's all. That's the alpha and omega of styles. In a very basic sense, styles are like templates. They let you put a pot-full of settings in one place, so you can work with them as a group.

One of the most important diagrams you'll find in this book is Figure 4.1. I hope it clears away some fog for you; hope it triggers that Aha! light bulb in your head.

There's a certain … asymmetry … in how WinWord really works. I'm not sure why it's lopsided; perhaps it just grew up that way. If WinWord's designers sat down and rebuilt it from scratch, perhaps the anomalies would disappear. But for now anyway, Figure 4.1 shows you the underpinnings of the real WinWord, warts and all.

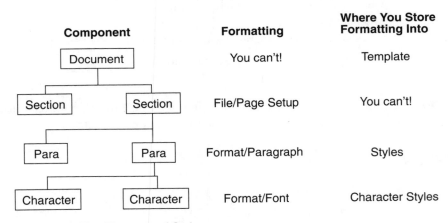

Component	Formatting	Where You Store Formatting Into
Document	You can't!	Template
Section Section	File/Page Setup	You can't!
Para Para	Format/Paragraph	Styles
Character Character	Format/Font	Character Styles

Figure 4.1 The Elements of Styles

Document formatting   Let's take Figure 4.1 from the top, starting with the document as a whole. As you've seen, WinWord doesn't have an easy way to format an entire document (aside from formatting a section and making sure the Apply To: box reads Whole Document, and I don't call that "easy"). It *does* have a bang-up way to store settings for an entire document—the template. We'll talk about templates later in this chapter.

Section formatting   Contrariwise, WinWord lets you format sections with great ease: simply stick your cursor in the section that needs changing, click on File, then Page Setup. Oddly, there's no easy way to store and retrieve section settings; there's nothing analogous to a template or a style for sections.

Paragraph formatting   Paragraphs reign supreme. Easy ways to store and apply paragraph format-ting have been available since the early days of WinWord 1.0; indeed, many would rightfully argue that comprehensive paragraph formatting is one of

WinWord's most endearing qualities. When you gather a set of formatting settings for a paragraph and name that set, it's called a style. (Some people call it a paragraph style.) When you apply a style, you merely copy all of those formatting settings over to the paragraph.

Finally, a relative newcomer on the WinWord scene, **character styles** are quite analogous to old-fashioned paragraph styles. They're a bunch of character formatting settings, gathered together and given a name, to make it easier for you to control the formatting of individual characters in your documents.

Character formatting

Building Character

So how does all of this fit together? Excellent question, and one that takes a bit of explaining.

Imagine you're in WinWord's shoes. Your mission, should you choose to accept it, is to look at the next character in a document and figure out how to put it on the screen or how to print it on a sheet of paper. The complexity of the problem may surprise you.

Alas, you won't really understand WinWord until you see how all these bloody settings bang against each other to produce the final character, so let's give it a shot. Actually, it's kind of a fun detective story, if you're of the sleuthing persuasion.

WinWord starts with a character number. If you typed an "a" on the keyboard, for example, WinWord starts with a number 97. WinWord must first flesh out the character itself, and in order to do that it must find the font, the point size, the "treatment," and all that.

WinWord looks to see if you've applied some sort of formatting directly to the character. Maybe sometime in the past you selected this character and forced it to be 12-point Arial bold. If it's been formatted manually, the character mystery is solved.

Manual formatting

If the character hasn't been formatted manually, WinWord next looks to see if you've applied a character style to it. With a character style in hand, all those messy character formatting settings are resolved. WinWord is ready to proceed.

Character style

If no character style has been applied, WinWord looks to the paragraph style. *Every* paragraph has a style. Without exception. The buck stops here; whatever character formatting is included in the paragraph style gets grafted onto the character.

Paragraph style

The precise method of nailing down a specific paragraph style's settings is a bit complex. It depends on something called style inheritance. We'll get to that shortly, with the Bilbo and Baggins styles.

Locating Character

Character is much easier kept than recovered.

Thomas Paine
The American Crisis, 1783

Now that WinWord knows what character is at hand, it must then discern *where* that character should go. This part is even tougher.

Character in the paragraph

First, WinWord has to figure out where the character goes in relation to the current paragraph. Using the three-step process mentioned earlier (looking for manual formatting, then character style, then paragraph style), WinWord checks to see if there's anything odd about the current character's location. It may be formatted Superscript, or the preceding character may have an unusual tracking (Spacing) setting, or it could be a tab character. The line may have just extended past the right margin, so there may be some word wrapping to do. A new page might be necessary. All sorts of fun stuff.

Paragraph on the page

Next, WinWord has to place the paragraph on the page, and that opens a real can of worms. WinWord checks to see if any manual formatting has been applied to the paragraph. You may have selected this particular paragraph and centered it, for example, or set up some oddball line spacing, or manually applied an indent. If it's been formatted manually, the location problem is solved and it's time to move on.

If there's been no manual formatting, WinWord picks up the formatting in the paragraph's style. Again, every paragraph has a style, so the buck always stops here.

Page on the paper

Finally, WinWord "places" the page on the sheet of paper (well, it doesn't really work precisely that way, but you get the idea). Headers, footers, and drawings are added at this point, too. Perhaps surprisingly, WinWord does *not* look at templates or styles while painting the page on the paper. It goes straight for the settings in the current section: the margins, paper size, and orientation.

See how that all fits together? If you've ever wondered why changing a style setting — say, making all Normal paragraphs double-spaced — suddenly changes your entire document, now you know. You also know why changing a template — say, making the margins smaller — doesn't do anything at all to your current document.

Defining Styles

A good style must, first of all, be clear.

> Aristotle
> *Rhetoric*, ca. 320 BC

There are two different kinds of styles—character styles and paragraph styles —and two different ways of telling WinWord how you want the styles set up.

I don't like the quickie method for defining styles, where you select something and type a new name in the style box on the Formatting Toolbar. The rules for what is defined and why and how are too complicated for my befuddled brain.

Just like Format Painting, which I discussed in Chapter 1, the shortcut simply loses too much and assumes too much. Besides, it doesn't work with character styles anyway. So I won't bore you with the quickie method.

The real way to set up a new style, or to change an existing one, is to click on Format, then Style, and then either click New or pick the style you want to change and click Modify. See Figure 4.2.

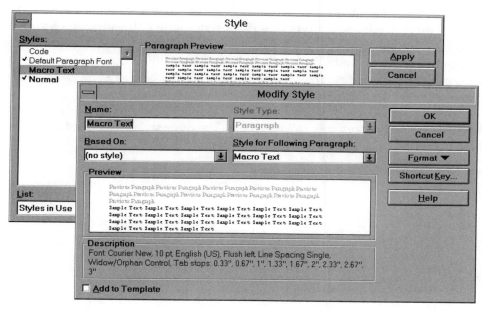

Figure 4.2 A Style Is Born

At this point you can click on Format and pick and choose whatever formatting you like. Click OK, then Close (or Apply if your cursor happens to be standing in the middle of a paragraph that you want to take on the new style), and you're done. There are a few nuances, however.

The Organizer button on the Style dialog "tunnels" to WinWord's template organizer. It lets you copy styles from other templates to the current template.

Style Gallery and AutoFormat

Microsoft makes much of the Format/Style Gallery menu option and the Format/AutoFormatting option (which is, more or less, just the Style Gallery applied automatically). Both of these options let you bring into your document massive numbers of predefined styles, all at once. They replace similarly named styles you've defined. I'll talk about AutoFormatting shortly.

Two other boxes are there, one marked Based On, the other marked Style for Following Paragraph. Behind those boxes lurks enormous power.

Inherited Style

> When we encounter a natural style we are always astonished and
> delighted, for we expected to see an author, and found a man.
>
> Blaise Pascal
> *Pensées*, 1670

Bilbo meets Baggins The phrase "Based On" is a touch misleading. That first box actually establishes a complex scheme of **style inheritance**, not unlike the inheritance you're accustomed to, the kind you studied in high school. Say you're setting up a new style called, oh, Bilbo. In this Style dialog box you set things up so Bilbo is Based On another style, say, Baggins. Unless you specifically change something, Bilbo takes on all the formatting settings of Baggins.

The Based On chain That's an incredibly powerful capability. Let me show you why. Say Baggins is Based On another style, oh, call it Gollum. The three styles look like Figure 4.3: Bilbo is Based On Baggins, which in turn is Based On Gollum.

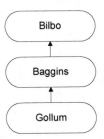

Figure 4.3 Lord Of the Styles

Let's say that you set up Baggins so that it centers paragraphs. That's all. In the Format/Style dialog box you click on Format, then Paragraph, and pick Centered. Easy.

Now, let's say that you set up Bilbo so that it italicizes everything. In the Format/Style dialog box you click on Format, then Font, and click Italic.

Instant inheritance Now you can monkey around with the formatting in Gollum, and both Baggins and Bilbo will change in lockstep. If you switch Gollum from Times New Roman to Arial, boom! Suddenly Baggins is Arial, centered. Bilbo is italic Arial, centered. The changes are inherited, through the Based On chain. And all the changes take place, like, *right now*.

If you carefully control which styles are Based On others, you can ripple changes through a document with just a few mouse clicks. It's one of WinWord's most powerful capabilities, but it's amazing how very few people know about it!

Makin' New Paragraphs

> Had I been present at the Creation, I would have given some useful hints
> for the better ordering of the universe.
>
> Alphonso X (the Wise)
> ca. 1270

The Style for Following Paragraph box in Figure 4.2 harbors another enormously powerful capability that few people seem to understand. It's a bit complicated, but it can really speed up your work, especially if you're a fast typist.

Every time you hit the Enter key, WinWord puts a paragraph mark in your document, ending one paragraph and starting another. A fundamental question arises: What style does the new paragraph take? As is so often the case in WinWord, the answer is: uh, it depends. **Formatting new paragraphs**

If your cursor is somewhere in the middle of a paragraph and you hit Enter, both the old and the new paragraphs take on all the formatting of the original paragraph. That's pretty much what you would expect.

If your cursor is immediately in front of a paragraph mark and you hit Enter, the new paragraph—the one you're starting—can be totally different from the original paragraph. (This is where the Style for Following Paragraph box comes in. When you hit Enter, WinWord takes a quick look at the Style for Following Paragraph box for the current style, and sets up the new paragraph with that style.

For example, if your Bilbo style has a Style for Following Paragraph of Heading 3, every time you hit Enter at the end of a Bilbo paragraph, you'll suddenly find yourself in a Heading 3 paragraph.

Two consequences are lurking here that may not be apparent. In fact, I'll bet one or both have bit you at some point. **The leading cause of weird tabs**

If your cursor is in a paragraph and that paragraph has tab stops set hither and yon, when you hit Enter, you create a new paragraph *with those same tab stops*. Starting a new paragraph does *not* reset the settings to those originally defined for the style; all the manually applied formatting is passed on to the next paragraph. Back when I started learning WinWord, I bet I lost a week's worth of work before I finally realized that's what was happening. Yeah, it's probably in the manual somewhere. But who reads the manual?

Here's the other strange thing. If your cursor is not immediately in front of the paragraph mark—if there's just one space between your cursor and the paragraph mark, for example—you won't pick up the Style for Following Paragraph style when you hit Enter.

WinWord ships with 74 prebuilt styles, ready for you to use. They're listed in Appendix B. **Bone-stock styles**

"Auto" Formatting

> Style is knowing who you are, what you want to say,
> and not giving a damn.
>
> Gore Vidal
> *Daily Express*, 1973

I don't often use the Style Gallery or AutoFormatting for two reasons. First, I'm not at all convinced that the predefined styles are any better than what you or I could come up with in just a few minutes. Second, I've seen situations where the styles that are automatically applied don't jibe with what I feel is right, for example, heading styles applied to sentences or vice versa.

To see what I mean, start up a new document and type:

What do you think about this?

I think it's pretty durn strange.

Now click on Format, then AutoFormat. See that? WinWord thinks the first line is a heading, which it clearly isn't.

 AutoFormat ain't too smart. There are lots and lots of examples of how AutoFormat gets confused. Yes, you can back out of AutoFormat's mistakes. But why bother? Do it yerself.

TEMPLATES

> If I believed in reincarnation, I'd come back as a sponge.
>
> Woody Allen
> *Seventeen*, 1972

Every new document you create is derived from a template. Like styles, templates let you establish a whole bunch of settings, give them a name (actually, store them in a file), and then call up those settings when you need them. Unlike styles, changes to a template don't automatically ripple through your document.

Template Raison d'être

> Art is the imposing of a pattern on experience.
>
> Alfred North Whitehead
> *Dialogues*, 1953

A bit of history   Way back at the dawning of WinTime, templates were document proto-types. Much as a stencil-style plastic template, they worked like simple cookie cutters, allowing you to crank out exact replicas of an original with minimal pain and fuss.

Instead of typing out the same boilerplate text, say, a template could be constructed to provide all the boilerplate as a simple consequence of creating a new document. Instead of copying all your font, paragraph, and margin settings to every new file, you could roll all of that into a template and never bother with it again. Instead of reinventing your styles with every new file, tediously reconstructing them from scratch, you could stick all your styles in a template and have them come along for the ride every time you created a new document.

It's an amazingly useful, powerful capability. You could build a template for your company's letterhead, say, then pass it around, and *boom!* suddenly everybody would be able to churn out similar-looking letters, taking advantage of all that prefab documents have to offer. You could create a prototype for all your invoices or internal memos. You could write little programs—macros—that let the computer take over, replacing hundreds or *thousands* of repetitive, error-prone keystrokes with a few lines of code.

Although templates could be used to enforce some semblance of uniformity in the office morass, they could do more than glorify slavish conformity. By simply reducing the repetitiveness of day-to-day document preparation, templates helped liberate people from the trivia that threatens to engulf all our lives. Their importance shouldn't be underestimated.

Beyond Big Brother

A well-built template could, and *can*, save hours of work every day. Over the years, life has become more complicated. The simple cookie cutter has been replaced by a multifaceted Swiss Army Knife of options, features, capabilities, and … confusion.

WinWord's implementation of templates differs from the old, dull cookie-cutter image in two important aspects.

More than a simple cookie cutter

First, WinWord put some decidedly fancy capabilities into its templates. Although WinWord templates include everything you would expect of a cookie cutter—anything you can put in a document, you can also put in a template—templates have a few extra bells and whistles that greatly magnify their usefulness. We'll talk about those extras in a moment.

Second, WinWord's designers decided they needed a granddaddy of all cookie cutters, a template that lurks in the background, omnipresent, omniscient, first among equals. It's the "global" template you've no doubt encountered—at least you probably *think* you've encountered it. Read on, read on.

Template Anatomy

A template is a super-duper document. It has all the characteristics of a document—size, margins, styles, text, headers, bookmarks, and all the other stuff that can go in a document—plus three extra goodies:

1. AutoText entries (Although, surprisingly, you can't put AutoCorrect entries in them.)

2. Your customized modifications to WinWord's Toolbars, menus, and shortcut keys

3. Macros (You can't do that with mere documents.)

I call them the Terrible Three. That's it. All of your angst about templates reduces to those three items, and the way they interact. Amazing, eh?

Static vs. Dynamic Stuff

> Have a place for everything and have everything in its place.
>
> H. G. Bohn
> *Handbook of Proverbs*, 1855

When you create a new document, you have to tell WinWord which template to use.

Doc as template   You might be surprised to discover that you can actually pick *any* WinWord document to be a template. WinWord will use a regular plain-Jane document as a template if you merely type the document's full name and path in the File New dialog. (See Figure 4.4.) That's an important revelation because it leads to a very simple conclusion that should clarify a whole bunch of things for you:

A "new" document is just a copy of the "template" file.

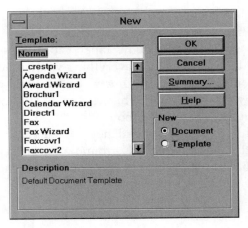

Figure 4.4 Pick a Template, Any Template

Since a plain document can't contain the Terrible Three—AutoText, customizing (Toolbars, menus, or keyboard assignments), or macros—those get left behind. But everything else is copied straight across.

Note how I didn't say anything about `.DOT` file names or `\TEMPLATE` subdirectories or convoluted inheritance schemes or any of the other mind-numbing complexities you've probably come to associate with the term "template." All of that is artifice, mumbo-jumbo invented in an attempt to explain something that, at its core, is quite simple: A "new" document is just a copy of the "template" file.

Since the "new" file is a copy of the template, you wouldn't expect changes in the template to change anything in your document, and, in fact, they don't. Once you start a "new" document, everything is copied from the template to the new file, and any subsequent changes to the template don't mean diddly.

Template changes are not propagated.

That's quite different from the way styles work. Styles are **dynamic**: if you change a style in a document, the changes propagate immediately throughout the document. But templates are **static**: once you've created a document based on a template, the document stands on its own two feet.

CONTEXT

> With ruin upon ruin, rout on rout,
> Confusion worse confounded.
>
> John Milton
> *Paradise Lost*, 1667

The most confusing part of WinWord tends to be the concept of context. Unfortunately it's one of the key concepts, something you have to "get" before you make the transition from novice to guru.

If you're trying to follow this discussion in the official docs, you're in for a rocky ride. The manual is wrong over and over again. It's a strange hybrid of how WinWord really should work and how the WinWord's original specs were probably constructed. Whatever the origin, WinWord doesn't act the way the docs say. Try it yourself and you'll see. If the folks writing the docs—accomplished WinWord fans all—couldn't get it right, you're to be forgiven if you get a bit confused.

You see, in WinWord 6.0, context is all screwed up. Let's try to take it a step at a time.

The Five Contexts

There is no god but Allah and Muhammad is the Rasul of Allah.

First of the Five Pillars of Islam

There are five **contexts**, five different sources of settings that can affect your document: the document itself; its template; the global template; other templates that live more or less on the "global" level; and built-in settings.

The document   We have a document on the screen, filled with words, paragraphs, styles, margins, fields, headers, footnotes, drawings, objects, and all those document thingies. Great.

Its template   Behind the document sits its template. The template is a super-duper document, almost always the progenitor of the document on the screen. If you don't pick a specific template when you start a new document, WinWord attaches NORMAL.DOT to it. You can change the currently active template by clicking File, then Templates, then Attach…

We don't really care about the document stuff that's in the template (like words, paragraphs, styles, and so on), but three things in the template matter a great deal: AutoText, customizing (Toolbars, menus, and keys), and macros. If you want to change any of those three things, you can't change them in the document —the document doesn't contain any of the Terrible Three. You have to go into the template and change them.

Global layer   Behind the doc's template sits the "global" template. Again, we don't care about the document-stuff in the global template. But the Terrible Three stored here — the AutoText, customizing and macros on the global level — control WinWord's behavior.

You might think that the global template is NORMAL.DOT, but you'd be wrong, despite what the documentation (and several dialog boxes!) say. It isn't quite that simple. There isn't a single global template; it's more like an amalgamation, a global layer, if you will. WinWord builds the global layer every time it gets going, based not only on NORMAL.DOT, but also on the contents of the \STARTUP directory.

\STARTUP   As best I can tell, here's what happens when you start WinWord, how the global layer is actually constructed. I won't swear it's gospel truth, but it's pretty close:

1. WinWord goes out and finds NORMAL.DOT. It sets up NORMAL.DOT as the first stab at a global layer. The Terrible Three (AutoText, customizing, and macros) located in NORMAL.DOT take over.

2. WinWord then shows the Tip of the Day. *<Don't ask me why, I only work here.>* About the same time it runs the WINWORD.EXE command line's /m switch.

That's why you can only specify macros in NORMAL.DOT on WinWord's command line. It's a bug, but if you don't understand it, don't worry about it.

3. After the Tip of the Day is cleared, WinWord starts looking at stuff in the \STARTUP directory. I think it loads .DOT templates first, in alphabetical order, followed by .WLL WinWord C programs (so-called "add-ins"), also in alphabetical order, but there may be some additional subtleties. \STARTUP can contain quite a few templates and programs. Thus, you may experience quite a delay after the Tip of the Day, before you get control of your machine. (Beats me why WinWord doesn't load these templates and additions while the Tip is on the screen.)

4. As each denizen of \STARTUP is processed, WinWord rolls changes in the Terrible Three (AutoText, customizing, and macros) into the global layer. They're cumulative. For example, if A.DOT in \STARTUP has an AutoText entry for the combination mnfffft, and B.DOT in \STARTUP has a different AutoText entry for mnfffft, the AutoText entry in A.DOT takes over.

At any time you can click on File, then Templates..., and add another template to this global layer (see Figure 4.5).

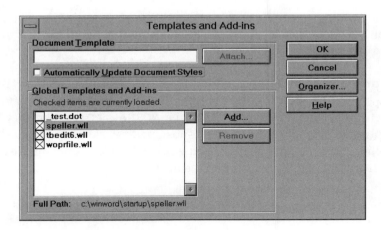

Figure 4.5 Adding a Template

The docs say that WinWord resolves naming conflicts (for example, where A.DOT and B.DOT both refer to mnfffft) by stepping through the templates in the global layer alphabetically, but that isn't true. If you add a template manually using File/Templates..., that newly added template goes to the end of the line, regardless of its position alphabetically.

Despite what the manuals say, this jockeying and conflict resolution isn't dynamic. WinWord doesn't go bopping through the global layer every time it's needed. I can only conclude that WinWord builds this global layer when it starts, begrudgingly tacking AutoText, customizing, and macros on if you manually add a template or `.WLL` add-in.

Finally, above all this, there are the settings that are built into WinWord itself. The terminology kind of craps out here. Sometimes these built-in settings, macros, and the like are called "built-in," which makes a lot of sense to me. Sometimes they're called "command level," "commands," "Word Commands," or "All Commands." Don't let the lousy flip-flopping terminology confuse you. The highest level (or lowest level, if you prefer) is built into WinWord itself.

How the Five Contexts Coexist

A friend in need … indeed.

"Pensées Pinecliffius"

A very strict hierarchy is at work here. To try to sort it out, I cobbled together Figure 4.6.

This is a rather idealized view of how WinWord *would* work if it worked logically; think of it as a starting point, something to hang your hat on while you go spelunking to greater depths.

I've drawn the Template box with dotted lines because sometimes there is no template level. Since `NORMAL.DOT` is a template like any other template, you can (and often do!) create a document based on `NORMAL.DOT`. When that happens, the template level kind of disappears, subsumed by the global layer. WinWord goes looking for the template associated with the active document, discovers it's `NORMAL.DOT`, and simply pops up to the next level.

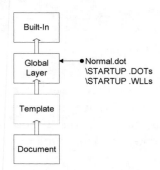

Figure 4.6 Context Interaction, First Cut

In Figure 4.6 I've labeled the Global Layer as a "layer" because it's more than a context. It's a jumbled-together heap of AutoText entries, customized settings and macros (or programs) that may have arisen from either the global template (NORMAL.DOT), or one of the templates or add-ins in the \STARTUP directory. What does Figure 4.6 *mean?* Ah, another good question!

When WinWord needs something, it follows a general pattern. Well, most of the time, anyway:

The hierarchy

- First, WinWord looks in the *document*. The document holds formatting information, styles, page settings, and the like—document things. But it doesn't hold any of the Terrible Three (AutoText, customizing, and macros), nor does it hold fundamental commands like those that open files or print on the printer.

- If WinWord doesn't find what it needs in the document, it looks in the doc's *template*.

- If it doesn't find what it needs in the doc's template (or if the doc's template is NORMAL.DOT), WinWord looks in the *global layer*. The global layer is the net result of smashing together two contexts: NORMAL.DOT and all the templates and programs in the \STARTUP directory. As mentioned earlier, the global layer is initially established when WinWord starts, and it can be modified by manually adding a new template or program (via File/Templates/Add).

- If all else fails, WinWord falls back on what was *built into* it originally.

As an example, say you're working on a document when you suddenly type the letters mnfffft and hit the AutoText button (F3 or <gulp> click the AutoText icon on the standard Toolbar). What, exactly, happens?

WinWord doesn't look in the document. If AutoText entries were stored in the document, presumably WinWord would look there. However, AutoText is one of the Terrible Three; no AutoText entries are stored in documents. Thus WinWord has to bump up one level to look at the document's template.

Document

If mnfffft is defined in the document's template, the search is over and WinWord can expand the AutoText entry. If mnfffft is not defined in the doc's template (or if the doc is based on NORMAL.DOT), WinWord gets bumped up to the global layer.

Template

The global layer, as I described earlier, is an amalgamation of NORMAL.DOT with the \STARTUP .DOTs and .WLLs thrown in, in alphabetical order, topped off by any templates or .WLLs that have been added manually since WinWord started. If WinWord finds an AutoText entry for mnfffft in the global layer, it's applied, and the work is done.

Global

WinWord doesn't look at the built-in level. No AutoText entries are defined at the built-in level, so there's nothing to look for.

Built-in

Key combinations

Custom key combinations work similarly. Every time you hit a key, WinWord has to decide if there's a special action it should perform. Say you type CTRL+F1.

No custom key combinations are assigned at the document level—again, key combinations are one of the Terrible Three—so WinWord immediately looks to the document's template. If CTRL+F1 is assigned at the template level, WinWord performs the action associated with the key combination. If CTRL+F1 is not assigned in the template, WinWord looks to the global layer. If the key combination is there, WinWord gets its marching orders. If the key combination isn't there, WinWord gives up because custom key combinations aren't defined at the built-in level.

Other customizing options

The other two customizing options, Toolbars and menus, work a bit differently, but then they really must. When WinWord needs to figure out what Toolbars and menus to display on the screen, it starts at the top and works its way down. First, the built-in Toolbars and menus get drawn, and then the modifications made at the global layer are rolled in. Finally, changes made in the document's template are applied. The resulting Toolbars and menus show up on the screen.

Macros

Finally, we have macros and commands. Whenever you press an established key combination, click on a Toolbar button, or click on a menu, WinWord goes looking for a macro or command with the associated name.

FileSave

If you click on File, then Close, say, WinWord goes looking for a macro or command called FileClose. If you click on the FileSave Toolbar button, WinWord goes looking for a macro or command called FileSave. Whenever you push the ALT+CTRL+F2 key combination (don't worry, I had to look it up, I can't remember all the weird key combinations either), WinWord goes looking for a macro or command called FileOpen. Of course, you can change buttons, menus, and key combinations to call up anything you like.

Build your own commands

In a stroke of pure genius, the folks who designed WinWord didn't hard-code the commands into the program. They let you change which buttons, menus, and key combinations call up which macro or command, and that's cool. But more important, they made WinWord so it would go through this context shtick when looking for *any* command.

So, when you click on File, then Close, say, WinWord starts by looking at the document's template for a FileClose macro. If none is there, it looks at the global layer for a FileClose macro. Only if there is no FileClose macro at a lower level does it resort to running the built-in FileClose command, which resides at the built-in level.

Control your destiny with macros

The result is enormously flexible. For example, you can write a FileClose macro and attach it to a template. Then, every time you close a document that's derived from that template, *your* macro will run instead of the built-in FileClose command.

Alternatively, you can write a FileClose macro and put it in a global layer template—either `NORMAL.DOT`, or any template in the `\STARTUP` directory. Your FileClose macro, being on the global layer, will always intercept a close. WinWord will never go up to the built-in level, where the standard FileClose routines reside.

Now you see why I don't like the macro/command terminology. There's almost no difference between the two. WinWord was brilliantly designed so that you can add your own commands to the program. The only difference between a macro and a command is that the latter resides inside `WINWORD.EXE`. That's it.

Macro vs. command

Final Word on Context

> Global citizens began it
> When Men-about-town became Men-about-planet.
>
> Christopher Morley
> *Toulemonde, 1944*

WinWord's context-sensitive capabilities and their associated context levels are shown in Figure 4.7. I hope you find this categorizing useful; far as I know, nobody has ever looked at them in quite this way.

	Toolbar	Menu	Key	Macro	Auto Text	Auto Correct
Built-In	X	X	X	*		
Global	X	X	X	X	X	X
Template	X	X	X	X	X	
Document						

*A built-in macro is called a "command."

Figure 4.7 Different Contexts' Capabilities

For example, Figure 4.7 tells you that certain keyboard assignments are built-in to WinWord and that they can be modified on the global layer or at the template level, but not in each individual document. Menus work the same way. Oddly, whereas you can reset keyboard and menu assignments in the Tools/Customize dialog, Toolbars are reset in the View/Toolbars dialog. Go figger.

Now that I've presented a somewhat rational view of what's happening with context, it's true confessions time. The WinWord world is not this orderly. There are glitches in all of this, and some of them are bloody hard to understand, much less explain.

I described what happens when you Reset the Toolbar, keyboard, or menus assignments in NORMAL.DOT. You just get the original, built-in keyboard and menu assignments. That's great.

You might think that a similar Reset in a template would wipe out all template-level changes and that the global layer Toolbar, keyboard, and menu assignments would always come through. Given WinWord's approach to context, you'd think that Reset would simply nuke all lower level assignments and let the higher level take over. Not so.

Hitting Reset in a template (other than NORMAL.DOT) *copies* the current NORMAL.DOT Toolbar, keyboard, or menu assignments to the template. If you subsequently change the Toolbar, keyboard, or menu assignments in the global layer, those changes may or may not "take" in documents based on the Reset template. Bizarre, but true.

If you've made changes in Toolbars, menus, or keyboard assignments in NORMAL.DOT and they aren't showing up when you use certain templates, chances are good you Reset the template's assignments at some time in the past. Another one they didn't warn you about, eh?

It's not just Toolbar, keyboard, and menu assignments. WinWord's designers decided to short-circuit the usual context rules with macros, too. I call this the WexBug because it was first brought to my attention by Ted Epstein and Julianne Sharer at WexTech Systems, two of the WinWord magicians who make Doc-to-Help.

Now I'll be the first to admit that there are powerful reasons for using this WexBug approach, but the change was slipped into WinWord 6.0, wasn't documented anywhere, wasn't discussed or debated (at least outside Redmond), and caused endless confusion among macro mavens.

The WexBug   When WinWord hits a command inside a running macro, you might think that it would apply the same context rules that pertain when you click on a Toolbar button or menu. For example, if you wrote a macro that uses a FileNew command, you might think that WinWord would go through the document-to-template-to-global-to-built-in sequence, in the same way that it does if you click on File, then New. Well, you'd be wrong.

When WinWord hits a command like that, it starts looking *in the template that contains the running macro*. The WexBug has other manifestations, but this bass-ackwards context is the easiest one to describe. This terribly complicated little nit won't affect many people, but it's yet another example of how Microsoft violates its own rules, of how you can't count on WinWord's underlying logical structure to think through problems, and of how, for better or

worse, you must rely on others' experiences and word of mouth. It's also a great example of why WinWord can be so damn frustrating. Really, anybody who says it's easy doesn't know what's happening.

By the way, if you ever want to construct a *document* that has its own macros, Toolbars, menu assignments, custom key combinations, or AutoText or AutoCorrect entries, it's easy. Simply create a new template. Close it. WinWord will force you to name it with the extension `.DOT` and place it in your `\TEMPLATE` directory. That's okay. Humor WinWord and do it the official way.

You *can* make a document smart

Then, *outside* WinWord, move the file wherever you like and rename it with a `.DOC` extension. Your new `.DOC` will act like a document in every respect, except it's really a template! The Toolbars, menus, macros, and everything else will go along with the "document," wherever it may venture. Nobody need ever know. It's that simple.

A Plaintive Plea

> Singularity in the right hath ruined many;
> happy those who are convinced of the general opinion.
>
> Benjamin Franklin
> *Poor Richard's Almanack*, 1757

There's an underlying symmetry to all of this that's just screaming to get out. I'd like to end this discussion of context with a plea for sanity, directed at The Primeval Creators in Redmond. Next time around, oh wise ones, would it be possible to make context a cardinal rule?

Why not put all six of the context-sensitive capabilities (Toolbar, menu, key, macro, AutoText, and AutoCorrect) in all five of the contexts (document, template, global, `\STARTUP`, and built-in)? It'd sure make WinWord a whole lot easier to understand, and I'd betcha bucks to buckaroos that it'd be easier to program, maintain, and support, too.

Make Resets that really work, by completely nuking the settings on a given level, not by copying stuff over. Finally, force everything to work according to simple context rules. No exceptions.

Foolish consistency may be the hobgoblin of little minds, but a little lousy consistency every now and then wouldn't hurt. Make this simple enough and youse guys might even put me out of a job. Scary thought, that. *Heh, heh, heh.*

FIELDS

Basic Birdsmanship is of course
to have the best pair of field glasses in any group.

Steve Potter
One-Upmanship, 1952

Like styles and templates, WinWord's fields are woefully underused. They should be a part of your everyday arsenal, a key ingredient in your guru's bag o' tricks.

WinWord's fields let you make like a duck: sailing along smooth, gracious, unruffled, by all outward appearances, belying the fact that you're paddling like hell underneath. Several of WinWord's niftier features, like Cross-References, Mail Merge, Insert Page Numbers, Date and Time, Object, Tables of Contents, Figures, Authorities, Indexing, and much more are just gussied-up pretty faces put on dirty, old, ho-hum fields.

Code vs. Result

I know why there are so many people who love chopping wood.
In this activity one immediately sees the results.

Albert Einstein

It's just a function.   A **field** is a miniature function, an honest-to-goodness computer program sitting at a specific point right inside your document. Like all good functions, a field pulls in things—numbers and characters and all sorts of bits and scraps of informational flotsam—mashes them around, and calculates a result.

For example, the {page} field takes a look around and finds out which page it's sitting on. That page number is the result of the {page} calculation. If you stick a {page} field on page number 127 of a document and tell WinWord to show you the results of field code calculations (as opposed to the field code itself), you'll see 127. Another example: the { = } field does arithmetic. The result of a field that looks like { = 1 + 1 } is 2. Rocket science again, eh?

Nested fields   You can mix and match fields and, with some restrictions, stick them inside of each other. It probably wouldn't surprise you to know that the result of the field { = {page} + 1} is the page number of the next page.

At any given moment, you can either have WinWord show you the field itself—the miniature program, like { = 1 + 1}, commonly called a field code—or you can have WinWord show you the result of the field, in this case 2.

Making Fields

> You love me!
>
> Sally Fields
> Oscar Awards

Although I use { squiggly brackets } (or "braces," if you prefer) in this book to warn you that you're working with a field, and in spite of the fact that WinWord displays the same { squiggly brackets } when you ask it to show you field codes, squiggly brackets do not a field make! The {} characters you see on-screen and in this book represent a very special pair of characters, called field characters. You can't simply type

{page}

in a document and expect WinWord to recognize that as a field code. It's a little more complicated than that.

The books tell you to use CTRL+F9 to put field codes in a document. I don't recommend that: it's too easy to screw up a field code when you're typing one in from scratch. In general, I recommend that you always follow this sequence when inserting field codes into a doc:

- First, make WinWord display field codes, not field results. If you made the changes recommended in Chapter 1, that's as simple as clicking on the standard Toolbar's ShowAll button. If you didn't make those changes, you'll have to click on Tools, then Options, make sure the that View tab is showing, check the Field Codes box, and click OK. Alternatively, you can stick your cursor inside a field, right-click on the mouse, and choose Toggle Field Codes.

- Then—and only when you can see field *codes*, not their results, on your screen—click on Insert, then Field…. You'll be greeted by the full array of available field codes, as shown in Figure 4.8.

Don't be intimidated by the wide choice. Figure 4.8 just cracks open the door. An entire programming language is lurking here, replete with tricks, traps, and all sorts of fun stuff, including more than a few bugs. I'll touch on a few of the biggies, but to really get into the nuances of fields, you'll have to consult a more detailed book, like the *Hacker's Guide to Word for Windows*.

Speaking of bugs. The official docs say you can toggle an individual field between showing its code and showing its result by putting your cursor in the field, clicking the right mouse button, and choosing Toggle Field Codes, or by

Whence the {field characters}

ShowAll

hitting `SHIFT + F9`. **Hey, maybe their copy of WinWord works that way, but mine doesn't. I couldn't find any way to switch between codes and results on anything but the entire document.**

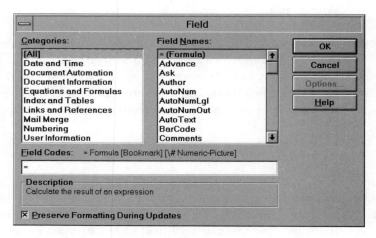

Figure 4.8 Insert Field, the Dialog

Oh. Lest you ever get confused. In the parlance, "make WinWord display field codes" and "turn View Field Codes ON" mean the same thing. Similarly, "make WinWord display field results" is synonymous with "turn View Field Codes OFF."

Using Fields

> Though all the winds of doctrine
> were let loose to play upon the earth,
> so Truth be in the field.
>
> John Milton
> *Areopagitica*, 1644

Stable fields   Some fields don't change very often. A field like {filename} returns the name of the current document, for example, `TUGWORD.DOC`. It isn't going to change unless you go outside WinWord and rename the file. Similarly, the {author} field produces the name of the author of the current document. It only changes if you go into File/Summary Info and change the line marked Author.

Changing fields   Many fields change values, though, and keeping up with the changes can drive you nuts. The {date} field is one of my favorites: not surprisingly, it changes every day. "Freezing" your letters and memos so they always show the date they were mailed falls into this changing-field-value category. If you put a {date} field in a memo, print the memo today, and then come back and print the same memo a week from now, the dates won't match. Fortunately a solution exists.

When the value of a field changes, you'll usually want your document to show the new value, not the old. Normally WinWord updates fields only when they're originally placed in a document. If you go into Tools, Options, pick the Print filecard, and check the Update Fields box, WinWord will also update fields prior to printing.

Updating

But that's it. Fields don't update themselves automatically, even if the underlying data (like the date, or the time, or whatever) has changed. You have to specifically tell WinWord that you want it to update the field. Fortunately updating a field is simple. Stick your cursor inside the field (or select more than one field, if you want to update more than one), click the right mouse button, and click Update Field.

Sometimes you actually want to prevent fields from being updated. That's at the root of the freezing {date} problem mentioned earlier. You want to put today's date in the document, but as soon as it's in there, you don't ever want it updated.

Stopping updates

WinWord gives you two ways to prevent field updates. You can *lock* a field, which simply tells the field to shrug off any attempts to update it. Alternatively you can *unlink* a field, which converts the whole field to text, right there, getting rid of the field entirely. "Unlink" is a lousy name. When WinWord unlinks, it's actually converting the field to text (or a picture), zapping out the field in the process.

Major Fields

Here are my favorite fields, ones I use all the time, in alphabetical order:

{ **any ol' thing** } returns the contents of the indicated bookmark. {Laurel} returns whatever is currently in the bookmark called "Laurel." This is actually the same as the {ref} field. For example, {ref Laurel} and {Laurel} produce the same result. (See the next section, on bookmarks, for details.)

{ **=** } calculates a number, often in conjunction with another field.

{**Author**} returns the name of the author of the current document, as shown in the File/Summary Info dialog box.

{**Date**} produces today's date, but you can muck around with formatting switches to give the day, date, time, and all sorts of other things. The field {date \@ "MMMM dd, yyyy hh:mm AM/PM"} turns into something like October 20, 1994, 03:42 AM.

{**Filename**}, {**Filesize**} gives the name and size of the current file. Note that the name comes out all caps, with no path information.

{**Gotobutton**}, when double-clicked on, immediately propells the cursor to the location of a specified bookmark. You can use {gotobutton} to create righteous hypertext-like documents, where users can double-click their way all over the place. (See the next section, on bookmarks, for details.)

{MacroButton} is the most powerful field. When a user double-clicks on this field, a specified macro is run.

{NumChars}, {NumPages}, and **{NumWords}** count the number of characters, pages, and words, respectively, in the document. Very useful for writers who like to put word counts in their work.

{Page} returns the current page number. If you reset page numbering in a section, that reset affects this number; in short, this is what you probably think of when you think of a page number. You might want to try using something like this in a footer: Page {page} of {numpages}.

{Print} tosses the indicated characters (usually obscure print codes) directly to the printer. Used to force printers to do things that can't be accomplished through "nice" means.

{SaveDate} can be used to keep track of revisions. {savedate \@ "MMMM dd, yyyy hh:mm AM/PM"} produces the date and time the doc was last saved.

{Seq} creates and maintains a sequential list of numbers. Most of its functionality now is easier to get at through the Insert Caption and Format Heading Numbering commands, but there are still many cases where you might use a {seq} field to keep a list of numbers running through a document.

Separate sequences are kept for different arguments. The first time WinWord hits a {seq foo} field, say, it gets the value of 1. The second time it sees a {seq foo}, it gets the number 2. And so on. You can keep multiple sequences going at the same time: {seq foo} produces a series of numbers completely independent of, say, {seq bar}.

{StyleRef} is another enormously powerful field. For example, {styleref "heading 1"} delivers everything that is included in the most recent "heading 1" style. You can use it to create running indices, as you'll see at the top of any telephone book. I used it to print the title of the current chapter at the bottom of each page of this book.

Even obsolete fields are used internally

Many of the other fields are pretty much obsolete nowadays, their functionality replaced by menus and dialog boxes that make life much simpler. Don't be surprised, though, when you tell WinWord to show field codes and all of these strange codes show up. Those fancy new menus and dialog boxes use field codes themselves!

Oddities

> 'Twas strange, 'twas passing strange.
>
> Shakespeare
> *Othello*, 1604

Fields can be pretty strange, at least at first. (Believe me, if you really dig down into them deep, they get *very* strange.) In general, the WinWord on-line help has good information and advice on the basic operation and settings for each field. Just look up the name of the field. To find help on, say, the {seq} field, hit F1, and Search for SEQ. It's that easy.

Before we leave the subject, there are a few traps, a few oddities, that I'd like to warn you about.

The {advance} field is a favorite of WordPerfect converts. It was designed to work the way WordPerfect's advance feature works, by reaching into the document and positioning text at specific locations on a page. Personally, I avoid {advance} like the plague. There may be certain situations where it's unavoidable, but I haven't hit one yet. If you can find a way to accomplish the same result using margins, indents, frames, or the drawing layer, you'll be much better off.

{Advance}

If you get to the point where you think the {ask}, {set}, or {fillin} fields look like a good solution, seriously think about using a macro. You'll find macros much simpler, more flexible, and more powerful. (One exception: if you need to, literally, fill in specific information for each record in a mail merge, {fillin} is probably the easiest way.)

{Ask}, {Set}, {Fillin}

None of these fields produce a visible result. They sit and lurk in your documents, manipulating text behind the scenes. {if} may or may not show a result. {Advance} produces a result, but only by moving other items around on the page. To see these fields, you have to tell WinWord to show field codes. There are no field results to see.

{Ask}, {Next}, {NextIf}, {Print}, {Set}, {SkipIf}

By contrast, {RD} (Reference Document, for linking together pieces of large documents), {TA} (Table of Authorities entry), {TC} (Table of Contents entry), and {XE} (Index entry) are formatted hidden. You have to tell WinWord to show hidden text—in the Tools/Options/View menu, or by clicking on the ShowAll button—to be able to see them. Perhaps surprisingly, these four fields do not appear when you tell WinWord to show field codes. Their appearance depends entirely on whether or not you are displaying hidden text.

{RD}, {TA}, {TC}, {XE}

The field that delivers the time and date the current document was last printed, {printdate}, is the only field I know that's updated even if you specifically tell WinWord *not* to update fields. It is *always* updated prior to printing, whether the Tools/Options/Print Update Fields check box is checked or not. This behavior is particularly surprising because {savedate}—a very similar field— is only updated when you tell WinWord to update it, regardless of when you save the document.

Nothing like a few exceptions to the general rule to make you feel more … secure, eh?

BOOKMARKS

> The only fun in this business for me is doing a show and turning it up
> real loud. The rest of it is all work.

> Frank Zappa*

WinWord's bookmarks have very few similarities to the old-fashioned card-board bookmarks you'll find in the real world.

Bookmark defined   Drag your cursor across a bunch of text. See how you highlight it, how you "turn it black"? Anything that's selected that way is called a ... uh ... selection. A **bookmark** is just a selection with a name.

In WinWordLand, bookmarks have two uses. First, they can mark a place in a document, just like that old-fashioned cardboard bookmark. You can use it to move directly to a predefined location. That's probably what you would expect from a bookmark.

The second use for bookmarks isn't so intuitive. WinWord gives you several methods for looking at and using the stuff that's *covered* by a bookmark. Since every bookmark is a selection with a name, it makes sense to talk about what is *in* a bookmark. That's not exactly what you might expect from an old-fashioned cardboard bookmark.

Bookmark Manipulation

Adding a bookmark   Creating a new bookmark couldn't be simpler. Just stick your cursor somewhere in your document (for a **point bookmark**), or select anything you like (for a **real selection bookmark**), then click on Edit, then Bookmark. (See Figure 4.9) Type in a bookmark name, and click Add. There. You now have a brand-new bookmark.

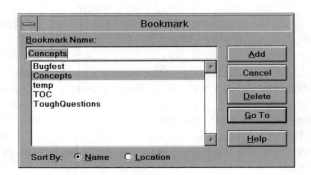

Figure 4.9 Edit Bookmark

---

*Zappa died while I was writting this book. A tireless defender of free speech, whether you loved him or hated him, you had to admire him. *Don't eat the yellow snow, Frank.*

Seeing all the bookmarks in your document is simple but of dubious value. If you click on Tools, then Options, bring up the View filecard, and check the Bookmarks box, WinWord shows you all your bookmarks. They're encased in giant, gray [brackets], scattered throughout your document.

Viewing bookmarks

That's fine, as far as it goes, but it overlooks a crucial part of bookmark futzing: given a pair of [bookmark brackets], you can't tell which bookmark they belong to. You can tell that there's a bookmark in your document, but you can't easily tell which bookmark it is. Worse, if bookmarks overlapp, you can't tell where one bookmark ends and another begins.

Worse, [if you[have over]lapping]

Figure 4.10 Overlapping Bookmarks

In Figure 4.10 I set up two bookmarks, and then used Tools/Options/View to show bookmarks. Here's a little intelligence test, pilgrim: Can you tell me which of these choices, A or B, correctly describes the contents of the bookmarks?

Choice A:

> In Bookmark 1: if you have over
> In Bookmark 2: have overlapping

Choice B:

> In Bookmark 1: if you have overlapping
> In Bookmark 2: have over

Bzzzzt. Time's up. The answer? You *can't* tell.

Now you know why I'm so ambivalent about showing bookmarks in the Tools/Options/View dialog. Yeah, it's kinda nice to know that a bookmark exists, but the amount of information you have on the bookmark, just by looking at it, hardly justifies the effort or the cluttered screen. I guess that isn't a bug, in the technical sense of the term, but it sure does make my life more difficult than it should be.

Bookmark as Location

> To a life that seizes
> Upon content,
> Locality seems
> But accident.
>
> Elizabeth Coatsworth
> *To Daughters Growing Up*

Goto   Despite the problems, bookmarks are nifty things for zipping around documents. Click on Edit, then Goto (or if you followed my biases in Chapter 1, click on the standard Toolbar's Goto button). Pick a bookmark. Boom! You're there. If the bookmark is a single point, your cursor is positioned precisely where you want it to be. If the bookmark is a whole selection, all of the stuff is selected, ready for you to go at it.

If you want to know precisely which bookmark is where, and where the bookmark begins and ends, this Goto approach (or its near identical twin Edit/Bookmark/Goto) is your only choice. Merely showing bookmarks via the Tools/Options/View dialog doesn't tell the whole story.

Hypertext   You can pair bookmarks with {gotobutton} fields to add hypertext-like links to your documents. If you click on Insert, then Field, and stick a field like this in your document:

{gotobutton SomeBookmark Double-click here to JUMP!}

you'll see this on your screen (providing you tell WinWord to show field results, instead of field codes):

Double-click here to JUMP!

and if you double-click anywhere in that sentence, WinWord immediately transports you to the bookmark called SomeBookmark.

Bookmark as Container

WinWord has several very powerful tools for manipulating what is inside a bookmark. When you work with those tools, you're usually much more interested in what the bookmark covers, that is what is between the [bookmark brackets], than where the bookmark sits.

{Ref} and bookmarks   You might want to use a bookmark as a container to replicate text throughout a document, using the {ref} field.

Say you have a report that goes out every month, and part of the report is the previous months' sales. That same figure needs to be repeated in ten different places in the report. The rest of the report changes a little bit, but it's mostly boilerplate. Typical management mumbo-jumbo.

Yes, you could use Edit/Replace, pick out the old month's figures and replace them with the new. But using bookmarks is easier, more accurate, and faster. Here's how:

1. Open up the document, and find the previous month's sales amount. You don't necessarily have to pick the first occurrence of the amount: just snag one that's easy for you to find.

2. Put a bookmark over it. Select the sales amount, click Edit, then Bookmark, type in something intelligent — say, Sales — and click Add. There. Now the bookmark Sales contains the previous month's sales amount.

3. March through the document. Every place you find the sales figure, delete it, click on Insert, then Field, choose REF, and go down to that little box at the bottom and make sure it says REF Sales. Click OK.

That's it. Next time you have a new sales figure, make WinWord show bookmarks (Tools/Options/View Bookmarks), put the new sales figure in the bookmark called Sales, select the document (Edit/Select All, or CTRL + click in the left margin), and update all fields (I would use F9).

Changing Contents

> A sensational event was changing
> from the brown suit to the gray the contents of his pockets.
> He was earnest about these objects. They were of eternal importance, like
> baseball or the Republican Party.
>
> Sinclair Lewis
> *Babbitt*, 1922

Scattering bookmark references through a document leads me to the toughest part of working with bookmarks: modifying their contents. If you only use bookmarks to mark locations in a document, this nasty won't ever jump up and bite you. But if you rely on the contents of bookmarks, you need to be careful. Changing what's inside a bookmark is notoriously difficult. When you start playing with them, you'll see what I mean.

There's a rule buried in here. If you type stuff at the beginning of a bookmark, whatever you type is added to the bookmark itself; the bookmark expands to hold all the new text you've typed. However, if you type stuff at the end of a bookmark, it is *not* added to the contents of the bookmark; that is, the bookmark does *not* expand to hold the new text.

The only decent solution I've found is to make sure WinWord shows you the beginning and end of all bookmarks, using the Tools/Options/View Bookmarks check box, and then ensure that you're sitting in the bookmark you think you're in by using Goto. If you go to all that trouble, you won't often clobber a bookmark, or leave text out that you thought had gone in.

FORMS

When I first saw the Forms capability built into WinWord 6.0, I was licking my chops with joy. Here, at last, I figured, was a chance to bring some computing power *into* my documents. Man, was I disappointed. It's an all-too-typical Microsoft "version 1.0" implementation. Yes, there are things you can use, but it could've been so much more.

Let me start by describing what this Forms feature *is*, then I'll explain what it *isn't*, and finally I'll bore you for a moment with what it should be.

The Formless Form

For years WinWord has had the basics of Forms production built into the product. They're called **templates**. In a very real sense, a Form *is* a template. Somebody constructs this fill-in-the-blanks form, saves it as a WinWord template, and the user creates a new file based on that template. If you want a blank Form—perhaps to send to folks in Timbuktu who don't have computers—you just print the template.

Conceptually WinWord 6.0 brings much new insight to the Forms problem. It has built-in ways to let users fill in the blanks they're supposed to fill in, while at the same time protect users from changing things that shouldn't be changed. (Er, what use is a Form if it can be changed willy-nilly?)

The form fields   Most importantly, WinWord 6.0 lets you put three new "form fields" into a document:

- Text fields, which let the user type into a document and provide some intelligence in editing what is typed (For example, forcing a "date" field to be a date.)

- Check boxes, which let the user check Yes or No by x-ing or clearing a box

- Drop-down lists, which let the user pick from a predefined selection of text values (For example, you can set up a list of all the people in your office and, instead of forcing the user to type in a name, simply let them select from the list.)

Those three form fields alone would bring enormous power to everyday documents, never mind the button bars and all the other bells and whistles WinWord bundles with its Forms capabilities.

Unfortunately there's less here than meets the eye. If you're counting on these forms fields to solve your everyday problems, better look before you leap.

A Gedanken Form Experiment

Let me show you what a hum-dinger drop-down list form field might be able to do, and at the same time show you some of the pleasures and pitfalls of Forms à la WinWord.

Click on File, then New. Make sure that the Template button is picked and click OK. There. You have a new template in front of you; we're going to turn it into a WinWord Form.

A quick overview of how to make a form

Hit Enter a few times. Presumably this is where the typical form stuff would go: fill-in-the-blanks, check boxes, whatever. Good. Now I want to put in an area where the user can type in a few paragraphs, and then have a drop-down box that lets the users pick their own name—kind of like a signature, down at the bottom.

Click Insert, then Form Field. We need a text field here, where the user can type things, so click the Text Box button and click OK, like Figure 4.11.

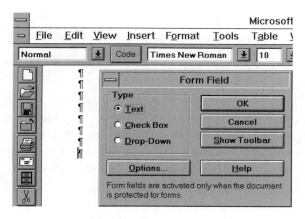

Figure 4.11 Text Form Field

See that gray blob that WinWord just put in your template? That's a text field, a place where people can type whatever they like.

Now hit Enter a few more times. Click Insert, then Form Field, click the Drop Down button, and hit Options. (See Figure 4.12.)

Adding a drop-down list

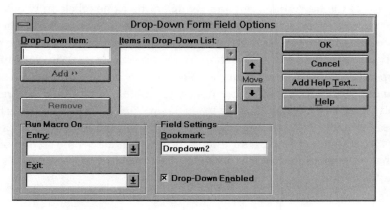

Figure 4.12 Drop-Down in Progress

Type in a name—say, Jane Smith—and click Add. Then type in another name—oh, John Smith—and click Add again. Click OK. Hit Enter again a couple more times, just for good measure. You should end up with a Form that looks more or less like Figure 4.13.

Figure 4.13 Test Form

Protect document

Good. That's a reasonable first stab at a Form. Now here's the trick. To make those form fields work—to turn the final field into a real, live, drop-down list, for example—you must "protect" the template. And that's where things fall apart. Click on Tools, then Protect Document, click Forms, and click OK. Then save your test form.

The Achilles Heel

What works

Create a new document based on your Form by clicking on File, then New, and picking the name of your saved test form. See how the cursor goes straight to the text field, so you can type things? Good. Type a few words. Then tab or move your mouse down to the list at the bottom. See how you can choose between Jane Smith and John Smith, with just a click? Great.

What doesn't

Get rid of the new document and create another one (click on File, then New, pick the name of your saved test form, and click OK). Now let's say you want to type a couple of paragraphs there at the top, in the text field. Type type type. Hit Enter. Type … type … ooops! See that? When you hit Enter, WinWord jumped to the drop-down signature list. Bummer. Wait. It gets worse.

Workarounds

You can work around the Enter-hopping problem a couple of different ways. Probably the easiest, ultimately, is to use WinWord's ability to Protect specific sections of a document; that capability is what awaits beneath the Sections button on the Tools / Protect Document dialog. If you create a whole *section* of a document that isn't protected, WinWord lets you type in it to your heart's content. Paragraphs galore.

Do you want to stick a bookmark in your form? No can do. Do you want to put in a picture, or frame something to move it around? Nope. You're faced with a fundamental dichotomy. If you want nifty stuff like the drop-down list box, you have to Protect the document. But if you Protect a document, you lose an enormous number of capabilities, everything from Edit/Select All, to footnotes, to captions, to inserting files, changing styles, to... believe it or not... word counts, envelopes, even the Tools/Customize dialogs!

Heaven help ya if you need to fill out an invoice form, and then make an envelope to go with it. Oy.

Hope for Forms 2.0

Take a look at that example I just tossed at you. Wouldn't it be loverly if you could stick drop-down list boxes in regular ol' documents? Or check boxes? Or radio buttons? Imagine being able to select from a bunch of predefined cc: lists, or from a collection of all your common memo TO: routings? The mind boggles. It could save tons of time.

Unfortunately you can't do that right now because you're forced to choose between drop-down lists and a ... uh ... laundry list of WinWord capabilities that are locked out when a doc is Protected.

Maybe Redmond will get it right next time.

5 Your Burning Questions Answered

The "silly question" is the first intimation
of some totally new development.

Alfred North Whitehead

Here's where I try to tackle the questions I hear most often, the things that seem to stymie the largest number of users, and give a few (sometimes surprising!) answers.

Unlike most of the other chapters in this book, you might want to look upon this part as a reference, not something you would normally want to tackle from beginning to end.

CRASHES

By compassion I subdue the demons.
All blame I scatter to the wind.

Milarepa
Tibetan sage

In a perfect world, there would be no General Protection Faults (GPFs), no computers that suddenly lose all connection with the outside world. As you know —if you've used the product for more than a day or two—WinWord does not live in a perfect world. WinWord crashes or freezes with alarming frequency, sometimes with completely bogus error messages. (Nine times out of ten, I have no idea why WinWord dies on me; so I should be telling you what to do, eh?)

Often you have no recourse once you're backed into a corner: your document gets hosed, maybe your whole machine freezes tight. Sometimes, at least, you can fix things so they don't crash again.

Buried deep within WinWord's soul are demons, gremlins that go flitting about whenever you load the program. Their eyes flash as they run by; their voices crackle while they trash your machine. You'll never catch one of the varmints in the midst of its havoc, so you'll have to settle for knowing that a malevolent sprite got you, even if you never learn its name. Indeed, the demons' creators generally have no idea why they exist or how to destroy them. It's the price we pay for progress.

Any time you see a box that says "So-and-so caused a General Protection Fault at xxxx" you've fallen victim to a programming bug (or, on rare occasion, a hardware problem). Either the folks who wrote WinWord made a mistake, or one of the myriad programs that support WinWord is out to lunch. You should never, ever get a GPF, and when (not if!) you do, *you* didn't do anything wrong: they're not your fault, they're the program's fault.

I cover fatal crashes, GPFs, weird lock-ups, in Chapter 6. Look there if WinWord just refuses to work, period. In fact, it would be smart to look in there and make the indicated adjustments *before* you crash. It's well worth your time.

SPEED

> All the speed is in the spurs.
>
> David Fergusson
> *Scottish Proverbs*, 1641

Hare tonic

You think WinWord runs as slow as a heavyweight tortoise on a molasses track, eh? Well, you aren't alone. Fortunately you can do a few things to speed WinWord up. Not all of them work, but what the hay.

The Minimum Machine

Microsoft will probably tell you that WinWord runs just fine on an 80286 with a couple of meg of memory. Don't know about you, but I gave up on the Tooth Fairy a few years back, when he gave me some bum stock options advice.

A fast 80386 at a minimum

The simple fact is that you need at *least* an 80386/25 with 4 MB of memory and 30 MB free on your hard disk before you should even think about running WinWord 6.0. Some folks grow gray waiting around for a 386/25 to run WinWord, but at least it's physically possible. If your machine isn't up to those standards, I'd strongly recommend that you find a copy of WinWord 2.0c somewhere. It's pretty well suited to 80386 systems, and it's fairly stable, all things considered. How's that for mincing words?

For day-in-and-day-out use, you should consider getting, at a minimum, a 486SX with 4 MB of memory, a local bus video card, and a fast hard drive with at least 40 MB free (you'll need 40 MB for WinWord, a permanent swap file, and ... oh ... you might even have some room left over for a few documents!).

You can see WinWord on a 640 × 480 screen, but just barely. The step up to 800 × 600 can save you tons of time; and 1024 × 768 could readily save you 30 minutes or more every day. To run 800 × 600, you'll need a flat 15-inch monitor, minimum—preferably a 17-inch—with 0.28 mm dot pitch or less. (Look in Chapter 7 of *The Mother of All Windows Books* for a lengthy discussion.)

The monitor

Memory Utilization

WinWord likes memory. Lots and lots of memory. WinWord eats memory like my son eats Tim Tams and my wife eats Brooklyn bagels. When WinWord wants more memory than you have on your system, your whole life can really get bogged down.

One of the most common memory-related sources of slow-downs is an engorged SmartDrive. SmartDrive, as you probably know, is a Microsoft product that caches your disk drives—provides a bit of fast storage area to serve as a go-between, reducing the amount of work your oh-so-slow disk drives must shoulder.

SmartDrive hogs memory

You may find that WinWord runs faster by actually *decreasing* the size of the SmartDrive cache. That's not exactly obvious, but it seems to work. You don't need a cache much larger than 1 MB most of the time, and if you have 8 MB or less of real memory, you should stick to a 1 MB or 512K cache size.

To decrease the size of the SmartDrive cache look in `AUTOEXEC.BAT` for a line like this:

```
C:\DOS\SMARTDRV.EXE 4096 1024
```

The line may be preceded by an LH or LoadHigh command, and all sorts of very officious-looking numbers. They don't concern us. The important numbers are the two on the end of the line, in this case, 4096 and 1024.

The first number is the size of the SmartDrive cache under DOS, in K; a value of 4096, as it is here, tells DOS to use a 4 MB disk cache. The second number is the size of the SmartDrive cache when Windows is running. In this case, a 1 MB (1024 K) SmartDrive cache is established when Windows starts.

Here are the values I would recommend for the second parameter on the `SMARTDRV.EXE` line:

- If you have 4 MB of memory or less, use 512.
- For more than 4 MB, up to 8 MB, use 1024.
- For more than 8 MB, try 2048.

Making your Windows swap file permanent, and getting to it with 32-bit access, also seems to help some folks. To do that, pop into Windows' Control

Swap file

Panel, double-click on the 386 Enhanced icon, click Virtual Memory>>, click Change>>, set up an 8 to 16 MB permanent swap file (no need to make it any larger, but 16 MB can come in handy if you're working with graphics), click OK, and make sure that the 32-bit disk access box is checked if it isn't grayed out. (If it is grayed out, check *The Mother of All Windows Books* for an explanation. It gets pretty complicated.)

BitmapMemory

If you have many graphics in your documents, particularly if you have many graphics, your scrolling times have gone to hell in a handbasket, and you have 8 MB or more of memory, open up `WINWORD6.INI` in your `\WINDOWS` subdirectory. Go ahead and use WinWord. Add this line to the [Microsoft Word] section:

> BitmapMemory=2048

then restart WinWord. Doubling the amount of space WinWord reserves for caching graphics, that is, raising the cache to 2 MB, may help speed WinWord up.

CacheSize

Similarly, if you work with big documents and have 4 MB or more of memory, you might want to open up `WINWORD6.INI` and add this line to the [Microsoft Word] section:

> CacheSize = 512

This quadruples the amount of memory WinWord sets aside to cache documents in general, bringing it up to 512K. If you have 8 MB of memory, you might want to jack that setting up to 1024.

Maximize Windows

The up-arrow

WinWord (actually, any Windows program) runs faster if it is maximized. Simply click on the up-arrow in the upper right-hand corner of the screen. Arrange for only one document to show at a time, and for it to take up the full screen. If more than one document is showing, click the document title bar's up-arrow.

Draft <Yikes!> View

Yeah, if you have to, Draft View is another option. It ain't pretty, but it works. This setting is buried a bit. Make sure that you're in Normal View (click View, then Normal), then click on Tools, Options, and check the Draft Font box. (See Figure 5.1.)

If the Draft Font box is checked, every time you pop into Normal or Outline View, you'll see things in the draft font. (Flip back into Page View, and everything is the way you'd expect.) The draft font is only used on the screen. WinWord can manipulate it very quickly. I've heard of some problems seeing curly quotes in the draft font, but I haven't found any solution.

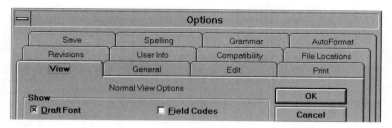

Figure 5.1 Draft Font

Fast and Auto Saves

WinWord's save methods can help or hinder your running speed.

With the Fast Save technique, WinWord saves an original doc, plus a short-hand form of all changes that have been made. Instead of rolling all the changes into a doc every time it's saved, and then forcing Windows to write the entire updated doc to disk, Fast Save lets WinWord store away the changes alone, and your saves really do speed up. **What's a Fast Save?**

What's the downside? Fast Saved documents can grow to twice the size of a "regular" document, even larger. TANSTAAFL*, eh?

To turn on Fast Save, click on Tools, then Options, bring the Save filecard to the fore, and check the Allow Fast Saves box. If you find that file size is more important to you than fast processing times, clear the check box.

Auto Save is a horse of an entirely different color, although it, too, can have a drastic effect on your processing time. As explained in Chapter 1, you can tell WinWord to automatically save a copy of your document every "x" number of minutes. The Auto Saved file does *not* replace the original file on your disk. Instead, it's stuffed into a specific place on disk. **Why Auto Save?**

Auto Save is mighty handy if you forget to save your document and all of a sudden WinWord (or Windows) crashes. WinWord has automatic hooks that force it to look for aberrant pieces of crashed-out files every time it starts.

There are two problems with Auto Save. First, it doesn't always work right. The Auto Saved file has been known to get scrambled (or deleted entirely; see Chapter 1 for warnings about the location of the TEMP file). Second, it really ties up all of Windows, sometimes for an extensive period of time, often when you really don't want it to.

If you remember to save your documents often, you don't need Auto Save or the all-encompassing interruptions it entails. On the other hand, if you only save about once every three days, you'd better turn Auto Save turned. To set it, click on Tools, then Options, bring up the Save filecard, and type in the number of minutes you want WinWord to wait between saves. **Setting Auto Save**

*There Ain't No Such Thing As A Free Lunch

Get a Faster Video Board

> Sign on the Temple bulletin board:
> Come early if you want to be sure
> Of getting a seat in the back.
>
> Leo Rosten
> *The Joys of Yinglish*, 1989

Having tweaked, twitched, and optimized WinWord to your heart's content, just about everybody comes to the conclusion that it isn't running as fast as they would like.

Accelerate!   If you reach that point, you should first consider buying an accelerated video board. You may find that it's a cheap, easy alternative to upgrading your computer as a whole. Several stable Windows accelerator boards are on the market, and they can be very effective.

Accelerator boards work by reducing the amount of stuff that has to flow between your computer's processor and the screen. The choke point between processor and video is one of the major roadblocks to reasonable Windows performance. The accelerator board alleviates—but doesn't solve!—the problem.

Changing from a "dumb" video card to an accelerated card (the Volante Warp series being my favorite at the moment, particularly because of their ultra-stable drivers) can triple or quadruple your scrolling rate. It's one of the few things that really can make your life better, get you home sooner at night, let you spend more time with the spouse and kids. If you don't have an accelerated card (or local bus video), it's time to get with the system.

Get More Memory

4 MB at least   WinWord 6.0 demands 4 MB. Give it any less and it's like a *Free Willy* orca wallowing in a cheap Mexican puddle: a travesty of the first degree. If you don't have at least 4 MB of memory and masochism doesn't run in the family, hie thee hence and get the chips!

If you run more than one Windows program at a time, you should seriously consider jumping up from 4 MB to 8 MB. WinWord and EXCEL together, for example, give the word "hog" a bad name. Giving them sufficient *lebensraum* should be your highest priority.

Get a Faster System

If you can't use the preceding ideas to tweak WinWord so it's fast enough for you, and an accelerated card and 4 MB of memory don't do the trick, it's time to ask Santa Claus, the Easter Bunny, the Office Nat, or <shudder> the boss for a new machine.

You'll pay for a 486SX in a nonce, simply because of all the time you'll save. With full 486 systems under $1,000, you have to ask yourself when it's time to stop tweaking and start paying.

PRINTING

Certainly one of the most, if not *the* most, frustrating aspects of WinWord is trying to get it to print what and how you think it should. Let's take a short walk through the printing minefield.

DeskJet

I don't mean to pick on the DeskJet. It's a great printer. I own one myself and recommend it to my clients and friends as the best inexpensive printer available. Perhaps it's because they are so popular—perhaps it's because DeskJet owners are so knowledgeable!—but for some reason, DeskJets seem to be having some difficulty co-existing with WinWord 6.0.

Some DeskJet users find that the Tools/Options/Print Printing Options Background Printing checkbox won't click on. WinWord insists on printing everything while you watch, instead of flipping to background printing and letting you get on to other work.

Background printing

The problem is in the driver. Certain versions of the DJ 500 and 500C printer drivers drop characters when run with WinWord background printing. WinWord disables background printing if it detects one of those drivers. Your best bet is to hop on the GO HPPER forum on CompuServe and see if HP has better drivers available.

There is a workaround, but you'll probably start seeing dropped characters; the cure is probably worse than the disease. But if you insist, go into WinWord's \MACROS subdirectory*, and open a file called MACRO60.DOT. Click on Tools, then Macro, and then double-click on SetPrintFlags. You'll see a dialog box like the one in Figure 5.2. See the line that says Disable Background Printing, +64? Uncheck that box and click OK. Yes, you do want to replace current settings.

---

*If you don't have a \MACROS subdirectory, you probably chose Typical Installation way back when you installed WinWord 6.0. Click on the Word Setup icon in Program Manager or break out the distribution diskettes, run Setup, pick Complete/Custom option, and add the \MACROS subdirectory.

```
┌─────────────────────────────────────────────────────────────┐
│ ▬                      Set Printer Flags                     │
├─────────────────────────────────────────────────────────────┤
│  ┌──────────────────┐              ┌──────────────────┐      │
│  │     Default      │              │        OK        │      │
│  └──────────────────┘              └──────────────────┘      │
│  Check box to modify settings on current printer ┌────────┐  │
│  HP LaserJet 4/4M: 64                            │ Cancel │  │
│                                                  └────────┘  │
│    □ TrueType as graphics for white on black text           │
│    ☒ TrueType as graphics for proper clipping around drawings│
│  ┌─Current Settings───────────────────────────────────────┐ │
│  │  □ Use Winword 2.0 bitmapped patterns to draw shading, +1│ │
│  │  □ Send mixed pages as multiple print jobs, +2         │ │
│  │  □ Simulate smart quotes & em dashes in non-scaled fonts, +4│ │
│  │  □ Request only standard paper sizes from driver, +8   │ │
│  │  □ Use low resolution bitmap patterns for hatched shading, +16│ │
│  │  □ Disable paper size and tray handling, +32           │ │
│  │  ☒ Disable background printing, +64                    │ │
│  └────────────────────────────────────────────────────────┘ │
└─────────────────────────────────────────────────────────────┘
```

Figure 5.2 Macro 60

Envelopes

> If you do your best, whatever happens will be for the best.
>
> WinWord 6.0 Tip of the Day
> *Would that it were so straightforward!*

Envelopes printing in WinWord 6.0 has so many problems that it'd be difficult to list—much less diagnose!—all of them. I sympathize with the 'Softies on this one. I've been writing WinWord envelope printing routines for years. It's a jungle out there.

In general, you can set some envelope options by clicking on Tools, then Envelopes and Labels... and clicking the Options button. But that's just the tip of the iceberg. Moving the POSTNET bar code is possible in some cases, but requires Herculean effort (see the WinWord User Manual). The addressee "grab" isn't very smart and will completely blow off almost any addressee that is formatted as a single paragraph (a common situation if your paragraphs are defined with an extra line after). Clicking the box to rotate an envelope 180 degrees doesn't work unless you create a custom envelope of the same size.

If you do a mail merge and WinWord hits a postal code it doesn't recognize (like any postal code outside the U.S.!), the POSTNET bar code doesn't print on the envelope. In its place you get a grand, bold **Error! Zip code not valid!** (This one is a "design feature." Honest. It was meant to work that way.) Headers in print merge main documents get stuck on attached envelopes (!). You can't use frames in the addressee style to move the addressee farther left than WinWord wants it. And on and on.

I once offered to write an envelope-printing macro for Microsoft, one that could be used by real people, in a real office, to get the mail out the door without all these mickey-mouse problems. I'm damn lucky Microsoft didn't take me up on the offer. I'd still be debugging the macro! Envelope printing is a nasty, complex problem. None of the major word processors come close to solving it.

Next time you get mail from Microsoft, take a look at the envelope. I'll betcha the sender used anything *but* the WinWord envelope printer to address it. That's the Gates-honest truth.

This is a crass commercial, but if you have envelope problems, here's your solution. I use the WOPR envelope printer (Enveloper, written by Vince Chen) and can't imagine working without it. (You wouldn't expect any differently, wouldja? WOPR's my pride and joy, my first-born done good out in the big city.) Look at the card in the back of this book for ordering info. Enveloper has been winning awards for years. Some folks have switched to WinWord just because of Enveloper. I'm serious about the 100% lifetime no-questions-asked money-back guarantee. And I won't mention WOPR again — even if WOPR *does* solve a large proportion of the problems mentioned in this book, and even if you *do* qualify for a steep discount 'cuz you bought this book—until we talk about add-ins in the final chapter. Promise.

Table Gridlines

If you see faint dotted lines around your table cells on the screen but don't get any lines on the printer, Table Gridlines is turned on (click Table, and look at the bottom of the list). In general it's easier to use tables if the gridlines are showing up on the screen, but it can be confusing when something on the screen doesn't appear on the printed page.

To draw lines around the cells in your tables, as in Figure 5.3, you have to use the Format, Borders command. Select the whole table, click on Format, then Borders and Shading, and click the Grid icon. Play with it a bit and you'll see how to adjust the thickness of the lines.

like	this

Figure 5.3 A Well-Celled Table

Tables
to align   Note that tables can be used for all sorts of formatting tricks, including lining text up side to side like this:

Part 1	Blah, blah, blah, blah, and blah again.
Part 2	Ipsum lorem cogitum sumo wrestler.

Tables
to draw   That's just a 2 × 2 table, with entries in the appropriate cells and no gridlines printed. Tables are also very useful for drawing rectangles and parts of rectangles like the ones in Figure 5.4

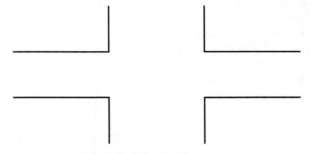

Figure 5.4 Parts of Rectangles

This is a 3 × 3 table with appropriate borders drawn in the corner cells. Tables can be quite versatile if you get the hang of them. We'll use a 3 × 1 table in Chapter 9 to draw crop marks.

Roving Callouts

If you've used callouts to draw lines and make annotations in your documents, you know how infernally fickle they can be. I had no end of trouble working with callouts in this book. You'll normally create callouts by clicking on the callout button, in the drawing Toolbar (see Figure 5.5).

This is the
Callout button

Figure 5.5 Callouts

Callouts flip-flop all over the place. At the beginning of a page, you might not *ever* get them to stay put. The reason for their peripatetic behavior lies in how the callouts are anchored to the text itself.

Drawings in WinWord live in a separate world called a **drawing layer**. Think of the drawing layer as a transparency that's superimposed on top of the document. You draw on the transparency. WinWord has to tack the transparency onto the document at specific points, like sticking a pushpin through the transparency and doc, binding the two together.

Those points where the transparency and the doc are tied to each other are called **anchors**. It's important that you be able to see the anchors; if you followed along in Chapter 2, you already have Show Object Anchors (in the Tools/Options/ View filecard) turned on. The anchors appear as, well, as anchors, typically in the margins of your documents.

An anchor looks like this:

The term "anchor" is an unfortunate one because these anchors float! When you insert a new callout (or anything else on the drawing layer, for that matter) or move the callout around, the anchor flits from paragraph to paragraph, apparently in an attempt to anchor the callout to the nearest paragraph. But *you don't want your callouts anchored to the nearest paragraph!*

I'm not absolutely sure—and can't tell for sure from the official documentation —but it looks to me as though WinWord anchors callouts to the paragraph nearest the callout box, the callout text. If that's true, it's a bug. A callout should automatically anchor itself to the paragraph nearest the end of the callout line. After all, that's what you're pointing to!

With very few exceptions, you'll want to anchor your callouts to the picture they're pointing at. You want the callout to travel with the picture, not with some chunk of text that just happens to be nearby. If you've been chasing callouts all over your documents, well, now you know why. Unfortunately the callout moves with paragraph text that's near the callout, rather than with whatever it's pointing to.

Here's how to make your anchors stay put:

1. Make sure anchors are showing. You'll have to flip into Page View and get the Show Object Anchors box in the Tools/Options/View filecard checked.

2. Arrange the callout so it's where you want it. When you're through futzing with it, the callout should be selected, and its anchor should appear somewhere near the callout text.

3. Click on the anchor and drag it to the left side of the paragraph that your callout is *pointing to*. That's where you want the anchor to be.

4. Double-click on the anchor (or click Format, then Drawing Object). Flip to the Size and Position filecard. Click the box that says Lock Anchor. There. Now your anchor behaves like an anchor—it'll stay put, locked onto the paragraph you've chosen.

The drawing layer can be very powerful. Maybe some day it will also be easy to use. We can always hope.

PRINTING SPEED

> Be wise with speed.
> A fool at forty is a fool indeed.
>
> Edward Young
> *Love of Fame,* 1725

If you think speed is a problem, and you think printing is a problem, you can just imagine what kinds of headaches printing speed might bring to the fore. The worst of both worlds. Here are my favorite tips for improving print speed.

Caches, Background Printing

WinWord and Windows give you all sorts of options for printing settings. That's because different folks look at the print speed problem differently. In fact, settings that are appropriate for everyday printing may not be the least bit appropriate for times when you have to get something off the printer, like, now.

There's fast, and there's fast

There are two different, conflicting definitions of the term "speed," and a few nuances between the two extremes. The fundamental dichotomy is simple. Are you more interested in getting the final page off the printer as quickly as possible, or is your primary concern getting back to work as soon as you can, even if it takes longer to physically get the pages out?

How to make the printer "release" faster

If you want to get back to work sooner and aren't too concerned about how long you'll have to wait to see the final printed page, try these steps:

1. Make sure that Print Manager is working. (If you have a different print spooler, like PrintCache, make sure that it's working.)

2. Go into Windows' Control Panel (probably in your MAIN group), double-click on the Printer icon, and make sure that the Use Print Manager box is checked. (See Figure 5.6.)

3. Look in your `AUTOEXEC.BAT` file, using something like SysEdit. Make sure that a `SET TEMP =` statement points to your fastest, cached hard drive, preferably with 8 MB or more free space. Print Manager uses this `TEMP` area to

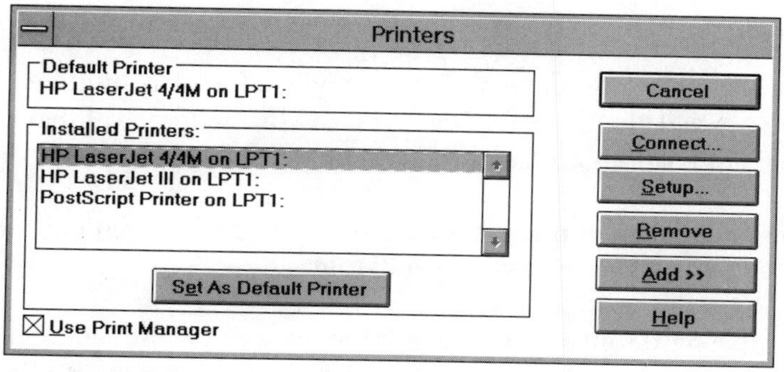

Figure 5.6 Print Manager

store print spooling files. If what you're trying to print doesn't fit into the temp area, all sorts of strange things can happen. Do not point TEMP to a RAMdisk; it'll work better if it's looking at a big, fast, cached hard drive. For details (it's complicated!), see Chapter 7 of *The Mother of All Windows Books*.

4. Inside Print Manager, click on Options, and set it to LOW Priority. That gives you and the work *you* do priority over the work that's sitting around ready to print.

5. Make sure background printing is enabled by clicking on Tools, then Options, then picking the Print filecard, and checking the Background Printing box. WinWord won't give you a very snappy response while it's printing—it has a lot of work to do behind the scenes and will take over your computer when you least appreciate it—but it's better than the alternative!

On the other hand, if you are going to stand and tap your foot until the output is ready—the boss is breathing down your back or you have to get to the post office before it closes—and you couldn't care less about getting back to working on your computer, try these:

How to get the pages off the printer faster

1. Turn Print Manager OFF. No, I'm not kidding. You'll run considerably faster without it, and changing back is easy. In the Windows' Control Panel, double-click on the Printer icon, and turn off the Use Print Manager check box. Look at Figure 5.6. If you have to use the Print Manager, click on Options, and set it to HIGH Priority.

2. Turn Background Printing OFF. Click on Tools, Options, get the Print filecard, and clear out the Background Printing box. (Actually, if you turn off Print Manager, WinWord is supposed to turn off Background Printing all by itself, but it won't hurt to check.)

If you're trying to get a document out quickly, background printing will just get in the way.

Hard Fonts

Break out your printer manual. Find out which fonts are built into the printer itself—the so-called "hard" fonts. See if you can live with one of them; hard fonts will *always* print faster than other kinds of fonts.

Hard fonts are faster. If there is a hard font that doesn't curl your toes, you should set it up as your normal (default) font.

Setting up a hard font as your default font is easy. Go into your \TEMPLATES subdirectory, open up NORMAL.DOT, click Format, then Style, Modify, then Format (again!), Font, and then pick the hard font you like from the list. Click OK all the way back out and close NORMAL.DOT.

TOOLBARS

> Power Toolbar: where drills and saws knock back a few brewskies.
>
> Pensées Pinecliffius

WinWord's Toolbar holds the potential to save you hours of work every week. There's no such thing as a "perfect" Toolbar; what works for you today may well be inadequate tomorrow. In the best of all possible worlds, you'll tweak the Toolbar whenever an opportunity arises. So it's important that you learn how to manipulate the Toolbar, and learn about its limitations.

Changing Button Assignments

> You press the button,
> we'll do the rest.
>
> Kodak ad

WinWord 2.0 made it pretty easy to change the command or macro assigned to a Toolbar button. Alas, WinWord 6.0 loses that nifty simplicity.

You can't simply change, you must delete, then add. The only way to change the command assigned to a Toolbar button is to first delete the button (along with its assigned command), and then add a brand-new button. (We did that in Chapter 1, when we changed the command associated with the FileNew button.)

In the process you'll lose any custom artwork you may have done to the button itself, unless you use some sort of graphics program to capture the old image before you delete it, and then go through the clipboard to paste it onto the new button. Bummer.

If you're a little rusty on the mechanics of changing Toolbar buttons, try reading through Chapter 1. It covers all the variations.

Status Bar Status

Once WinWord's shining light, the status bar has gone to seed.

Why isn't the status bar treated like every other Toolbar? Why all the wasted space, with no customizing? Why can't you put your mouse in the status bar and right-click to look at other Toolbars? Why can't you move it someplace other than the bottom of the screen? Why do you have to know that its presence is controlled by the View menu? Why can't you take something off the status bar—say, the clock—and put it on a different Toolbar? The answer, my friend, is blowin' in the wind .... C'mon Redmond. The status bar has become an underachiever joke. It's just another Toolbar. Give us the tools so we can work with it!

And while you folks are at it, give us something more than page and column numbers, okay? Why not a Free Systems Resources monitor? Or the name of the active printer? Maybe a quick summary of print jobs? The size of the current file? Or the current directory? Maybe a MOM-style hot switch, to flip to another application? An enormous amount of information could be placed on the status bar, but we still don't have the hooks.

Formatting Button Confusion

In every previous version of WinWord, you could tell at a glance whether the currently selected text was bold or italic or both. If nothing you selected were italic, for example, earlier versions of WinWord would show the Italic button "unpushed." If all of the selected text were italic, you would see a "pushed" italic button. And if they were mixed, you'd see a "hollow" italic button, as in Figure 5.7.

Figure 5.7 Three Faces of Italic

That was pretty neat, especially if you were working with a low-resolution monitor or a small bit of text where it was hard to see if the text was italic or not.

Unfortunately WinWord 6.0 doesn't have the same capability as its earlier incarnations. In fact, the hollow button face has disappeared entirely. When folks ask me what happened to it, the best I can do is extend condolences. WinWord has lost some of its functionality, and nothing you can do will bring it back.

Microsoft claims this change was intentional; they say they did it to make WinWord act more like EXCEL. It ain't a bug, it's a feature. That makes a whole lotta sense to me. Every software manufacturer should remove a word processing

feature in your word processor so it acts more like your spreadsheet. Maybe they should take charts out of EXCEL so that it works more like WinWord. I mean, since EXCEL limits cells to a max of 255 characters, maybe WinWord should limit pages to 255 characters.

Vertical Vertigo

Why do buttons change *function* when they're in a vertical Toolbar? The Undo button loses its multilevel function when it's on a vertical Toolbar; you can only undo one level at a time. Same for the Redo button. The View Zoom button brings up a dialog box instead of a simple drop-down list.

It isn't a question of implementation: WinWord's programmers and designers can do it. The Insert Table button, for example, works the same way whether it's on a vertical or a horizontal Toolbar. Why not Undo? Redo? Zoom? When folks ask me about the changing functions, I just shrug my shoulders and mumble something about superior intelligence.

HUGE FILES

WinWord files expand to fill every vacuum. If you add a picture or two and link in an object, you can turn a simple two-page memo into a 1 MB behemoth. I've worked with book chapters that run 10, even 12 and 14 MB; all it takes is a reasonable collection of illustrations, and your files can bloat beyond all recognition.

Big files are more than just a pain in the neck. They take up more disk space than necessary. They're more expensive to send over the phone lines. And I'm absolutely convinced that huge files make WinWord less stable.

To reduce the sheer size of your documents, here are two steps you can take:

No fast saves
- If Fast Save is turned on (Tools/Options/Save filecard/Allow Fast Saves box), try turning it off. WinWord's fast save records changes to a document by keeping the original document intact and appending the changes to the end of the document. That makes saving faster—your computer doesn't have to write back all of the original document—but it also swells file sizes.

- Working with pictures involves significant overhead for each picture put inside a document. Consider "linking" the pictures to your file. If properly coaxed, WinWord sticks a "link" in your document, instead of the picture itself, saving enormous amounts of space.

You link a picture by clicking the Link to File checkbox in the Insert Picture dialog box and then unchecking the Save Picture in Document box. You have to do both, in that order. (See Figure 5.8.)

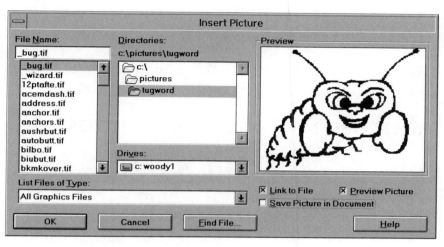

Figure 5.8 Linking Picture to File

I've encountered several problems using links and not saving pictures in the document: **The downside to links**

1. It's slow. Scrolling can be painful because you have to wait while WinWord brings in each picture. I've often been tempted to reboot my machine, thinking that WinWord had frozen, when it was just trying to get a linked picture onto the screen. You can work around that by only showing picture placeholders: click Tools, Options, bring up the View filecard, and click the Picture Placeholders box. **Slow scrolling**

2. Transporting the doc is a pain in the neck. You must move the doc and the pictures separately, of course. There's no easy way to tell WinWord to "just link to pictures in the current subdirectory." You must duplicate the file structure on the second machine, ensuring that the pictures are in the same subdirectories. If you linked `_BUG.TIF` in `C:\PICTURES\TUGWORD` on the first computer, then you must make sure that `_BUG.TIF` is also in `C:\PICTURES\TUGWORD` on the second computer. **Moving the doc**

3. I've hit General Protection Faults when activating a second program at the same time WinWord is trying to bring in a linked picture. I can't reliably reproduce the bug, and I'm not sure if it's WinWord or the converter that's screwing up, but it does happen. Linking is not as stable as sticking the picture in the doc.

4. Sometimes WinWord has trouble updating the display, especially when you scroll quickly. Hundreds of times I've scrolled to a page and the linked picture

just doesn't appear. Usually I can get the picture to show up by scrolling up or down a page or two, and then waiting for the converter to bring in the picture.

Whatever you do, don't use Master Documents. You can read all about it in Chapter 6.

OTHER PROBLEMS ... UH ... OPPORTUNITIES

An optimist sees an opportunity in every calamity.
A pessimist sees a calimity in every opportunity.

Anonymous

Here's a grab bag of additional problems I hear about almost daily.

Weird Stuff on the Screen

The symptoms of this problem are legion. Sometimes your Toolbar buttons go a little crazy; they lose their color or develop strange bands. Sometimes pictures get stripes in them or big characters grow bizarre shading. Occasionally the monitor starts flickering like a firefly in heat. You may click OK on a box, and only part of the box will go away (that's called a remnant).

You may have discovered quick fixes. For example, I often found that weird screen stuff like that would go away if I simply minimized and then maximized WinWord. And I ignored it until I started spending more time miminizing than I did typing!

Almost always the problems disappear if you switch over to the standard Windows VGA video driver: double-click on the Windows Setup icon (probably in your MAIN group) and pick the plain-vanilla VGA driver. If things suddenly start working right, you've found the culprit.

The bad news is that there's a 99.9% chance that the source of your problem is a buggy video driver. Microsoft can't do anything about it! You'll have to contact the video board manufacturer directly. See the discussion of GPFs in Chapter 6 for a few tips. And good luck. I've been there many, many times.

Conversions

Who to call   WinWord does a pretty good job of converting back and forth among several file formats. If you're having trouble with a specific conversion, first make sure you have the Supplement File Conversion disk (call Microsoft USA at 800-426-9400, or your local office), get on CompuServe's GO MSWORD forum, or call the Microsoft bulletin board at 206-936-6735. Converters are being updated constantly.

The TIFF import filter in WinWord 6.0 has caused no end of problems, with GPFs and lockups common. Many have endless headaches with the .PCX filter as well. Microsoft promises these converters will be improved in version 6.0a. I remain skeptical.

If you run into an industrial-strength conversion problem, you'll need an industrial-strength converter. I've had a lot of good luck with the Word for Word converters from MasterSoft, 6991 E. Camelback Road, Suite A320, Scottsdale, AZ 85251, voice 602-277-0900.

Password Protection

> It's no secret that's known to three.
>
> Irish proverb

Encryption and password protection (File/Save As/Options/Protection Password) is a strange topic. As of this writing anyway, dear ol' Uncle Sugar has bizarre export laws that prohibit companies like Microsoft from selling a product with an encryption technique that's too good. I guess that might've made some sense a couple decades ago, but now it's just plain stupid.

Anyway, the folks at Microsoft have to take into account American export restrictions when designing products like WinWord. As a result, password protection of WinWord docs isn't anything close to being secure. If you think a password is going to keep your data from prying eyes, well, you're sadly mistaken. It'll keep a very naive person with a hex file viewer from seeing what you've written, but anybody who's determined will be able to crack your documents. **Password, yes Protection, no**

Passwords *are* good at one thing, though. They let you shoot yourself in the foot, real good. They practically load the gun, cock the hammer for you, and beg you to pull the trigger. It's a real crap shoot. Will you suffer more by leaving your docs "unprotected," or will you suffer more when you—inevitably!—forget your password?

Microsoft will tell you that passwords can't be cracked. (Eh, you expect them to say anything different?) Microsoft isn't about to help you decipher a "protected" document. Imagine the implications: if they help you, they'd have to help somebody else. And if they helped somebody else, what good is password protection?

Fortunately, if you password protect a document and forget the password, a solution is not far away. There's a company called AccessData Recovery, located in WordPerfectLand, 87 East 600 South, Orem, Utah 84058, voice 801-224-6970, fax 801-224-6009. They sell a product called WDPass that's designed to crack WinWord passwords. I won't guarantee that WDPass can crack any WinWord 6.0 document. But I *do* know that it's cracked every WinWord 2.0 document I've ever fed to it. If you ever put passwords on documents, you need this package. It's really that simple. **WDPass**

Real protection   Oh. The best way to password protect a doc? Just work on it normally. When you're done for the day, copy it to a floppy, delete it on hard disk, and stick the floppy in your pocket. If you're the paranoid type, nuke the version on hard disk with a utility that overwrites data sectors on hard disks. Norton works fine.

ProgMan Working Directory

> It's all in the day's work,
> as the huntsman said as the lion ate him.
>
> Charles Kingsley
> *Westward Ho*, 1855

In Windows' Program Manager, you can set a **working directory** for every application. It's a nice, easy way to get an application kick-started looking at the correct directory for documents. You might set up different Program Manager icons to bring up WinWord with different subdirectories loaded and ready to roll.

Unfortunately, in WinWord 6.0, working directory doesn't work.

WinWord 6.0 overrides the Program Manager working directory setting with something called a DOC-PATH. Click on Tools, Options, pick the File Locations filecard and you'll see it listed under Documents, as in Figure 5.9.

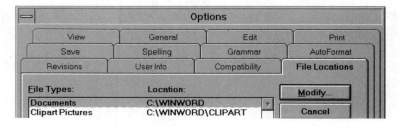

Figure 5.9 The Nefarious DOC-PATH

But there's a trick. Ah, yes. If you click on the Modify button and completely wipe out the Documents entry, WinWord suddenly finds its manners and refers to the working directory that Program Manager established for it.

Tables Break Incorrectly

> Spread the table
> And the quarrel will end.
>
> Hebrew proverb

Sometimes the top row of a table falls at the bottom of the page, and the next row continues at the top of the next page: the top row becomes a widow. Bummer. How can you keep the first row along with the rest? Easy. Select the entire top row. Click on Format, then Paragraph, and pick the Text Flow filecard. Check the Keep With Next box.

First row widow

Delete Key Won't

If you find yourself selecting something and hitting the Delete key, and WinWord asks, down in the status bar, "Delete Block? No (Yes)", you had the misfortune of installing WordPerfect Help. When WordPerfect Help is active, WinWord insists on asking this question, apparently in an attempt to mimic (and thereby help?) reformed WordPerfectionists.

Delete block?

To get rid of the pesky question, click Tools, then Options, bring up the General filecard, and uncheck the Navigation Keys for WordPerfect Users box. (This is a navigation key?)

Key Assignments

Ever wonder which keys are assigned to what functions? Me, too. There's a simple way to see all your custom key assignments. (Yeah, it's in the manual, I'm sure.) Click on File, then Print, and pick Key Assignments out of the list box. If you want to see WinWord's standard key assignments, check out Appendix C.

Print key assignments

Eradicating WinWord 2.0

If you installed WinWord 6.0 over the top of WinWord 2.0, chances are good that most — but by no means all! — of the vestiges of WinWord 2.0 have been eliminated from your system.

If you're done with WinWord 2.0 and it's completely off your system, you should take a minute to pop into `WIN.INI` and delete everything in these sections:

.INIs

```
[DCAConv]
[MacWordConv]
[Microsoft Word 2.0]
[MSWord Editable Sections]
[PCWordConv]
[PCWorksConv]
[TextLytConv]
```

You won't be needing anything in those sections, ever again. *Make sure that you don't delete the* `[MSWord Text Converters]` *section, though! WinWord 6.0 uses it.*

If you have a file called `WINWORD.INI` in your WinWord directory, you can delete it, too, but do *not* delete `WINWORD6.INI` in your Windows directory.

REG.DAT   WinWord 2.0 also puts stuff in your Registration Database, `REG.DAT`, but I think that WinWord 6.0 cleans it up pretty well; besides, I haven't found a reliable way of removing those entries.

Other files   WinWord 6.0 installs all sorts of new, updated files into many different nooks and crannies of your system, everything from a new PostScript driver to bug fixes for OLE 2.0. Just in case you need to track down the latest version of all those system files, Appendix D lists the files that WinWord 6.0 installs.

6 Bugfest 6.0—What Docs Dare Not Tell

Women Who Run With WinWord
And the Men Who Hate Them

Working title for *The Underground Guide*

Everything in this chapter is a bug to my way of thinking anyway. Instead of distracting you, visually, with dozens of pictures of bugs, I'll do it once right here and get it out of my system. There. I feel better now.

Once again, I'm writing this chapter to correspond to WinWord 6.0, the original shipping version. You can tell which version you're running by clicking on Help, then About. Some of these bugs may be fixed in subsequent releases and/or bug patches—*man, I hope so!*—but even still it's important that you know what can and does go wrong in any version, should you find yourself stuck with an old version that goes belly-up. Besides, if history is any predictor, many of these bugs or their vestiges will dog WinWord 6.1, and 7.0, and 8, and 9....

I think you'll also find it instructive, seeing how to think through a WinWord "bug" problem, struggling to find a workaround. I'll show you one example, in all its gory detail, shortly.

ENTOMOLOGY

Here Skugg lies snug
As a bug in a rug.

Benjamin Franklin
1772

There are two main reasons for listing bugs. First, if you hit a known bug, at the very least you'll know that there's no reason to keep banging on it; in the best possible case, a workaround may be available. Second, as this chapter attests, there are so many bugs that—should you hit one that isn't yet documented—you're more likely to realize that *you aren't going crazy*. That's a rather … uh … important realization, eh?

Definition   So, you may ask, what *is* a bug? Good question. As far as I'm concerned, a bug is anything that doesn't work the way *I* think it should—and I would urge you to adopt a similar definition. There's a great campaign button that made the rounds at one of the early WinWord conventions. Quite an observation: "It's not a BUG—it's a *feature*." I keep that button on my desk; it's one of my prized possessions.

Some of the things I call bugs are entirely intentional: the 'Softies insist WinWord is *supposed* to work that way. So be it. You can call them "design flaws" if you like. It won't bother me any. But when the rubber meets the road, intentional bugs aren't any better than unintentional ones, in my experience. If it walks like a duck and quacks like a duck…

Where did they all come from?   This chapter is the distillation of thousands of man-months (er, organism-months) of beating on WinWord 6.0 by the bug catchers listed in the introduction to this book. It is by no means an exhaustive list, but I've gone to great pains to make it as accurate as I could. Collecting bugs is a challenging pastime. Reproducing bugs is an art, and the folks listed in the introduction are artists of the first degree.

When I was gathering this information, Microsoft was running almost 1000 messages *a day* through its GO MSWORD CompuServe support forum. That has to be a record of some sort. Oh, yes, there are bugs. Lots of them. Some of these bugs have workarounds. Many do not. When I (or one of the bug catchers) could figure out a way to fix or avoid the bugs, it's here.

BUGS UNVEILED

There are lots of different kinds of bugs.
Like grasshoppers.
They have to be captured.

Justin Leonhard, age 5
12/23/93

No doubt you've read in the press that WinWord 6.0 is loaded with bugs. If anything, that's an understatement. I firmly believe that WinWord 6.0 is the buggiest piece of software Microsoft has ever released (though some would disagree, citing WinWord 1.0 as the likely recipient of that award—small consolation, eh?).

Why weren't the bugs caught in testing? Why would the Redmondians release such a buggy product? How can they get away with it? Three excellent questions, pilgrim. Let me show you what's going on behind the scenes.

Mushroom Beta

Yeah, bugs like these are supposed to get squashed during prerelease testing. Almost all major software manufacturers these days send advance copies of new software to folks outside the company to assure the product is thoroughly tested before it's put on the shelves. That's called a **beta test**. You've probably heard the term.

The Beta

Usually the manufacturer sets up some mechanism for beta testers to report problems, typically a bulletin board or a CompuServe forum, where beta testers can talk to each other, work through problems, and bounce ideas off the developers. Most of all, communication among beta testers is vital to avoid reinventing the wheel. If somebody has already reported a bug, there's no reason to dig deeper until a developer works out the kinks. Communication is key to an effective beta.

Beta communication

Well, the WinWord 6.0 beta wasn't conducted in the usual way. There was no open communication among beta testers. Indeed, Microsoft threatened WinWord 6.0 beta testers within an inch of their professional lives should they speak to anyone about the product—*even other beta testers!*

I call it the Mushroom Beta, in honor of Mushroom Management, a technique with which you are, no doubt, familiar. You can see the consequences in every nook and cranny of WinWord 6.0.

Getting Away With It

Impunitas semper ad deteriora invitat.*

Legal maxim

Why did the folks at Microsoft think they could get away with releasing such a buggy product? *Because everyone else is doing it!*

I don't think anyone (outside Orem, Utah, anyway) would argue with the statement that WordPerfect 6.0 for Windows, released a month or two before WinWord 6.0, is the buggiest product WordPerfect Corp. has ever released.

When your number-one competitor eschews quality control, you lose a lot of incentive to do things right. Microsoft played follow-the-leader, marching to the tune of Orem's deleterious drummer. Chris Peters, VP of Microsoft's Business Unit, is quoted in *InfoWorld* as saying that WinWord 6.0's horrendous bug problems are "typical or slightly less than typical of modern software." Chilling thought, that.

The computer press, with precious few exceptions, doesn't want to talk about bugs. WinWord 6.0 was no exception. The big magazines don't want to publish detailed exposés, and in many respects it's hard to fault them.

*Impunity encourages worse offenses.

Imagine what would happen if *OB Magazine* came up with a feature article that trumpets all the problems with Bandersnatcher 6.0. Then, the day before the issue hits the stands, the president of BandersnatchInk calls a press conference. He announces that the Bandersnatchies know all about the article, and they've already fixed every bug mentioned. That's an editor's worst nightmare. Well, one of them. (Of course I'm just crazy enough to think that readers would want to know about the bugs anyway, but that's another story.)

Microsoft had to weigh the expense of releasing a buggy product and its inevitable fixes against the cost of delaying the product until it was ready. They opted to ship early, and ship buggy.

<Sigh> Here's the clincher: *they were right!* Man, do I hate to admit it. WinWord 6.0 sold like mad. The black eye WinWord took in the press disappeared in a few weeks. Consumers—like you, like me—either didn't know about the bugs or didn't care. And we all got what we deserved: the shrink-wrapped beta, called version 6.0. Oh, well.

FATAL BUGS

> One should accept the truth from whatever source it proceeds.*
>
> Maimonides
> ca. 1200

All too frequently, WinWord locks up—sometimes with a General Protection Fault, sometimes just everything freezes—and there's bloody little you can do about it. These are the bugs from hell: mean, snarly, snappy little buggers that will make your life miserable.

General workarounds   Sometimes you can save your work, snatch it back from the jaws of permanent perdition, and retrieve at least *some* of what you have done. If WinWord starts producing weird error messages that you've never seen or don't understand, it's time to bail out. Now! Before permanent damage can be done. Here are a few general guidelines:

- Save often, save well. Please. And keep backups, too. Yeah, if you're looking at this, it's probably too late, but do it next time, okay?

- Select the whole document and copy it to the clipboard, if you can.

Copy it to something outside of WinWord   - If you got the doc copied, open up Windows Write and paste everything in there. Save the doc in Windows Write before trying to go back into WinWord and salvaging the doc. You'll lose your formatting, but that's a minor nit compared to losing an entire document.

*From the extraordinary *Great Jewish Quotes* by Noah benShea.

- Try File/Save. If that doesn't work, try File/Save As. If that doesn't work, try File/Exit. Rarely, you can get the accelerator keys to work (for example, `ALT+F`, `S`) when the mouse freezes.

- If you have Auto Save turned on, I suppose there's a very slim chance that if you wait the "save" amount of time (typically 5 or 10 minutes), WinWord might Auto Save a fresh copy. But don't count on it.

- If all else fails, go for the three-finger salute, `CTRL+ALT+DEL`. Get out of WinWord completely.

- If Auto Save is turned on, exit and immediately reenter Windows, then immediately restart WinWord. If you're lucky, you'll snag onto WinWord's automatic restore sequence. If you're extremely lucky, the Auto Save file will contain some of your more recent work in a form you can retrieve.

  Auto Save sometimes does

- If Auto Save is not turned on, hit the big Reset button on your computer. Without Auto Save, there's no chance you'll be able to retrieve anything. Might as well start out clean.

That's my best advice. It should help minimize problems, but it sure as corruption won't eliminate them.

GPFs

> He who overlooks one fault invites another.
>
> Publilius Syrus
> *Sententiae*, ca. 50 BC

WinWord can trigger General Protection Faults for all sorts of reasons, but by far the largest percentage—well over half, maybe three-quarters—of all GPFs can be traced to lousy video drivers.

If you get a message that says "`WINWORD.EXE` caused a general protection fault in module xxx.dll at location yyyy:yyyy" and the module in question looks as though it's associated with your video board, you're in for fun times. Start by jotting down the exact text of the message. Then call the manufacturer (or drop them a line on CompuServe) and tell them precisely what happened and when. Include the text of the GPF message.

No, that won't always solve the problem, but it's a fighting start. You can also hop on the GO MSWORD forum on CompuServe and complain to Microsoft, but —and I'm telling you straight—there's very little they can do about it.

Segment Load Failure

I had never encountered the Segment Load Failure error message in Windows until I started working with WinWord 6.0. Segment load failures appear randomly, for absolutely no reason I can discern, and they're fatal. You'll be kicked out of WinWord, tossed back into Windows with a bunch of Free System Resources gobbled away, and Dr. Watson probably won't even notice.

There's one thing I've found that helps. Maybe I'm crazy... naw, I *am* crazy, no maybe about it... but after hitting a long string of segment load failures—8 or 10 in an hour—I tried something that eliminated them. They haven't come back. Yet. It may be coincidence, but ...

I shut down my computer completely and dug into the beast. My motherboard has a DX2/66 chip in a ZIF socket. No, not a Ziff socket. "ZIF" is just techno-gobbledygook for saying that the big 486 chip is stuck in a holder with a little flip-handle.

Move and cool the chip
Most computers have their main chips pushed down into a fixed socket. It's difficult to remove the chip, and nigh on impossible to put it back without bending a pin or two. The ZIF (zero insertion force—*ugh!* what a lousy name) socket has a clip that grabs onto the chip and holds it in place; flip the handle up, and it's easy to take the chip out. More importantly, it's easy to put the chip back in.

That's what I did. I flipped up the handle, pulled the chip out, and put it back in. Figuring that the segment load failures might be attributable to heat problems, I left the case off the machine (which is a fire hazard and a shock hazard and voids the FCC certification and violates every cannon of common sense and nobody should ever be so stupid and I'll get my butt sued if I don't say this loud and clear: I do *not* recommend leaving the case off your machine!). I stuck a big fan next to the case, pointing it straight at the chip. Noisy as a dog in a hen house. But ... my segment load failures disappeared. It worked. So far, anyway.

Next time I get into town I'll pick up one of those big internal fans, and figure out a way to aim it at the chip. I'm convinced that *my* segment load failures, at least, are not caused by a bug, but by an overheated chip. Either that, or the WinWord gremlins liked to dance on a hot heat sink.

Kick-Starting WinWord

Interdependence absolute, foreseen, ordained, decreed.

Rudyard Kipling
McAndrews Hymn, 1893

Not all bugs are WinWord bugs! So many things are floating around in your computer that it's often impossible to sort out exactly what is causing which problem. That being the case, I offer my own little list of actions to perform if WinWord suddenly stops working. Try each, one at a time, trying to crank up WinWord each time. If you find one thing doesn't work, *put it back how you found it* before proceeding with the next step.

If you follow these steps, in order, I do believe you stand the greatest chance of getting back up, in the least amount of time:

- Using Windows Setup (probably in your MAIN group), switch over to the plain, standard VGA video driver.

- Move everything in your WinWord \STARTUP directory to some place safe.

- Start WinWord with the /a parameter, to keep automatic startup macros from running. In Program Manager, click File, then Run, then type in C:\WINWORD\WINWORD.EXE /A (or whatever it takes on your machine to get WinWord running), and click OK.

- Using the Windows control panel, switch to the most generic printer driver you can find (typically Generic/Text Only). There are several old, stable drivers: I've found the LaserJet II driver that originally shipped with Windows and the latest LaserJet III driver to be particularly solid.

- In your Windows directory, rename WINWORD6.INI to WINWORD6.OLD. (Remember to put it back the way it was—copy WINWORD6.OLD over the newly created WINWORD6.INI—if this doesn't solve your problem! You should be restoring everything after you try it and it doesn't work, remember?)

- In your WinWord directory, rename NORMAL.DOT to NORMAL.OLD.

- Double-check your AUTOEXEC.BAT and CONFIG.SYS. If you're running DOS 6.0 or later, try using this for CONFIG.SYS (make a copy of the old one before trying a new one!):

```
device = c:\dos\himem.sys
files = 60
buffers = 30
stacks = 9,256
```

where the DEVICE= line points to your latest version of HIMEM.SYS, typically in C:\DOS or some such. If you *aren't* running DOS 6.0 or later, get with the system and get the upgrade, okay?

Microsoft says you should run BUFFERS = 10 if you have SMARTdrive going because there's a performance hit if you have 30 buffers defined with SMARTdrive. So be it. I'm superstitious. I'll take the performance hit, rub my good luck charm, and leave buffers at 30.

- If that doesn't work, try this for **AUTOEXEC.BAT** (assuming you have 10 MB or more of room on your **C:** drive; Windows for Workgroups users need not include the share line):

```
set temp = c:\temp
share /L:500 /F:5100
```

- Microsoft recommends that you scour your **SYSTEM.INI** and **WIN.INI**, eliminating any non-Microsoft entries on **LOAD=**, **RUN=**, and **SHELL=**, and to make sure the line **SYSTEM.DRV=SYSTEM.DRV** appears in the [boot] section of **SYSTEM.INI**.

  There's good reason for that: third-party shells can be very … uh … problematic, and that's being charitable. The initial release of Norton Desktop for Windows version 3.0, for example, gave WinWord 6.0 terminal indigestion, in many different ways. Unfortunately getting rid of third-party products often isn't as easy as scanning those lines and changing them. You may have to contact the manufacturers involved to get a safe uninstall.

- Yeah, you're gonna hate me. Unstack your drive (or undoublespace it), and ditch QEMM and 386^MAX, and say good-bye to PrintCache and any of those system thingies that have a nasty habit of getting in the way. Take everything out of your Windows startup group. Don't worry; it's only temporary. Again, if this doesn't work, put everything back before embarking on the next step.

- Finally, try starting Windows in standard mode, that is, type **WIN /S** at the DOS prompt.

Those are all the tricks I know about. Betcha that more than half the time switching to the VGA video driver will solve your problem.

Doc Brain Salad Surgery

> Logic is neither a science nor an art, but a dodge.
>
> Benjamin Jowett
> 1870

What you're about to read just happened to me, in real time, as I was writing this book. The chapter you see right now was snatched from the jaws of WinWord defeat and reconstituted on the fly. Instead of complaining to Microsoft—they've heard enough of my gripes!—I decided to recount my tale to you. Perhaps you'll see something of yourself here. Maybe, just maybe, this glimpse into my sheer terror may help you pull out of a problem, too.

So I'm running a couple weeks late on the delivery of this manuscript, battering my head against the wall and trying to pull all the bug reports together and fashion them into what you see in this chapter. Pretty normal, around here. This isn't Pournelle's Chaos Manor; this is the Ninth Ring of Dante's Hell—though admittedly the scenery is better.

Four o'clock in the morning. Monday morning, no less. Fresh coat of snow on the ground. About 10 below outside, considering the wind chill factor. I stumble into the office, flip on some lights, adjust the heat, turn on the machine, crank up WinWord, click File, then Open, and open up TUGWORD.DOC. (Catchy name, eh?)

I run over to the office fridge while WinWord is loading TUGWORD.DOC. Pop open a can of ice-cold Diet Pepsi. Rinse the sleep out of my throat and pounce on my chair. There's the *Underground Guide*, up and ready for business. So I hit SHIFT+F5, to go back to where I was working. This usually takes a minute or two, so I lean back in the chair and wait. And wait. And wait. And wait. **Really, this is what it's like**

What the hell? I click around a bit. The mouse is frozen. The keyboard is frozen. WinWord won't do diddly.

Hoo-boy. This I don't need. I hit CTRL+ALT+DEL (I'm still trying to figure out how to do that and flip the bird at the same time), get out of WinWord, and restart Windows. Bring up WinWord. File. Open TUGWORD.DOC. Scroll around a bit. Move the cursor. Hey, everything is working fine. Move down a couple pages, type in some stuff, and hit Save.

Bang! Or should I say, whimper? Nothing happens. No whirring disk. No flashing red light. Zip. Nada. And the mouse and keyboard are frozen again. CTRL+ALT+DEL time.

Well, I checked everything. I mean *everything*. Windows was working fine. WinWord even seemed to be okay. Other docs came in and lollygagged around, just like usual. The mouse was connected to the back of the PC; the keyboard cord was plugged in. So I opened TUGWORD.DOC again, played with it a bit, things were going fine, and suddenly once again, Bang! the whole thing froze.

Panic started playing with my head, sneaking up my spine, curling up the sides of my medulla oblongata. Absolute sheer barking terror. I had a backup, but it was a day old. I'd *never* be able to re-create all the info I had typed the previous day on bugs and workarounds and all that. Much of it was done by experimenting, banging away at things over and over again, and relying on reports from dozens of people. The work was gone. **What would *you* do?**

I was torn between picking up the phone to scream at any randomly selected Microsoft employee, and just simply putting my head down on my arms, to cry. Really. Then it struck me there *weren't* any Microsoft employees on the phone at 4:00 AM.

People ask me why I write books like this one, why I'm not satisfied trying to explain how things are *supposed* to work, why little ol' me will take on multi- **Interlude** billion-dollar corporations and their products, *mano y mano*, instead of waffling and glossing over the gory parts—especially when it would be so much easier to toe the party line, pull the tough punches, and write a "nice" book. Lemme tell ya why. It's because of times like this, when products start screwing up, and I get so mad I could spit nails. Dammit, I've lived through it. I know how it hurts; I've felt the pain in my gut, just like you. My son won't being seeing his dad tonight because some computer program isn't smart enough to skip over the bad stuff when it hits something it doesn't understand. Okay. Okay. My vented spleen is showing. Soapbox OFF.

The five p's   When things start going bonkers like this, what do you do? The easy answer is that there's no easy answer. You *push* and you *pull* and you *poke* and you *prod*—and most of all you *pray* that something works.

I tried changing video drivers. Print drivers. Pulling everything out of the WinWord \STARTUP subdirectory. Renaming WINWORD6.INI. Renaming NORMAL.DOT. Starting WinWord with the /a switch (WINWORD.EXE /A from Program Manager) so that it would bypass the usual startup routines. I double-checked my SHARE parameters. Stripped AUTOEXEC.BAT and CONFIG.SYS down to bare bones. Got rid of everything in the windows Startup Group, and on the RUN= and LOAD= lines in SYSTEM.INI. I went into Tools/Options, brought up the General filecard, and unchecked Update Automatic Links at Open.

I mean, it's *embarrassing* when you're supposed to know what you're doing, and you can't get the infernal thing to work!

Scrambled doc?   The only thing I could imagine was that the .DOC had somehow become corrupted—a flipped bit, binary brain salad surgery. The doc had shown no prior flakiness: I'd been working on it for weeks. But it was strange that WinWord would load it, wait a while, and then crash. If I had a corrupt doc, I'd expect WinWord to work around the bad bit or two, even if it hit me with an inscrutable error message:

> Error=199.8234; Cannot defloogle the whozamajiggers. Probable corrupt file. OK to skip the 64 characters starting at line 23 on page 1046?

I'd expect that. Might even lose a bit of formatting. Fair enough. But a lockup? That's unforgivable.

I thought about trying to convert the file to a different format, but if the converter crashed, it wouldn't really tell me anything. Converters crash all the time.

So I copied the file to a floppy and hauled it down to my son's computer, copied the file to hard disk (I *never* unleash WinWord on a floppy file), cranked up WinWord, opened the doc, played with it for a minute, and Boom! There it goes again.

Well, that's progress. If two different installations croaked the same way—what techies call a **reproducible bug**—chances are very good it's a problem with this file, and how WinWord interprets it.

So I started playing with it. I must've spent half an hour poking it. I finally found that WinWord hung around page 51. How did I come to that conclusion? Well, I opened the file and did an F5 real fast to jump to a page number toward the end of the document. WinWord would show its repaginating message down on the status bar:

Word is repaginating TUGWORD.DOC, page xxx, Press Esc to Cancel.

Cool. But then it would hit page 51, and WinWord would stop. Freeze dead in its tracks. The whole machine locked up. I ran over to my son's machine and tried the same thing, with the same result. Voilà!

Now what to do? I knew it froze on page 51, but if I sat around long enough to copy everything from page 1 through page 50 into the clipboard, WinWord would freeze again … Aha! But of course. WinWord must be freezing because it's *paginating in the background*; as soon as it hits page 51, it's bye-bye.

And, of course ("Of course," he says, though it took nearly an hour to figure it out!), the way to circumvent the problem is to clear out the Tools/Options/Background Repagination box, open the doc, then switch to Normal View real quick, before WinWord had time to paginate down to page 51. Ah, Houdini ain't got nuthin' on these pinkies.

That much worked: I could open the doc, and it wouldn't suddenly freeze. Unless I tried to do anything on or near page 51, anyway.

By an excruciating scroll-and-guess process, I found out just how far above page 51 I could go without sending WinWord into the land of nod. Then I found that if I moved all the way to the end of the doc (without scrolling), I could move *up* the doc, closing in on page 51 from below. It won't work if you scroll down from above, even if you F5 to jump to, say, page 53. WinWord counts the pages as it goes down, and it froze on page 51; for some reason, it does not count the pages as it goes up. I got lucky. That took me more than an hour because each time I tried scrolling a line too far and WinWord froze, I had to restart Windows, not just WinWord.

Once I'd scoped out how far I could go—roughly to the end of page 49, and a little above the beginning of page 53—I simply selected the stuff I could grab and copied it to a new document. The working part of the fix took all of about 30 seconds. I lost a little over two pages, and I was done just in time for a late breakfast. Five hours lost to a WinWord bug, a bug that causes WinWord to freeze dead in its tracks on a corrupt file.

If WinWord can display the page immediately before the bad bit and the page immediately after the bad bit, and I can copy all that stuff to a new document, why in all-fired tarnation can't WinWord just skip over the bad bit?

Sorry, Bill and Chris and Peter, but *this* is where we need some IntelliSense! The flashy stuff is nice, and it wows the reviewers fer sure. You get check marks in all the right boxes. But the meat 'n taters, day-in-and-day-out stuff—

like robust error recovery—is where we folks in the trenches really need some intelligence.

Maybe you'll hit the same situation some day. If you do, I hope you'll remember this little story. Even if you don't hit this precise problem, though, I'll guaran-damn-tee that, sooner or later, you're going to come across something that's straight out of the Twilight Zone. As sure as death and taxes.

When something like that hits, you need to strap on those hip waders and get working. You'll find that Microsoft tech support (they call themselves PSS; and there are some mighty fine folks working for PSS), helpful as they can be at times, won't have a clue. You have to take WinWord into your own hands and … *cut out its heart and stomp on it.*

Cannot Save or Create File

Frae saving comes having.

Scottish proverb

This is a terribly destructive bug that should strike fear into the hearts of every WinWord 6.0 user. Here's what happens. You're typing along, minding your own business. You've got a lot of work up there on the screen. So you click File, then Save. WinWord hits you with this message:

Cannot save or create the file.

Make sure the disk is not full or write protected.

If you've read this far, it shouldn't surprise you one little bit that 90% or more of the time this error has *nothing at all* to do with your disk being full or write protected. (If you disk is full or write protected, by all means, clean it out or take off the write protect tab! *Jeeeeez….*)

This same bug can also cause WinWord to spew such bogus messages as:

File is in use by another user.

Cannot open document.

Word cannot open the document.

The "another user" message is particularly hilarious—or infuriating, if you prefer—because it can appear on nonnetworked systems.

If you're lucky, you may have hit a benign variant on this bug. You might be able to save everything if you close all your WinWord documents and then ALT+TAB through all your other applications, closing down all files exiting any running applications. But if you hit the full-fledged killer bug, it's another story entirely.

The killer form of this bug is an SOL* bug, as bad a bug as I've ever seen. The only oddball responses that occasionally seem to work are:

You can't recover.

- Go into Tools/Options/Save and make sure that the Allow Fast Saves and Embed TrueType Fonts boxes aren't checked. Then try to save the file.

- If that doesn't work, John Notor (thanks, John!) reports some success saving the doc in a different format. He has successfully fended off this bug by saving in WinWord 2.0 format, quitting WinWord, starting it again, then bringing the offending doc back in, and saving it in WinWord 6.0 format.

- As a last resort, if your document contains embedded objects, delete them and try to save. If that works, Insert them without "linking" them; that is, uncheck the Link To File box.

These are known as "voodoo workarounds." Some folks report that they work, sometimes, heaven only knows why.

Other than those three very rare possibilities, this Cannot Save or Create File error message is fatal. If you get it, you're hosed. You won't be able to save any of your work, and there ain't a bloody thing you can do about it. Hit CTRL+ALT+DEL and pray that your last backup is at hand.

The problem stems from something called a **file handle**. Like so many other wonderful remnants of the DOS era, file handles are set up in one, fixed-size pool, whenever you boot your machine. If WinWord suddenly discovers that it needs more file handles than you have available, it croaks with this error message and takes your work with it.

WinWord uses an enormous number of file handles: dozens of times as many as a typical DOS program. It has temporary files flying all over the place; the new segmented document architecture requires files like politicians need PACs. You'll never see all those files, but they're there. And each one needs a file handle.

Unfortunately, if you're running Windows 3.1, there's only one way you can give WinWord enough handles: you have to bump up the parameters on the SHARE statement. (If you have Windows for Workgroups 3.11 and its VSHARE.386, you won't hit this problem, or several other SHARE problems, for that matter.) Make a backup copy of AUTOEXEC.BAT, just in case you get hopelessly turned around. Then open up your AUTOEXEC.BAT and find the line that looks like this:

SHARE is usually the culprit.

```
C:\DOS\SHARE /L:500 /F:5100
```

(The path to SHARE may be different on your machine, of course.) An LH or Loadhigh may be in front of the SHARE, and some inscrutable numbers may be

*Supremely Outta Luck

floating around. Get rid of them. If you're having SHARE problems, the last thing you need to do is load SHARE into high memory.

The trick here is in the /L: and /F: parameters. If you've been playing with your SHARE parameters, or if another program has munged* them, or if somehow you restored an older version of AUTOEXEC.BAT, your SHARE may not reserve enough room. Make sure /L: is at least 500 and /F: is at least 5100. If you use Master Documents, you may want to bump /L: up to 1000. Larger numbers take up more space in conventional memory (that is, memory below the 640K border), but there doesn't appear to be much of an alternative.

Some folks recommend that you put SHARE in your CONFIG.SYS instead of AUTOEXEC.BAT. Try a line like this (making sure you point to your latest version of SHARE):

```
INSTALL=C:\DOS\SHARE.EXE /L:500 /F:5100
```

While you're in your CONFIG.SYS anyway, double-check and make sure you have at least FILES=60 and BUFFERS=30. Nobody really knows why that helps, but some people who understand these things swear it does.

Microsoft reports that it has also hit this bogus Cannot Save or Create File error message with folks running MasterWord (restart WinWord with the /a command line switch so it bypasses MasterWord), Adobe Type Manager (get a more recent version), QEMM (if you put SHARE in upper memory), if your TEMP= directory doesn't have enough room (see the next topic), and if EMM386.EXE isn't set up correctly (good luck). Users have reported problems along these lines, even though they've tried everything Microsoft could throw at them. It remains a perplexing bug.

Networkers beware! If you're running on a network, beware! Even though your networked stations may have a good, big, fat, SHARE setting, you might blow away your server unless it is beefed up, too.

TEMP = too small

6 to 8 MB minimum for TEMP Sometimes the preceding error message (Cannot Save or Create File) is triggered when WinWord doesn't have enough space in the TEMP= directory. Microsoft recommends that the TEMP= line in your AUTOEXEC.BAT point to a place with at least 6 to 8 MB of free space.

I, personally, have never hit this problem, but it would behoove you anyway to keep TEMP= pointed at some place with at least that much free space. You may cause a GPF, or at least start getting weird Out of Memory errors.

---

*munge /*muhnj*/ v.t. To destroy, usually accidentally, occasionally maliciously. *New Hacker's Dictionary* (MIT Press, 1992)

PATH = too big

The WinWord 6.0 tutorial triggers a GPF if the `PATH=` statement in your `AUTOEXEC.BAT` file is more than 128 characters long, that is, if there are more than 128 characters, including spaces, after the equal sign. You can't make a `PATH=` statement that long with MS-DOS, but NDOS and 4DOS do allow it. Only solution I know is to shorten the `PATH=` statement.

128 characters maximum

Too Many Edits/Out of Memory

> Everyone complains of his lack of memory
> but no one his lack of judgment.
>
> La Rochefoucauld
> *Maxims*, 1665

Too Many Edits/Out of Memory errors crop up from time to time, and for no reason I can discern. I don't have any good solution for either, except the general workaround given at the beginning of this session.

If it helps any, I discovered while writing the original *Hacker's Guide to WinWord* that the Too Many Edits error often cropped up in WinWord 2.0 when WinWord's Undo facility got overwhelmed by the number of changes made to a document. If that's what causes the problem in WinWord 6.0, there's probably nothing you can do about it except to close the document, get out of WinWord, and then start it again. If you can.

Undo buffer full?

Similarly, I found that the Out of Memory error had absolutely nothing to do with memory — again, this is in WinWord 2.0 and may not apply to WinWord 6.0. Sometimes the Out of Memory error reflected an inadequate amount of Free System Resources (FSR). If you aren't conversant with FSR and the methods for reclaiming them (primarily, close and restart all of Windows), look at the lengthy description in *The Mother of All Windows Books* or some other good Windows book.

Free System Resources?

Here's the kicker. Back in those days (and probably still, today), Out of Memory was the error WinWord slapped up on the screen when it didn't know what was going on — when it encountered an error that didn't fit any of its predetermined problem conditions. It's the "default" error message. So if you see an Out of Memory, don't take it too seriously. Just get out of what you're doing *now* and restart WinWord.

Master Document

> I am glad the old masters are all dead,
> and I only wish they had died sooner.
>
> Samuel Clemens
> 1867

You might've noticed that I didn't mention WinWord's Master Document capabilities anywhere in this book. That was intentional. Why? Because I *still* don't believe that by the time you read this Microsoft will have all the bugs out.

The Master Document concept is a good one. Take a big document and have WinWord break it into smaller pieces, automatically, based on heading levels. (You can read about the details in the official WinWord User Manual.)

It had (and probably still has) one minor problem: WinWord's Master Document capability was broke, and broke bad. It would work with a few files, or small files, or (preferably) a few small files. But as soon as too many sub-documents profilerate, and they get big enough, WinWord would start coming up with bogus Too Many Files messages and completely trash your documents. Parts of your document would end up willy-nilly in dozens of poorly marked files, and you'd have Hobbes time trying to reassemble them.

This isn't an isolated incident. I've heard of four real, honest-to-Gates WinWord gurus—people who really know their stuff and can work their way out of *any* difficulty—who have lost days' worth of work with Master Document going bye-bye and taking their changes with it.

Avoid Master Document, pilgrim, at all costs. Even if Microsoft puts out a bug fix that specifically deals with Master Document and announces that all is well in a multimillion dollar press conference. I don't care if Word Program Management hires the pope to do the demo, *you should be very skeptical.*

File Find vs. WINWORD.EXE /N

If you start WinWord with the /n command line switch (so no document comes up), do a File Find, and then pick Preview from the View list, you'll trigger a GPF. No known solution or workaround.

Saving in WinWord 2.0 Format

No footnotes in TOCs   If you have a document with a footnote, annotation, or endnote in a Table of Contents, you'd better not try to save it in WinWord 2.0 format! WinWord 6.0 will crash and burn with a GPF, and it'll take your document with it.

You'll get a similar reaction if you have a footnote, annotation, or endnote in a Table of Figures or an {embed} or {link} field. Those are pretty rare, but an annotation in a Table of Contents isn't unusual at all.

OLE 2.0 Move-By Shooting

This Object Linking and Embedding problem is supposed to be solved in the first bug fix release of WinWord, which should be available by now, but you never know for sure.

If you Insert an Object into your document, move it, and then save the doc, sometimes the object will go haywire and not allow further editing. The next time you try to save the document, you may get a totally bogus Disk Is Full Writing to Drive C: message or maybe a There Are Too Many Edits In This Document or a This Operation will Be Incomplete/Save Your Work.

Disk Is Full, Writing to Drive C:

This bug only crops up when you do a full ("slow") save. When WinWord does a fast save, all is well, and the bug doesn't bite you. Therefore, Microsoft recommends that you turn on Allow Fast Saves (on the Tools/Options/Save filecard) when working with OLE objects. But even with Allow Fast Saves turned on, WinWord occasionally does a full save. It flashes a The Fast Save Limit Has Been Exceeded message on the status bar and reverts to a full—and potentially deadly—save. So you can't avoid the problem entirely.

Fast Save as the culprit

When the bug hits, you have a choice of two equally lousy responses:

- Click once on the object and hit the Delete key. You'll lose the object, but at least you'll be able to save the doc.

- Close the file without saving your changes. If you haven't copied any part of the doc into another document, you'll just lose the work you've done since you last saved the doc. If you *have* copied or moved part of the doc, the object is totally screwed up.

It's hard to believe that WinWord 6.0 shipped with a bug this deadly—and common!—but it did.

Equation Editor Under Windows NT

WinWord has all sorts of problems running under Windows NT. One of the worst: If you try to crank up the Equation Editor while under NT, WinWord can spontaneously GPF! Again, this is supposed to be fixed in the release available by the time you read this.

DANGEROUS BUGS

> When there is a possibility of danger,
> do not depend on a miracle.
>
> *Talmud*, Kiddushin

These are bugs that won't cause GPFs or data loss. They aren't quite as severe as the preceding bugs, but you can still find yourself losing lots of time trying to deal with them.

Paste at End of Doc, *Not*

The final paragraph mark is sacred.

Have you ever copied something onto the clipboard, pasted it onto the tail-end of a WinWord document, and suddenly had everything go to hell? Page settings. Section settings. Headers and Footers disappear. All sorts of fun stuff.

The best workaround Microsoft can offer at this point is to warn you not to paste anything into the final paragraph in a doc. That's a pretty lame suggestion, but, alas, it's the best one I know.

If you need to insert something at the end of a document, make sure you add a couple of paragraph marks to the very end of the doc, and then back up a paragraph or two before moving it in.

Revision Marking Updated Fields

All updated fields are revised, aren't they?

All fields, when they are updated, are marked as revised, whether their value changes or not. They're even marked revised when the updating is automatic, as may happen before printing. That can lead to no end of headaches.

Moral of the story: if you rely on revision marking, you'd better not use fields, or at least you'd better keep a very close eye on them.

Vampire Paragraph Marks

Paragraph marks in WinWord 6.0 take on a life of their own. Sometimes it seems as though you can't kill them without waiting for them to return to the casket so you can drive a wooden stake through their hearts. So put on your strand of garlic, dust off that copy of Nosferatu,* grab a crucifix, read up on the Chronicles,** and try this fun little experiment:

ShowAll

1. Make sure that paragraph marks are showing. (If they aren't showing, click the Show All button.)

2. Type in a couple of paragraphs. (Any paragraphs will do.)

3. Select an entire paragraph and hit the Delete key. The paragraph disappears.

4. Select a paragraph mark (or put the cursor in front of a paragraph mark), hit the Delete key, and it disappears, too.

5. Select some (but not all) text in a paragraph, plus the paragraph mark at the end of the paragraph, and hit the Delete key. See that? The paragraph mark remains! Back from the bit bucket. Ve vant to trink yuur blooood …

---

*F.W. Murnau's *Nosfretu*, a silent 1922 movie, may be the most horrifying vampire flick ever made. Check it out.

**The Vampire Chronicles*, three novels by Anne Rice, are stunning works.

Vlad the ParaImpaler has another manifestation: if you select an entire paragraph and move it into the middle of another paragraph, everything comes along, including the paragraph mark, its style, the whole nine yards. That's as it should be. But if you select anything less than an entire paragraph — just miss the first character — the paragraph mark stays put!

Paragraph marks come and go, for no apparent reason.

I have no idea why Microsoft did that. And I find it *very* confusing. It's probably the result of some usability lab test result conducted on Electric Pencil aficionados.

Hidden Characters

> I am invisible, understand, simply because
> people refuse to see me.
>
> R. Ellison
> *The Invisible Man*, 1952

Hidden characters do all sorts of weird stuff. These kinds of stupid hidden pet tricks look like parlor magic that is of dubious interest to the serious WinWord user, until one of them jumps up and bites you. It happens all the time, and it's most unnerving.

It's easy to accidentally delete hidden text.

Type in four paragraphs, one after the next, like this:

abc¶
def¶
ghi¶
jkl¶

Select the third paragraph and click on Format, then Font, and make all the characters Hidden. Click OK. Poof! They disappear. (Equivalently you can hit CTRL+SHIFT+H.)

Put your cursor at the beginning of the document. Hit SHIFT+DOWN. The first paragraph will be selected. That's great. Now hit the plain ol' down-arrow. See how the cursor jumps to the start of paragraph *four*? Bizarre.

While you have that third paragraph formatted hidden, try a few other things:

- Select the fourth paragraph and format it hidden by holding down CTRL+SHIFT+H. *Hah!* All of a sudden, paragraph three reappears, and paragraph four is still visible.

- Format paragraph three as hidden again. Then select all the paragraphs and number them. You'll see paragraphs numbered 1, 2, and 4, which is a bit strange, but reasonable. Put your cursor in the fourth paragraph and hit the Home key. See how you get stuck in front of the number? Paragraphs 1 and 2 don't work that way.

- It gets better. Stick your cursor in front of the 4, and then hit the backspace. Not only do you knock out the hidden paragraph number 3, you also lose numbering on both paragraphs 2 and 4!

Be extremely careful when navigating—and especially deleting—anything around hidden characters. Here thar be tygers.

Bogus Margins, Missing Footers

WinWord seems to have a hard time printing in Landscape mode (where the long side of the paper is on top) with custom paper sizes, on LaserJet 4ML and 4MP printers running with the HP-supplied PostScript drivers. I've seen reports of WinWord actually *changing the margins* on pages destined for a LaserJet 4P. The solution? Contact HP for an updated printer driver.

Frames blast out footers

Speaking of bogus margins. If you put a frame on a page, and then add text to the page above the frame, the stuff in the frame may get bumped down, so it obliterates whatever may appear in your footer. I've seen the same thing happen to callouts.

Footloose and Fancy Freenotes

Gratuitous space in footnote

Footnotes still have many problems inherited from earlier versions of WinWord, and at least one new bug—an important one, at that. You can't create a footnote number that is only one character wide: WinWord, in its infinite wisdom—and in defiance of most style conventions—insists upon sticking extra space* down at the bottom of the page, after the footnote number or character, before the footnote text.

Footnote numbers look terrible up in the main body of the document when they're followed by any kind of punctuation mark* . Again, there's a fixed-width space inserted, gratis, by WinWord.

My footnote overfloweth

Finally, if you have many footnotes on one page, some of them may appear on an entirely different page from the one on which the reference occurs. If that happens, the **continuation separator**—the bar that separates the body from the footnotes that are supposed to be at the bottom of the continuation (second) page —appears on the first page.

* Like this. There's an extra space after the *. See it?

* . See how the double-width footnote character looks lousy next to a period?

That's a bug. If you feel lost in the middle of WinWord's footnoting terminology (jeeeez, what *is* a continuation separator?), you aren't alone. As this bug demonstrates, WinWord's designers get confused, too.

If that flip-flopping onto a second page happens *and* you're generating table of authorities entries, the overflowed entries won't even appear in the TOA! That's a dangerous bug that's bound to bite more than a few attorneys.

A Re-Kerning Problem

> Let there be spaces in your togetherness.
>
> Kahlil Gibran

Here's another one of those problems that's supposed to be solved in the first maintenance release of WinWord 6.0, the bug fix, which should be available by the time you read this. All the more reason to pick up the phone and get the update, now!

WinWord lets you kern fonts (see Chapter 3), by choosing a Points And Above size on the Format/Character/Kerning for Fonts filecard. In theory you pick a point size—say, 14 points—and all characters 14 points and above will be kerned; that is, specific pairs of characters will be squished together by an amount recommended by the font's designer.

Points And Above sorta

In practice, it doesn't work that way. Although the screen shows proper kerning, WinWord only *prints* the correct kerning on fonts with that specific point size. If you choose 14 points, say, as the Points And Above amount, 16-point characters appear properly kerned on the screen, but they won't be kerned when the doc prints! Ooooops.

Of Widows and Orphans

> At six I was left an orphan.
> What on earth is a six-year-old
> supposed to do with an orphan?
>
> Anonymous

Widows and **orphans** are the single lines that can appear at the end or beginning of a page. Unless you've done something to change it, WinWord keeps your docs from having widows and orphans.

I didn't believe this until I saw it, and it doesn't always happen. If you have Widow and Orphan control turned on (Format/Paragraph/Text Flow, and the Widow/Orphan Control box is checked), WinWord may swallow an extra line from the bottom of the page!

Widow/Orphan control can do strange things to page breaks.

Try it. Open any WinWord document. Find a paragraph that extends over two pages, preferably several lines in either direction. Make a mental note of where the paragraph breaks, which line is at the top of the second page. Stick your cursor in the middle of the paragraph, click Format, then Paragraph, bring up the Text Flow filecard, and clear the Widow/Orphan Control box.

If you have this problem, the lines jump around; the first line on the second page becomes the last line on the first page. I have no idea what causes this or how to cure it. But it sure can screw up a carefully crafted document!

Flipping Floppies

Here's a Cardinal Rule of WinWord Sanity:

Never, ever use WinWord to open a file on a floppy disk.

Yeah, it's supposed to work. Yeah, WinWord 6.0 is supposed to be better than earlier versions of WinWord, which would freeze up tight sometimes when working on a floppy. Sure.

Ubiquitous temporary files

WinWord plays around with all these temporary files, and some of them get stuck in the "current" directory. No doubt you've seen WinWord's temporary files, with names like ~WRD001.TMP: they're probably scattered in half the subdirectories on your hard disk right now.

WinWord has always had problems with weird files sprouting up all over the place. If you open a file on a floppy, all of a sudden that floppy drive becomes your "current" directory, and WinWord can hurl all sorts of chunks in its direction.

Don't droppy that floppy.

If you find yourself violating that Cardinal Rule of WinWord Sanity, at least avoid the Veritable Venal Sin:

Don't ever, ever pull a floppy diskette out of a drive until you've closed every file on that drive.

It isn't good enough that you pull in a copy and play with it, or that you don't care about changes made to the file on floppy. Doesn't matter. If you pull that floppy out, WinWord hounds you mercilessly until you put it back in.

If you do open a file on a floppy and then remove the diskette, don't be surprised if WinWord crashes.

Keep With Next Doesn't

It's always something.

Gilda Radner

Sideheads

If you have a sidehead or callout (or any frame) attached to a paragraph, and the preceding paragraph is marked Keep With Next, often the frame is considered "next" and appears on the same page as the preceding paragraph, but the following paragraph—the one you would expect to be bound by the Keep With Next— flops over to the next page. (See Figure 6.1.)

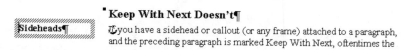

Figure 6.1 The Frame Factor

To WinWord's way of thinking, the stuff inside a frame *precedes* the paragraph it's anchored to, regardless of where it's located, physically, on a page. In Figure 6.1, the word "Sideheads" is in a frame, anchored to the paragraph that starts "If you have a …". As far as WinWord is concerned, that frame precedes the paragraph. So if the heading "Keep With Next Doesn't" is formatted to Keep With Next, and the page breaks in just the right way, the sidehead may stay with the heading, and the paragraph that anchors the sidehead may flop onto the next page. It's really ugly and, if you don't know what's happening, very confusing.

Keep With Next loses its meaning when faced with frames; WinWord's concept of "next" is probably quite different from yours.

There's a solution, at least for sideheads. Format the stuff inside the frame as Keep With Next as well so that WinWord is forced to keep it on the same page as its anchoring paragraph.

TOC Doesn't Pick Up Line Feeds

Any line feeds (Shift+Enter) in a heading aren't brought forward to the Table of Contents. The whole heading is strung together on a single line and the line feed is ignored. I haven't found a good solution to this problem. You pretty much have to fix the TOC manually.

> The line feed just disappears.

Manually applied formatting in the heading doesn't get picked up in the Table of Contents, either. If you have a foreign word italicized in a heading, for example, the Table of Contents entry comes up without the italics.

> Character formatting doesn't make it, either.

That presents some interesting possibilities for headings formatted as Hidden text, by the way. Play with it a bit and you'll see how you can automatically create "phantom" entries in the Table of Contents, headings that don't show up in the text but appear in the TOC.

Flakey Flip-Flop

If, after I depart this vale, you ever remember me and have thought to please my ghost, forgive some sinner and wink your eye at some homely girl.

H. L. Mencken
Epitaph, 1921

This one really bothers me. It only seems to happen on large documents, and it may be a video driver problem. I can't replicate it. But it's been dogging me for years, through many versions of WinWord — since WinWord 1.0 — on many machines, and with several different manifestations. Most recently, it's taken on a form that I call The Flakey Flip-Flop.

Apparition I   I'll be typing along, in a document with, oh, 20 or more pages, in Page View. While in the middle of a paragraph, I encounter the end of a page, and I keep typing. The cursor moves on to the next page but the first line on the new page— the line I'm typing on—suddenly disappears! The cursor is still there, moving across the page, following along as I type, but no text is behind it. Very eerie. And it only happens sometimes.

Apparition II   There are other manifestations. Sometimes when I start a new paragraph and it's the last line on a page, the paragraph disappears. Completely. It vanishes into thin air. The display starts flashing, as though WinWord is having trouble deciding which page the line should go on. If I pause for a minute or so, the display catches up and my characters suddenly appear, but in the interim it looks as though everything I've typed has dropped off the end of the earth.

Apparition III   This one just happened to me. I was typing along, working on a paragraph that extends to a second page. The line on the second page disappeared, as in Apparition I. I wasn't sure if I had mistyped something, so I scrolled down a page and then back up, hoping that WinWord would display the line. When I came back, I had two cursors, one at the end of the upper page and one directly below it on the next page! I typed in something and saw black blotches on the second page. Very bizarre.

If those things happen to you, well, you aren't going nuts, and your computer isn't headed south. Your document is probably just fine. It appears to me that WinWord just works this way, even on the fastest souped-up PCs available. I have no idea why.

Slow down and WinWord will catch up.   Usually WinWord catches up by the time you finish typing a few lines. If you absolutely must see what you've typed, you can scroll down a page and back again, and it'll appear. But if you're expecting to see what you typed on the screen as you type it, WinWord will not oblige.

Section Numbers

I call this the Wharmbug because it was first brought to my attention by Eileen Wharmby. Eileen now has a number of fonts *and a bug* named after her; she graciously served as Tech Editor for this book as well.

Another foolish (in)consistency   If you select a bunch of stuff in a complex document, and then look down at the status bar, you'll see that the At, Ln, and Col information all pertain to the beginning of the selection. The Page, Sec, and xx/xx page number information all pertain to the end of the selection.

Except sometimes. For reasons I don't understand, if you select the final paragraph mark in a multisection document, sometimes the status bar (and, worse, WordBasic macros, via SelInfo(2)) tell you that you are in section number 1. I have seen WinWord flip-flop between the correct number and the bogus 1, on the same document, in a matter of moments. Scary.

PITA BUGS

> Those that do not feel pain seldom think that it is felt.
>
> Samuel Johnson
> *The Rambler*, 1750

These bugs aren't going to break your documents or keep you flipping through the manual to find any way out of a desperate situation. They're just general pain-in-the-neck bugs, the kind of things you'd never think could appear in a program as big and expensive as WinWord, or from a company that prides itself (I'm told) on fit and finish. I'm listing them here so you'll know that WinWord really does work this way. In some cases, I've also been able to figure out workarounds.

Dialogs Won't Stifle

Most of WinWord's dialogs fit into the general Windows mold; they use the typical Windows conventions for how dialogs should look and feel. For example, WinWord dialog boxes are usually smart enough to know that double-clicking on a selection is the same as clicking once on the selection, then clicking OK. I'll bet you double-click a dozen times a day: double-click on a file name, say, to open the file, or double-click on a picture's name to insert the picture. Great. **The Windows Way**

Unfortunately some of WinWord's dialog boxes don't work the way they should. It's almost as if Microsoft rushed these dialog boxes out the door, paying no heed whatsoever to how they'll be used. *You're* the one who pays for their haste: *you're* the one who wastes time moving the mouse around and clicking where a click should not be necessary.

In techie patois, most of the problem hinges around which dialog boxes are "modal" and which "modeless." To the typical user, it's a question of whether the folks who designed this stuff actually tried using it!

Click on Insert, then Cross-Reference. You'll see a dialog like that shown in Figure 6.2. If this dialog behaved anything at all like a normal Windows dialog box, you'd be able to double-click on the For Which Caption reference—say, the line that says Figure 6: Linking Picture to File—and have the cross-reference inserted into your document. Ba-da-boom ba-da-bing, it'd all be done. **Insert Cross-reference**

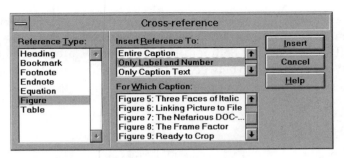

Figure 6.2 Insert Cross-Reference

Unfortunately it doesn't work that way. The only method available for putting a cross-reference in your document is to click once on an item in the For Which Caption dialog box, then click Insert, and finally click Close (the Insert button turns into a Close after you've inserted something). This is a PITA bug for folks who use Insert Cross-reference manually. The same bug in a slightly different guise shows up in WinWord's macro language, though, and there it can be quite mystifying … even destructive.

Notes from the underground usability lab

If the folks designing the Cross-Reference dialog box had actually used it on a good-sized document, they would've discovered that you almost always want to insert a reference to the *last* heading, bookmark, footnote, endnote, equation, figure, or table that went into the document, so the For Which Caption lists should appear in reverse order.

Insert Symbol

Insert Symbol has several problems. I'll talk about the dialog box problems here, then pick up on the rest of the sorry InsertSymbol story in the next section.

Click on Insert, then Symbol. You'll find something like the dialog box shown in Figure 6.3.

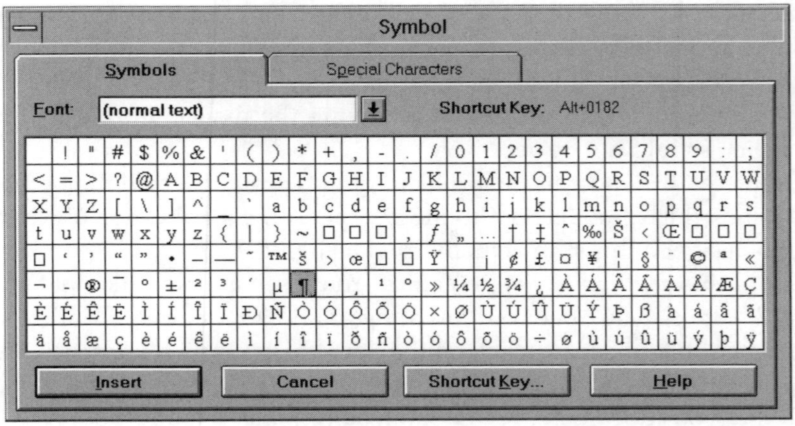

Figure 6.3 Insert Symbol

You might assume that double-clicking on a symbol would insert it into your document and then close the dialog box. It doesn't. Double-clicking on a symbol is the same as clicking the symbol once, then hitting Insert, but it doesn't shut down the dialog box. The dialog box just sits there with its ugly face hanging out, waiting for you to close it.

If WinWord users commonly inserted two or more symbols into a document back to back, I could live with this violation of standard Windows practice. But it's a rare day, indeed, when I insert two symbols in a row—and I'll bet it's the same for you, too.

Fortunately there's a solution to the Insert Symbol dialog box problem. Click on Tools, then Macro. Make sure that Macros Available In shows `NORMAL.DOT`. Type InsertSymbol (no space), and click Create. WinWord shows you the standard InsertSymbol macro:

```
Sub MAIN
Dim dlg As InsertSymbol
GetCurValues dlg
Dialog dlg
InsertSymbol dlg
End Sub
```

Here's the utterly screwy part. You want to make a change to that macro, almost *any* change, so that WinWord will think you've altered the macro, but you don't want to change what the macro *does*. I stick a space after the word MAIN. Just about anything will work as long as it doesn't interfere with the actual text of the macro. Click File, then Close. Yes, you want to save changes.

Try it out. Get into a document and click Insert, then Symbol, and double-click on the symbol you like. It's inserted, just as it should be. Then, poof! The dialog box disappears, as it should. Incredible, eh?

I have no idea why this works; I just bumped into it while playing around. There should be absolutely no difference between the macro with a space after MAIN and the macro without a space after MAIN. Somehow, though, if you make your own InsertSymbol macro (which is what we did by faking WinWord out, making it think that we had something different from the standard macro), WinWord doesn't keep the dialog box on the screen.

Fortunately that cleans up this bug. Unfortunately the same trick doesn't work for the InsertCrossReference sticky dialog box that I discussed earlier. And it doesn't work on EditGoto. Which brings me to the next infernal sticky box.

Click on Edit, then Goto. You'll see a dialog box like that in Figure 6.4.

That's a very nice dialog box, carefully crafted with a lot of thought, and it works well, too. Except the lousy thing won't go away! Don't know about you,

Goto won't stifle

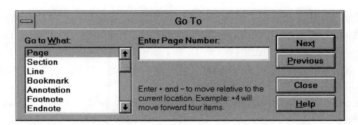

Figure 6.4 Edit Goto

but when I jump to a certain page in a document, I want to get down to work. Instead of letting me get to work, WinWord insists on keeping the Go To dialog box up on the screen, getting in my way.

Next is dumb.

Worse, after I've Gone To wherever it was I wanted to go, WinWord leaves the "focus" on the Next button. If I then hit Enter, WinWord jumps to the Next occurrence of whatever I happened to type. This makes a lot of sense.

For example, say I hit F5, bring up the Go To dialog, type in, oh, 7, and hit Enter, I'll go to page 7. Then if I hit Enter again, I'll go to page 7. Hit Enter again, and I'll go to page 7. Geeeee, I want to do that all the time! You get the idea. Obviously, whoever designed this never used it on a real document.

My pet peeve: Double-clicking on a bookmark name in the Go To dialog box doesn't go *anywhere*.

Worst of all, though, the Close button doesn't have an accelerator key. To close the dialog box, I have to go running for the mouse to click the Close button! There's no way a touch typist can easily Go To page 7 and start working.

Edit Find ain't so bad.

Edit Find works the same way. In this case, though, the behavior isn't quite so offensive. Since sometimes you *will* want to Find the same thing, over and over again, leaving the dialog box up on the screen does make some sense. I wonder why the folks in Redmond don't give us a choice: leave the dialog box open or shut it when it's done?

Alas, I don't have a good workaround for the InsertCrossReference or EditGoto sticky dialog box problems. I just hope that bringing them to your attention will help you feel a little less frustrated; at the very least you'll know that there are other folks who think this stuff is tiresome.

The Symbol Debacle

> As the development of the mind proceeds, symbols, instead of being employed to convey images, are substituted for them.
>
> T. B. Macualay
> 1828

When you use Insert/Symbol to put a symbol in your document, WinWord takes great liberties with your actions, stuffing some incredibly obscure junk into the document.

Here's a little experiment. Open up a document, any document. Click Insert, then Symbol, scroll down to the Wingdings font, and put any Wingding symbol in your document. (When I'm exploring the bleeding edge like this, I like to use the Wheel of Dharma, just to keep things in perspective, but you can use whatever you like.)

Now put your cursor at the beginning of the document, click on Edit, then Find, and find that Wingding symbol. Go ahead. I dare you.

Guess what? *You can't do it.* No way, no how. Well, I take that back. If you want to write a 612-line macro, kinda off-the-cuff, doncha know, I guess you could find the symbol. Maybe. But anything short of that is an exercise in futility.

If you're really up on this stuff, you'll know that there's a macro in Microsoft's `MACRO60.DOT`* file called FindSymbol that will find symbols like this. But if you're a typical user, you're just SOL. (For what it's worth, FindSymbol is a simple 612-line macro that goes through all the gyrations necessary to find symbols. Easy, huh?)

Why is it so tough? Because WinWord uses a Kludge—*mit kapital "K"*—to put symbols in documents.

Recall in Chapter 3 how we went over characters and character numbers and all that. When you see the letter "a" on your screen, for example, you're really dealing with character number 97 in some given font. The "Z" is character number 90. You know the tune.

When WinWord 6.0 puts an Insert/Symbol-style symbol into your document, it doesn't really stick the *symbol* in there. Instead, it sticks a character number 40 in the document and uses some sort of back-room shenanigans (which I don't profess to understand) to make sure that the impostor character number 40 appears on screen and that the chosen symbol comes out on the printer. Given any character on your screen, there is no way to tell by looking at it whether you have an Insert/Symbol-style symbol or a regular ol' everyday character.

This is difficult to explain because there's nothing to see! All the funny stuff goes on behind the scenes. Let me demonstrate with a simple example. Start a new document. Click on Insert, Symbol, then scroll to the Wingdings font, and put a two finger V-for-Victory "peace sign" into your doc. Good. Hit Enter a couple of times. Type the letter "A". Select it and, using the Formatting Toolbar, change it into the Wingdings font. You should have something that looks like Figure 6.5.

The Wingding Wheel of Dharma

A symbol by any other name would smell so sweet.

---

*`MACRO60.DOT` should be in WinWord's \MACROS subdirectory. If you don't have the file, or the subdirectory, you'll have to break out the installtion disks, go through a Custom/Complete install, and install all of the WinWord "sample" macros.

Let's call the first kind of symbol, the one generated with Insert Symbol, an **Ersatz character**. I'll call the second kind, the one that's been formatted directly in the given font, a **Real character**. (Immediately begging the Firesign Theater question, "Which real?" Gack!)

This Wingdings character was generated by Insert Symbol: ✌¶
¶
This is an "A" formatted with the Wingdings font: ✌¶

Figure 6.5 Ersatz on Top, Real on the Bottom

Appearances can be deceiving. See how there is no difference in the appearance of the Ersatz peace symbol, compared to the Real one? But they're very, very different, underneath, down where it counts. The Ersatz character is a character number 40 formatted in the current font (in this case, Times New Roman). The Real character is a character number 65, formatted in the Wingdings font. They are *not* the same. Just for starters, here's why:

- You can't search for an Ersatz character—one constructed with Insert Symbol—in your document, unless you're willing to scout out FindSymbol and get it going, and wait and wait and wait for it to work. By the way, FindSymbol will only find Ersatz characters; it won't find Real characters.

- If you search for a left parenthesis, using Edit Find, you'll come up with a match on *any* Ersatz character! Doesn't matter what the character looks like, which font, or anything else. The left parenthesis always matches Ersatz characters. You might've guessed that the left parenthesis happens to be the *real* character number 40, in most fonts.

- If you double-click on an Ersatz character, you'll get the Insert Symbol dialog box. If you double-click on *the same character* that's simply been formatted—a Real character—you'll select the character and any surrounding text. Since there's no way to know ahead of time whether you're looking at an Ersatz character or a Real character, this behavior can be quite... disconcerting.

- Several WinWord IntelliNONsense settings behave differently, depending on whether you're working with an Ersatz or a Real character. Try turning Automatic Word Selection on (in the Tools/Options/Edit dialog box) and play with it. You'll see. Ersatz characters are treated like left parens. As well they should, because they are!

If you've ever wondered why symbols behave one way sometimes, and quite differently other times, well, now you know. It's very confusing, bothersome, and complex. There's no Field Code you can hide or show, no oddball Format Font setting that will show you which characters are Ersatz, and which are Real. It's all hidden, way back where you can't get at it.

For the life of me, I don't understand why Insert Symbol doesn't, simply, put a symbol with the selected font into the doc.

Navigation

> Laissez faire et laissez passer.*
>
> De Gournay
> 1750

Flipping back and forth between View Field Codes and View Field Results can land your screen three or four pages away from where you started. The cursor is still there, but the screen has gone fishin'. Sometimes the same thing happens when you switch into and out of Page View, or Outline View.

Can't see the cursor?

There's a simple trick. If you need to find the cursor, hit the right arrow, then the left arrow. WinWord snaps to attention and scrolls to the correct location.

It Always Repaginates

Man, this is infuriating. WinWord picks the worst possible times to go into its repagination paroxysms. Repaginating a good-sized document can freeze things up for a minute or more, and really destroys your (or at least my!) train of thought.

I've tried and tried to nail down what causes WinWord to decide it needs to repaginate. No luck. It seems almost random.

The only solution I know is the obvious: work in Normal View and turn off Background Repagination on the Tools / Options / General filecard. You won't be able to see what your document will look like, but at least you won't grow old watching WinWord do its repagination thing.

Autonumbering Slowdown

> I am not a number — I am a free man!
>
> Number Six
> *The Prisoner*

I figure this is a bug because *nothing* should be this slow. If you use WinWord automatic numbering to put numbers on many paragraphs (say, hundreds), scrolling through your document becomes an study in slow motion. I don't know

---

*Liberty of action and liberty of movement.

why, but the auto numbering (Format/Bullets and Numbering) is so slow I wonder if WinWord isn't recalculating all paragraph numbers on the fly.

The {seq} trick

Fortunately, this one has a solution. Instead of using auto numbering, create your own numbers using WinWord fields. Every place you want a number, click on Insert, then Field, click on Seq, and type in a name like ParaNumber. That puts a {seq ParaNumber} field in your document, and {seq } fields, for some reason, update much faster than auto numbering.

If you do a lot of numbering like that, you can write a simple macro to insert the {seq} field. Click on Tools, then Macro, make sure NORMAL.DOT shows in the Macros Available In box, type a reasonable name like InsertSeqParaNumber, click Create. The macro should look something like this:

```
Sub MAIN
InsertField "seq ParaNumber"
End Sub
```

Click on File, then Close. Yes, you want to save changes. Then drag the macro over to a Toolbar by clicking Tools, Customize, bringing up the Toolbar filecard, making sure NORMAL.DOT shows in Save Changes In, scrolling down to Macros, then click and drag InsertSeqParaNumber. From that point on, whenever you want to add a sequence number, stick your cursor where the number should go, and click on that Toolbar button.

Stops on Ruler Won't Move Right

> I was thrown out of college for cheating on the metaphysics exam;
> I looked into the soul of the boy next to me.
>
> Woody Allen

Tab stops and indents can get sticky

This is one of those "just so you know you aren't going crazy" bugs. Sometimes you can't simply click and drag the tab stops or indent marks on the Ruler. You have to click twice before they'll move. I have no idea why. It just works that way.

Similarly, if you click either down-arrow on the formatting Toolbar (the one next to the style, or the one next to the font), you won't be able to grab onto anything in the Ruler. You have to click once in the document, to roll up the list, before clicks on the Ruler "take."

Toolbar Amnesia

Top and bottom border

Some Toolbar buttons just don't work. Here are two easy ones. Click on Tools, then Customize, pick the Toolbars filecard. On the left scroll down to Borders, click and drag the top and bottom border buttons to any convenient Toolbar.

Now type in some text, select it, and click one of the buttons. See that? Nothing happens. Zip. The buttons don't work, period.

Style and Font Hot Zones

Put your mouse up on the formatting Toolbar, somewhere between the style name and its down-arrow, or between the font name and its down-arrow. See how the yellow Tips box pops up? With the Tips box up, you'd expect you'd be able to click and have either Styles or Fonts at your command. Not so. Click and drag, and you'll move the *Toolbar*!

Tutorial vs. Dr. Watson

Windows' knows-all, sees-all Dr. Watson hiccups sometimes when you leave a tutorial session or screen (Help/Examples and Demos). Dr. Watson reports an error, even though there isn't one. Ignore it. The wizened one has been dipping in the 7% solution.

More Dumb Bullets

> The fundamental cause of trouble in the world today is that the stupid are cocksure while the intelligent are full of doubt.
>
> Bertrand Russell

Remember in *Who Framed Roger Rabbit?*, how the detective pulled out a 'Toon revolver and started loading it with 'Toon bullets, but then the bullets started screwing around so much, he threw up his hands in disgust? "Dum-dums," he said. Well, you're about to enter WinWord's ToonTown.

If you select a bunch of paragraphs that start with numbers, like this:

Bulleting numbered lists

1. Larry
2. Moe
3. Curly

and then try to bullet the paragraphs, WinWord asks if you want to get rid of the numbers at the beginning of those paragraphs. That's a neat feature. But if you select a bunch of paragraphs that start like this:

U.S. Navy

U.S. Department of Commerce

and then try to bullet it, you'll get the same message! WinWord seems to think that you are trying to convert a numbered list. Man, that's dumb.

This one's worse. If you bullet or number a series of paragraphs, and then right-mouse-click to remove the bullet or number for one of the paragraphs, every time you go in to change the bullet or number style (to make the bullet bigger, say), the paragraph you skipped gets its bullet or number back!

Manual formatting zapped

And here's a related killer: as soon as you remove the bullet or number from a paragraph, you lose all manually applied indent formatting.

When you have a bulleted list or a numbered list, the character formatting of the bullet or list number (for example, bold or underlined) depends on the character formatting applied to the paragraph mark. You can actually make a bullet in a list bigger by formatting the paragraph mark for that item as bold!

This is an intelligence test. Type in these three paragraphs:

> We at Frumious Bandersnatch, Inc., expect:
>
> 100% compliance; and
>
> Immediate notification of any problems.

Format Number

Select the two final paragraphs, and click on the Format Number button on the Formatting Toolbar. What would you expect to get? *Heh, heh, heh.* I'm not going to tell you what really happens. You won't guess it in a hundred years. Try it yourself and see. Betcha even the programmers who wrote this part of WinWord won't know the answer to this one!

Microsoft should take bullets and numbering back to the drawing board.

Phont Phunnies

> Woody ... must be absolutely barking mad. This realization ... helped me restrain myself from hurling [the book] across the room when I reached a section on the "Phont Phunnies."
>
> Tim Nott
> *Windows User*, June 1993

WinWord 2.0 suffered from a terrible, debilitating bug known as the Phont Phunnies. This particular affliction would spontaneously change fonts, without any participation by the user. It didn't appear until folks had spent quite a bit of time with custom styles; the bug didn't unveil itself immediately after release of WinWord 2.0, it took many months before Phont Phunnies started rearing its ugly head. I have my fingers crossed that the worst incarnations of the Phont Phunnies won't appear in WinWord 6.0.

That said, one version of the Phont Phunnies is alive and well, and living in WinWord 6.0. It's "by design"—WinWord's designers mean for it to work this way. Maybe you think this is right, but I sure don't.

Let's say you have A.DOC, with the Normal style defined with, oh, 18-point Arial. You create a style—let's call it FooStyle—based on Normal. It, too, is 18-point Arial. **Copying styles**

Now create a new document. Copy a FooStyle paragraph from A.DOC into the new doc. It's FooStyle. It's 18-point Arial. That's fine. Click on Format, then Style, and it's based on Normal. Fair enough.

Go back into A.DOC and change Normal so it's, oh, 10-point Times New Roman. See how FooStyle changes? Yep. That's how it's supposed to happen. The styles are all interconnected.

Now change Normal in the new document. Make it 10-point Times New Roman. Since FooStyle is based on Normal, and Normal is changed, you'd expect the FooStyle stuff to change, wouldn't you?

Well, it doesn't. Somehow the Based On box in the Format Style dialog lies. FooStyle in the new document isn't based on Normal at all; it kind of floats out there in the WinWord ether. Consistency defeated once again.

Won't Work With ...

> The art of living lies less in eliminating our troubles
> than in learning how to live with them.
>
> Bernard M. Baruch

As of this writing anyway, WinWord just won't work with:

- The HP LaserJet Fax. You get a bogus "Printer is busy. Try again when the printer is available." message. Neither RapidFAX nor WinFAX Pro seem to work. Many fax drivers and/or macros need updating specifically for WinWord 6.0 (specifically, Delrina should have a new macro by the time you read this).

- ATI Crystal Fonts. Nobody seems to know whether WinWord or the ATI driver is at fault. Last-minute workaround: ATI reports that Crystal Fonts will work if you choose a PostScript printer and use Type 1 fonts. Good luck.

There are many other odd problems:

- Several fonts don't work right. Bookman Old Style Bold, some of the Minions, and AGaramonds. It's not clear what's going on.

- Many of the templates and most of the macros that shipped with WinWord 2.0 won't work with WinWord 6.0. So much for the "automatic" converters. If you want to use the WinWord 2.0 templates (which were pretty nice!), you'll have to get updated versions from Microsoft. They are available on the CompuServe GO MSWORD WinWord forum.

- If you have a VGA gray-scale monitor, you may not be able to see some of the text in the grammar checker. It fades into the background, displaying black on black.

- WinWord 6.0's tutorial won't even run under Windows NT. No way, no how, don't even bother trying.

As usual, your only hope is to contact the manufacturer and see if they have a fix, even if the manufacturer is Microsoft!

Little Things

> The Way is Form without Form.
>
> Lao-tzu
> *Tao Te Ching*, ca. 250 BC

There must be hundreds of other, minor bugs.

- Accept revision marks in a document, then print it. The revision marks will print in footers and figure sequence numbers.

- Many form fields don't act right. There's no drag 'n drop. Selection rules are a bit different. For some reason known only to Microsoft, you can't do a File/Page Setup while your cursor is in an unprotected section of a form. And so on. Forms and form fields aren't nearly up to the standards of the rest of WinWord. Truly a version 1.0 implementation.

- Here's one of my favorites. (Thanks, Keith!) Create one paragraph that looks exactly like this:

    "A b, c, d".¶

Now select everything from the "b" to the end of the line, including the paragraph mark. Toggle case (Initial caps, all caps, etc.) using SHIFT+F3. *Heh, heh, heh.*

- Speaking of Change Case, the SHIFT+F3 key combination only goes through three of the Format/Change Case choices. Using SHIFT+F3, you only get ALL CAPS, all lowercase, and First letter cap. You don't get the two other Format / Change Case options, Initial Caps (which Microsoft calls Title Case) or tOGGLE cASE. Skipping the latter isn't any big deal, but the former can be useful, for example, when toggling caps on names like JOHN DOE. Using SHIFT+F3, you will never be presented with the option John Doe.

- WinWord still scatters .TMP files all over the place. From time to time you should leave WinWord, scan all your disks (hard drives, floppies, the works) and delete all the outstanding ~*.TMP files.

- Sometimes the Go Back key combination `SHIFT+F5` doesn't work. If you make several changes in a doc, open two more docs and move around, then close those two docs, `SHIFT+F5` probably won't take you to the last change in the original doc.

- Outline sometimes "forgets" recently added headings. Put a heading in a doc, flip to Outline View, and it may or may not be there. Sometimes Outline View doubles up headings. Cut stuff from one level and put it in another and the + and - signs aren't updated correctly. All of this is very ephemeral: you'll never be able to reproduce some of it. But it *does* happen.

- The .PCX converter has the devil's own time getting colors right, particularly with Paintbrush pictures. Solution? Avoid using Paintbrush!

- If you have a style that includes a frame, and you make the Style for Following Paragraph any style without a frame — say, Normal — WinWord won't turn the frame off. You type, hit Enter, and your cursor stays inside the frame.

- The ruler goes crazy in tables sometimes. If you create a doc with a mirror margin (File/Page Setup) and you insert a table, and then a page break, then another table, the ruler works fine on the first table but really goes crazy in the second table.

- Table headings — where you tell WinWord to print the top row of a table on every page — can get all confused if you only select part of the table while clicking Table, then Headings. I've seen headings disappear with the Headings menu item checked, and vice versa. Solution? Select the whole table when changing the headings.

- When you use Equation Editor 2 to insert an equation into a WinWord doc, OLE kicks in the way its supposed to. However, when you click back in the document, the border around the equation flip-flops around and you're greeted with an error "ding." Doesn't seem to hurt anything, but it's sure unnerving.

- You should be able to highlight a bunch of stuff and drag it wherever you like, but I'm forever getting stuck. WinWord won't scroll above the current page for love nor money. Move the cursor up above the Toolbar and it turns into a circle-and-slash "can't do" shape. The only solution I've found is to drag the selection *down*, below the status bar. That unfreezes things, and suddenly WinWord lets you move up.

- Similar drag 'n drop problems have been reported when dragging stuff from other Microsoft apps, for example, EXCEL 5, into WinWord. WinWord refuses to scroll as it should.

- Some of the key combinations don't seem to work right. For example, `SHIFT+END` extends the selection to the end of a line, as it should. But if you keep the Shift key down and hit the End key again, the selection does not extend to the end of the next line. Except—and this is mighty strange—if you keep the Shift key down, and hit the down arrow, suddenly the End key starts extending the selection!

- When you SaveAs in a new format—for example, saving a WinWord 6.0 document in WinWord 2.0 format—and immediately leave WinWord, you get an extra, totally bogus prompt that asks if you really want to save the doc in the new format *even though you haven't made any changes.* The first time that happened to me, I was sure I had hosed the doc. Ends up it's another "feature."

- Somehow cross-references gets doubled sometimes when you have revision control turned on and use hidden text for deleted text. Figure 3, for example, might appear as Figure 33, until you accept all changes and update all fields.

- Templates are so much harder to use than documents, and they shouldn't be that tough. If you SaveAs a template, trying to put it in another directory (outside the \TEMPLATE directory), you have to type in the whole path. You can't SaveAs a template in a different format. There's no reason in the world why you shouldn't be able to save a template as text or RTF—I would've used that capability a hundred times in the course of writing this book.

- Create the field {gotobutton zappo Double-Click Here To Jump}. Show field results (not codes) and you'll see Double-Click Here To Jump. Great. Now select the field and unlink it. Care to guess what you'll see? WinWord truncates it to Double-Click. The rest gets tossed in the bit bucket. It's hard to believe, but true.

Finally, man, you *have* to be worried about a program that lists ax in the dictionary but not axe; OLEO but not OLE; upchuck but not uncheck, and on and on....

Next time you hear that WinWord doesn't have any major bugs in it, or that the folks who gripe about WinWord's bugs are a small 0.01% minority of all users, you have my permission to guffaw. The worst part? Many, many bugs don't appear until months after the product ships. This is the tip of the iceberg, pilgrim.

7 Macros

appakā te manussesu ye janā pāragāmino athâyam itarā
pajā tīram evânudhāvati*

Dhammapada
ca. 500 BC

Ah, WordBasic. The bane of my existence. For years folks have asked me to write an "Intro to WordBasic." Here it is. My best shot.

I think it's important that you understand the *why* behind macros before you even think about the *how* of putting them together. So bear with me a bit, and I'll try to ease you into the topic.

If you're afraid of "programming," if you're tempted to turn to the next chapter, resist the urge, okay? You will find that the time and effort you spend learning how to write and run WinWord macros will repay itself many, many times over, every working day. Any time you find yourself repeating the same actions, you've found a good candidate for a macro.

Don't turn that page!

Look at it this way. You can mow your lawn with a pair of pinking shears, or you can mow it with a 250-horsepower WhizNZapper. Yeah, it takes a while to learn how to use the WhizNZapper, and the first few times you use it the results will be a bit crude. So what? Even if you haven't mastered the machine, it'll get the job done, and done well.

As you get more experience, you'll wonder how you ever managed with the pinking shears. And, although you may spend more time mowing the lawn with a WhizNZapper when you first try, by the time you run it the second or third time, you'll more than pay for the investment.

*Few cross over to the further shore; the multitudes who remain run to and fro on this shore. (Translated from the Pāli by Dr. H. Kaviratna.)

Oh, speaking of investments. In WinWordLand, the WhizNZapper is free. You needn't buy a thing. There's nothing to add on, no form to fill in, and no waiting for a package from Redmond. The 250-horsepower beast is already built into WinWord, and it's humming away just below the visible surface. All you need to do is spend some time learning how to speak its language. And it ain't that tough!

From the very first version, WinWord has harbored a built-in programming language, WordBasic. You can call it a "macro" language if you like, but WordBasic in a very real sense has revolutionized the way Windows users look at their applications. It's raised the bar—set the standard—for how Windows programming languages should work.

WordBasic brings the full power of WinWord to anybody who can handle an IF statement. Talking heads on TV like to gab about "empowerment." Hey, they ain't seen nuthin' like this. WordBasic is empowerment on steroids.

I'm proud to be something of a WordBasic pioneer. (I've got the arrows in my back to show for it!) I hope that this chapter gives you a glimpse of what I find so fascinating about the language. It can be ... seductive.

WHY SHOULD YOU CARE?

Power is precarious.

Herodotus
Histories, ca. 430 BC

This is power, and it's power *you* can use. Anything you can do in WinWord, you can do with a macro. Many things you *can't* do in WinWord, you can do with a WordBasic macro. Indeed, as Vince Chen demonstrated in his seminal DLLAccess article in the 12/21/93 *PC Magazine*, anything you can program into Windows itself can be done with a WordBasic macro. The full range of Windows programming—from simple offerings for the Windows Gods, to complex delving into Windows innards—is at your beck and call from a WordBasic macro. Mind boggling.

Genesis

WordBasic as Frankenstein I'm convinced that WordBasic's original designers had no idea what astounding power they were unleashing on an unsuspecting world. They made a few design decisions, way back in the dawn of WinWord time, that laid the foundation for a stunning plethora of possibilities. WordBasic was woven into the very fabric of WinWord, and it was granted power to control WinWord in ways no macro language had ever experienced.

WordBasic grew out of the confluence of two very different visions of a "macro language." One part is old fashioned macro-style keystroke recording; the other, the language-style constructs of Basic. Let's take a look at each.

Keystrokes

I cut my teeth on 1-2-3 macros a decade ago. The old 1-2-3 macro language begins and ends with keystrokes. You tell 1-2-3 which keypresses you want repeated, and it fakes out the program, making 1-2-3 believe that you're sitting at the keyboard, pressing those keys. That's neat. If you get the keypress sequence right, you can save yourself hours—even days—of work, letting the computer press the keys for you.

Keystroke macros

As macro languages got more sophisticated, some brilliant programmer figured out a way to "record" macros. Instead of forcing you to write down the keypress sequences in some weird language—something like, oh, {down}{backspace}789{enter} —a macro recorder would actually look over your shoulder as you pressed a bunch of keys and replay the key sequence at your command.

Recorder: monkey see, monkey do.

Recording Macros

> Surrounding yourself with dwarfs does not make you a giant.
>
> Yiddish Folk Saying

The mechanism for macro recording is pretty simple, and it's virutally identical in every computer application.

There's a macro Record Start command, not unlike pressing the Record button on a tape recorder or VCR: "Yo! Computer! Start collecting the keys I'm pressing!"

Start

There's a macro Record Stop command, "I'm done! Stop right now."

Stop

There has to be a way to store the recorded macros—generally by giving them a name, however cryptic—and a way to replay a specific recorded macro.

Play

The very best macro recorders let you dig into the middle of a recorded macro and play around with it. For example, you might record a macro that selects the word "McZee," deletes it, moves to the next line, and turns that line bold. A good macro recorder should give you the ability to alter the macro, so, for example, you can delete "McZee" and turn the next line bold throughout an entire document.

Alter

Programming Language

As soon as you talk about modifying recorded macros, you bump into the problem of a programming language. An inscrutable macro recorder (say, the old Windows macro recorder) produces gibberish that's very difficult to decipher and modify. That's where Basic comes into play.

I'm an unabashed fan of Basic, and I'll say it to your face, even if you think of Basic as a "toy" language. Basic is a remarkably expressive computer language that's easy to understand and easy to use, particularly in its more recent incarnations. Yeah, it has its shortcomings. What doesn't? When it comes to bringing computing power to the people, Basic is the premier choice.

Keystrokes and Languages

Here's the first stroke of genius, one of the astounding design decisions made by WordBasic's creators:

WinWord records its macros in Basic.

That means you can record a macro, then look at it, and stand a fighting chance of understanding what's going on. Instead of struggling through gobble-dygook that looks like {down}{backspace}789{enter}, recorded WordBasic macros look more like this:

```
LineDown
CharLeft
Insert "789"
InsertPara
```

The appearance of the macro makes a big difference. If you've recorded the macro, and then decide that you want to run it ten times, say, there's no telling what modifications have to be made to get the {down}{backspace} 789{enter} keystroke macro to run ten times. But in WordBasic, it's pretty straightforward:

```
For i = 1 to 10
LineDown
CharLeft
Insert "789"
InsertPara
Next i
```

When WinWord's designers decided to record all macros in Basic, they established Basic as the *lingua franca* of WinWord, supplanting simple keystrokes. Since a macro recorder must be able to record every valid action in WinWord, it follows as night unto day that anything you can do in WinWord, you can also do in WordBasic.

That simple fact has had enormous repurcussions. Indeed, the computer industry is only beginning to understand how fundamentally applications' embedded programming languages have changed the way people like you and me interact with computers.

The Second Seal

> When you teach your son,
> you teach your son's son.
>
> Talmud
> Kiddushin

Embedding Basic inside WinWord was the first brilliant decision WinWord's designers made. Second, and just as important, they decided to make WordBasic programs run like any other WinWord programs, even *supplanting the built-in operations of WinWord itself.* Think about that for a second. It's quite important. Fundamental, in fact.

If you don't like the way WinWord works—not just the stuff on the surface, but the underlying behavior, way down in the guts of the program—you can change it so it works *your* way.

What's the mechanism for changing how WinWord works? Why, a little macro! A simple, powerful, Basic program. This is the genius lurking just underneath WinWord's surface.

You don't need to rip out WinWord's guts or write a 100,000-line C program. No need to hire platoons of programmers or spend months slaving over an inscrutable "production" programming language. You can change the way WinWord works by writing a little Basic program. Your ten-year-old would understand it. You'll probably find it simpler than programming your VCR. I sure do!

VBA (Visual Basic for Applications)

> I base most of my fashion sense on what doesn't itch.
>
> Gilda Radner

Why should you take the time to learn WordBasic when VBA (Visual Basic for Applications) is destined to replace it? Ah, yet another good question.

A bit of perspective. EXCEL 4.0 had a macro language called XLM. Though XLM has its partisans, I always found it terribly cumbersome, not even half a step above the old keystroke style macros. With EXCEL 5.0, released in January 1994, Microsoft stopped supporting XLM entirely, replacing it with a new macro language called VBA, or Visual Basic for Applications. Although old XLM macros would work with EXCEL 5.0, Microsoft had clearly let XLM out to pasture.

XLM goes the way of the dodo.

The same thing is supposed to happen to WordBasic. Microsoft claims that WordBasic, just like XLM, will be replaced by VBA. No definitive word yet on when that will happen, but it'll probably arrive in WinWord 7.0, whenever that appears.

I am underwhelmed by VBA's current capabilities, as demonstrated in EXCEL 5.0. It's an unwieldy, underpowered, cantankerous language that shows all the hallmarks of a Microsoft version 1.0 release. That doesn't mean it won't improve with age—far from it!—but the initial release of VBA isn't in the same league as, say, Visual Basic or WordBasic. Vince Chen and I moan about VBA's shortcomings in our February and March 1994, columns in *PC/Computing*; you can look there for details, if you're curious.

Is VBA worth the wait?

VBA is no VB.   It remains to be seen if the WinWord version of VBA is any better than the EXCEL 5.0 version of VBA. Frankly I'm skeptical. But Microsoft has committed to improving VBA, even bringing it up to Visual Basic's power (which is saying something!) in the near future. If that's the case, VBA may some day rule the Windows application programming roost. But I'll bet it doesn't happen until late in the decade, if then.

In the meantime, you won't lose a bit by learning WordBasic. Even if Microsoft declares WordBasic dead — as it has with XLM — almost all of WordBasic's underpinnings will emerge in the WinWord VBA. Microsoft simply has no choice. WordBasic has evolved to take control of every nook and cranny of WinWord. For VBA to take on WordBasic's mantel, it'll have to poke into those same nooks and crannies, and the exact dialect for doing so can't be much different from WordBasic's.

It's a long jump from XLM to VBA. The concepts are entirely different, the method of expressing ideas miles away. But it'll be a short hop from WordBasic to VBA. The concepts will be similar, and the language is nearly identical already. You're better off climbing on the WordBasic train now. It'll make the transition to VBA much easier.

GETTING STARTED

> Beware of religions that have waterslides.
>
> Rubber stamp
> Inkling Stamp Company
> Santa Barbara, CA 93140

We won't be recording too many macros.   Books on WordBasic tend to start out by showing you how to record keystrokes. If you're stuck in the monkey-see, monkey-do keystroke recording frame of mind, that's probably the best way to start, and you're better off learning WordBasic from one of those books. I'm going to try something a little different.

To me, the easiest way to learn how to do something is by watching somebody really *do* it, then diving in and playing with it a bit. That's one of the reasons why you'll find macros scattered throughout this book. They aren't carved in stone; they're there for you to play with.

I'll go through the WordBasic basics in this chapter. Then, in Chapter 8, I'll give you additional examples — real, working, useful macros — and step you through custom dialog boxes.

Just Do It

> WordBasic is not a spectator sport.
>
> Pensées Pinecliffius

So much for the preliminaries. Let's dive right in.

Get your butt over to your computer. You can't do this while sitting in the cafeteria or commuting on a train. You have to get your hands dirty, plunk at the keys, and *feel* what's going on.

Crank up WinWord. Click Tools, then Macro. Make sure that Macros Available In shows `NORMAL.DOT`. Type in a name—I'll use temp—and click Create. You'll get something that looks like Figure 7.1.

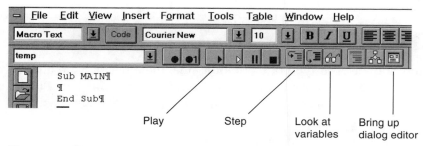

Figure 7.1 The Macro Pane

Figure 7.1 is called, variously, the WinWord macro pane, the macro editing pane, the macro window, or the WordBasic editor. I don't know why they call it a "pane." (Hmmmm … maybe they used a cognate?) I just call this place "home." You will, too, as you get more conversant with macros.

Macros have their own Toolbar. You can see it in Figure 7.1. With rare exceptions, I only use four of the buttons on the macro Toolbar; they're marked in the figure. We'll use them all extensively in this chapter.

> **A macro Toolbar orientation**

- The right-wedgie button, which is supposed to like a VCR Play button, runs ("plays") a macro.

- The first loopy-arrow button steps through a macro, one command at a time.

- The spectacles take a look at variables and their values.

- The button on the end that looks like an ATM machine brings up the WinWord dialog box editor.

Hello, Word!

Every WordBasic program starts with a Sub MAIN (presumably "this is the MAIN subroutine") and ends with an End Sub ("this is the end of the subroutine"). Don't ask me why, that's just how it's done. Between Sub MAIN and End Sub you get to work your magic.

When you create a new macro, as we've done here, WordBasic supplies you with Sub MAIN and End Sub and then sticks your cursor between the two, ready for work. Nice touch.

Let's start with an easy macro, one that puts the message "Hello, Word!" in a box on the screen. That box is called a **Message Box** (rocket science time again, eh?), WordBasic calls it a MsgBox, and the text you want to put in it is "Hello, Word!". The macro you need looks like this:

```
Sub MAIN
MsgBox "Hello, Word!"
End Sub
```

You only need to type in the middle line; the other two are already there, compliments of WordBasic. Type in that one line. Then hit the "Play" button. Perhaps not surprisingly, you'll see your message on the screen (Figure 7.2).

Figure 7.2 WordBasic to Earth. Anybody Home?

Save macro   Click OK. Let's save the macro. Click File, then Close. Yes, you want to save changes. We'll be using your temp macro, Hello, Word!, shortly.

Oh. The Hello, Word! message box macro you just wrote? There's no way to record that macro using WinWord's recorder. You're already swimming out among the beyond-keystroke sharks.

WHERE DO THEY LIVE?

Each Nutch in a Nitch knows that some other Nutch
Would like to move into his Nitch very much.
So each Nutch in a Nitch has to watch that small Nitch
Or Nutches who haven't got Nitches will snitch.

Dr. Seuss
On Beyond Zebra, 1954

Local macros,   WordBasic macros reside in templates. Period. As you saw in Chapter 4,
global macros,   WinWord has many different *kinds* of templates—local, global, and a potentially
add-on macros   huge collection of add-on templates—and macros can sit in any kind of template.

When you write a new macro or copy over a macro from someplace else, you'll always be putting the macro in a template. That's the only place WinWord will keep them.

Although it's true that you can grab hold of a macro and stick it in a regular ol' everyday document, it won't run from the document. Macros have to be set up in a special way, and that way is through the Tools/Macro command (or copied through the Template Organizer).

We're going to work with global macros in this book, the kind that are stored in NORMAL.DOT. As you get more adept at writing and running macros, you'll want to learn about the other places you can stick them, and for that kind of exploring I strongly recommend *The Hacker's Guide to Word for Windows*.

HOW CAN I CALL THEE?

> I call a fig a fig, a spade a spade.
>
> Menander
> ca. 300 BC

You can run your macro, bringing your macro to life, in many different ways. Some of those ways are pretty complex, and I won't go into the more bizarre methods here. However, there's a core collection of straightforward ways to run macros that you should understand.

Let me count the ways

Tools/Macro

Do you have the temp macro sitting around? Good. Click on Tools, then Macro. Make sure that Macros Available In shows NORMAL.DOT. Now double-click temp. Hello, Word! should greet you.

Double-click to run

That's the simplest way to run a macro, although it's far from the most convenient. You can also click on Tools, then Macro, click temp once, and click Run. Whoop-dee-doo.

Key Combination

You can also assign a specific key combination to trigger your macro. Click on Tools, then Customize, and bring up the Keyboard filecard. Make sure that Save Changes In shows NORMAL.DOT. Over on the left, under Categories, pick Macros. On the right, under Macros, pick temp. Your screen should look like Figure 7.3.

Stick your cursor in the Press New Shortcut Key box, and hit some oddball key combination. (When I'm testing out macros, I use CTRL+F1 because it's easy to remember, and WinWord doesn't assign anything to that particular key combination.) Click Assign, then Close. *Make sure that you click Assign before you click Close.* I always forget that part!

Assign temp to CTRL+F1.

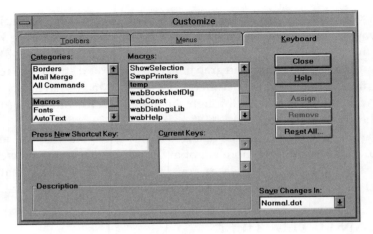

Figure 7.3 Tools Keyboard

Now hold down the Control key and hit F1. WinWord knows that you want to run temp. Hello, Word! pops right up, eh?

On the Menu

Similarly, you can put your macros on WinWord's menu. Say you want to stick a line, oh, under the Help menu that says "Run My Temp Macro." Clicking on that line should run temp. Piece o' cake.

Click Tools, Customize, bring up the Menu filecard, and make sure that Save Changes In shows NORMAL.DOT. Under Categories, pick Macros. Under Macros, pick temp, just as you did for the keyboard assignment. (See Figure 7.4.)

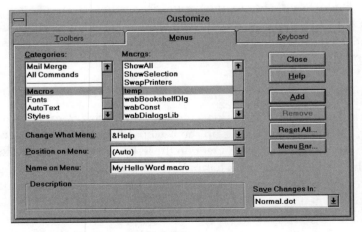

Figure 7.4 Temp on the Help Menu

In the Change What Menu box, pick &Help. (In case you were wondering, the &Help (No Document) choice you'll find farther down the list is for the menu that WinWord displays when there is no active document.) And in the Name on Menu box, type something like My Hello, Word! macro.

Click Add, then click Close. That's all it takes. If you look on your Help menu, you'll find a line at the bottom that says "My Hello, Word! macro." If you click on it, temp runs, and you'll see the Hello, Word! box on your screen.

Toolbar Button

You put macros on the Toolbar several times in Chapters 1 and 2, but if you want to brush up, it's easy to put temp on a Toolbar. Click Tools, then Customize. Make sure that Save Changes In shows NORMAL.DOT. In Categories pick Macros. Under Macros pick temp. Click on temp and drag it to whichever Toolbar you'd like. Pick a picture and click OK.

Whenever you click that Toolbar button, temp runs, and you'll get the Hello, Word! box.

Calling From Another Macro

No macro is an island, apart from the main. You can have macros that start other macros, which in turn start other macros. It's easy to write a macro that calls temp.

Click on Tools, then Macro. Make sure that Macros Available In shows NORMAL.DOT. Type in a name—oh, how about CallingTemp—and click Create. WordBasic springs forth, with a Sub MAIN and End Sub ready for you. If you simply stick the word "temp" on a line, WinWord knows that you want to run temp. Try it:

```
Sub MAIN
temp
End Sub
```

Now click the right-wedgie "Play" button. See that? When WinWord hits the line

Play it again, .SAM.

```
temp
```

it knows that you want to run the macro called temp, and it does so. In turn, temp flashes the Hello, Word! box up on the screen. Neat, huh?

CUCKOO MACROS

The common cuckoo of Europe, Asia and Africa lays its eggs in other species' nests where they are reared by their foster parents.

New American Desk Encyclopedia

Global vs. built-in

Chapter 4 explained how WinWord, when searching for a macro or command, looks at the global level before looking at the built-in level. Earlier in this chapter I raved a bit about the WinWord designers' brilliant decision to let you take over WinWord's workings and bend it to your own devices. That's a bit esoteric. Let's make it more concrete.

Preparation

First, I want to make sure you don't clobber anything that's already installed on your computer. So bear with me for a second while we back up some stuff that could go boom.

Click on Tools, then Macro. This time, make sure that Macros Available In shows All Active Templates. Yeah, I know, we've never done things this way before. Hang on. I just want to take a look at all your macros, okay?

Scan the list. If no macro appears in the list called EditGoto, you're home free. In fact, I chose EditGoto because there aren't too many products that glom onto that name. I'd guess that your chances of having a macro called EditGoto were less than one in a thousand.

You only need to do this if you have a macro called EditGoto.

However, if you do have a macro in that list called EditGoto, I want you to rename it. Click Organizer, click once on EditGoto (it could appear either on the left or the right), click Rename, and type in something you won't forget, like WoodyMadeMeDoThis. Click OK, then Close.

After you're done with this little experiment, you'll have to come back and put EditGoto back together again. Click on Tools, Macro, All Active Templates, click Organizer, click on WoodyMadeMeDoThis, click Rename, type EditGoto, click OK, and click Close. Whew.

Execution

He was but as the cuckoo is in June,
Heard, not regarded.

William Shakespeare
King Henry the Fourth, 1597

We're going to turn your temp macro into a cuckoo and drop it into one of WinWord's nests. In particular, we're going to rename temp so it's called EditGoto. And then you better strap on your seatbelt, bucko.

Click Tools, then Macro, then Organizer. The box on the left or the box on the right (or possibly both, see Figure 7.5) will be labeled NORMAL.DOT.

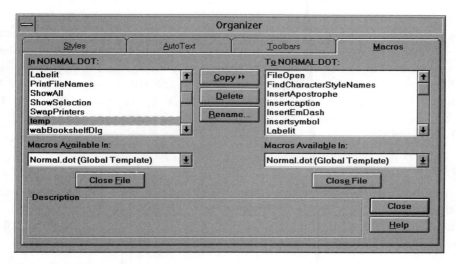

Figure 7.5 Getting Normal Organized

Scroll down to temp, and click the Rename button. Type EditGoto just like that, no spaces, no quotes, just plain EditGoto. Click OK, then click Close. Congrats. You've just renamed temp so that it's now known as EditGoto.

Rename temp to EditGoto.

For what it's worth, that whole Tools/Macro/Organizer/Rename exercise took but two clicks in WinWord 1.0. Back when version 2.0 came out, WinWord's creators decided that macros were too hard for everyday users, so they took macros off the menu, replacing them with Tables. Now you have to wade through six layers of boxes and bull to get anything done. Oh, well. That's progress.

Goto No More

Congratulations. You've just replaced WinWord's Goto function. Completely. Everywhere. (Don't worry, it's easy to switch back.)

Give it a try. Do anything you can think of to run WinWord's built-in Goto function. Click Edit, then Goto. *Ha!* Temp is sitting there. Your Hello, Word! dialog box pops up.

Goto replaced on the menu

Do you have Goto on your Toolbar, as I showed you in Chapter 1? If so, click on it. Boom! There's temp again, with its Hello, Word! box.

Goto replaced on the Toolbar

What about F5? That's the key that WinWord automatically assigns to Goto. Hit it. Zap! Once again temp takes control.

Goto replaced on the keyboard

WinWord also assigns CTRL+G to Goto. I'll give you one guess as to what happens when you hit CTRL+G. Yep. It's temp again.

Grok that one for a moment. You've just replaced WinWord's built-in Goto function, something buried in a thousand lines of C code spread over a dozen subroutines somewhere in the bowels of `WINWORD.EXE`, with your very own one-line macro. Your macro can do anything it bloody well pleases. And any time WinWord goes looking for its built-in Goto function, it's going to run *your* macro.

I think you can see now how WordBasic macros give you nearly complete control over your WinWord destiny. I hope you've also come to appreciate the brilliant simplicity in this design. You can pick and choose what you want to change, write a little (or a big!) WordBasic macro, drop in your changes, and the resulting customized version of WinWord runs your changes as if they were part of WinWord itself.

Restoration

Rename EditGoto as temp

Naturally you want your Goto back! Not to worry. Click on Tools, then Macro. Click Organizer. Click EditGoto (which may be on either the left or the right, or both). Click Rename. Type in temp—again, no quotes, no space, no nuthin'. Click OK. Click Close. There. Everything is back to … uh … normal.

SOME PRACTICE MACROS

> Oft bend the bow, and thou with ease shalt do,
> What others can't with all their strength put to.
>
> Robert Herrick
> *Hesperides*, 1648

That's the grand scheme of things, the big picture, the way WinWord and WordBasic can work together. I think your understanding WordBasic's place in this universe is more important than the language itself. You can always look up the WordBasic commands. You can't always see how they fit into the larger context. That said, let me get you started with the language.

Sprechen Sie?

Computer languages vs. human languages

Computer languages, like human languages, don't unveil themselves immediately. You have to memorize little snippets—"Hello, how are you?" or "Where is the bathroom?" or "I can count to ten"—and then work on tying the snippets together.

Computer languages, like human languages, have all sorts of rules and conventions. There are phrases that "sound right"; there are phrases that don't quite go together, even if they do work.

You wouldn't expect to learn French in one sitting. It amazes me how many folks get frustrated because they can't learn Basic in one sitting. In many ways, Basic is more difficult than French. Of course, in other ways, it's considerably simpler. (You don't have to pinch your nose while you're talking, for starters.)

No royal road to Basic

If you concentrate on getting the feel of a language—again, human or machine—you'll often find that the nit-picky rules fall into place, sooner or later. You'll get better at it with practice. That's precisely the method I think you'll find easiest for learning WordBasic.

Let's go back over the macros you wrote in the first four chapters, and then we'll toss in a couple of interesting, useful critters for you to play with.

General Approach

In general, if you hit a macro you'd like to play with, click on Tools, then Macro. Make sure that Save Changes In shows `NORMAL.DOT`. Click once on temp (or type in a new name, if you prefer). Click Edit (or Create, if it's a new macro). Then start typing away.

Whenever you want to test the macro, hit the right-wedgie button. If things start going by too fast, don't use the right-wedgie. Instead, click on the floppy-arrow button, and step through the macro one line at a time. If you're curious as to which variables have what values, click on the spectacles.

Testing

To save the macro, just click File, then Save, or Close, same as you would with any document. They'll be stored away in `NORMAL.DOT`.

Feel free to keep bunches of macros floating around. You might see a slight performance drop—most likely measured in fractions of a second—if you keep hundreds of macros in `NORMAL.DOT`, but you'll probably never notice.

How many is too many?

If/Then/Else

> Learning without thought brings ensnarement.
> Thought without learning totters.
>
> Confucius
> ca. 500 BC

The most fundamental control statement in practically any language, the If statement, tells your program to do one thing if an expression is true, another thing if it's false. Here's the first macro you hit in Chapter 1:

```
If ViewFieldCodes() Then
  ToolsOptionsView .FieldCodes=0
Else
  ToolsOptionsView .FieldCodes=1
End If
```

Built-in function   ViewFieldCodes() is a built-in WinWord function (of which there are hundreds) that looks at the current document and returns True if WinWord is showing field codes, or False if it's showing Field results.

Built-in command   ToolsOptionsView is a built-in WinWord command that ccrresponds, more or less, with the dialog box you see when you click Tools, then Options, the View. Generally a "1" means that the corresponding box is checked; a "0" means it's unchecked.

In this particular instance, the macro flips WinWord over so that it shows field results, or so that it shows field codes—in other words, it "checks" or "clears" the Show Field Codes box—depending on the value of ViewFieldCodes().

On Error

Refinement   If you recall, we refined the macro just a touch to take care of the situation where it's inadvertently run while a macro is in the top window—when the question "Are field codes showing, or are results?" has no meaning.

```
Sub MAIN
On Error Goto HeyYoureInAMacroTurkey
If ViewFieldCodes() Then
  ToolsOptionsView .FieldCodes=0
Else
  ToolsOptionsView .FieldCodes=1
End If
HeyYoureInAMacroTurkey:
End Sub
```

Labels   The On Error statement also controls how WinWord skips through a macro. If it hits an error—in this case, if ViewFieldCodes() croaks because the "Are field codes on?" question has no good answer—it jumps down to the indicated label, in this case, the label I've called HeyYoureInAMacroTurkey:.

Insert

InsertEmDash   WordBasic can do much more than manipulate WinWord's settings, of course. The macro we put together to insert an em-dash into a document uses the WordBasic Insert command to put stuff in a document at the current cursor location.

```
CurrPoints = FontSize()
FontSize 6
Insert " "
FontSize CurrPoints
```

```
Insert Chr$(151)
FontSize 6
Insert " "
FontSize CurrPoints
```

The macro also manipulates font sizes and demonstrates a couple of ways to move around inside a document.

You might've noticed an oddity ... oh, hell, might as well call it a bug ... in how InsertEmDash behaves. If you stick your cursor in the middle of a word, then run InsertEmDash (by hitting the number pad's minus key, if you set it up that way), you've no doubt seen how InsertEmDash insists on turning everything into 6-point text.

Fortunately the solution is pretty simple. I didn't want to go into all the gory details back in Chapter 2, but you're accustomed to gore by now.

The problem lies in the way WinWord applies font formatting changes. If nothing is selected and you change font formatting—turn on italics, say, or change the point size—WinWord takes it upon itself to change all adjacent characters so that they take on the new formatting. The line in InsertEmDash that says FontSize 6, run when there is nothing selected and the cursor is inside a word, turns the whole word into 6-point mush.

The solution lies in putting the spaces into the document, selecting them (using the command CharLeft 1, 1, which moves the cursor left one character, selecting the character as you move), and formatting them at 6 points. A better InsertEmDash looks like this:

```
Sub MAIN
SelType 1
CurrPoints = FontSize()
Insert " "
CharLeft 1, 1
FontSize 6
CharRight
FontSize CurrPoints
Insert Chr$(151)
Insert " "
CharLeft 1, 1
FontSize 6
CharRight
FontSize CurrPoints
End Sub
```

To make those changes to your copy of InsertEmDash, assuming you already have it on your system, click on Tools, then Macro. Make sure that Macros Available In shows NORMAL.DOT. Click once on InsertEmDash, click Edit. Then make the indicated changes. When you're done, click File, then Close. Yes, you want to save changes.

PrintFonts

Let me close this collection of small, useful macros with a sentimental favorite, one I think you'll find very valuable.

This is a classic WordBasic macro.

I first wrote about PrintFonts back in the days of WinWord 2.0a and told the rambling story of my trials and tribulations with the macro in the original *Hacker's Guide to Word for Windows*. Think of Arlo Guthrie's troubles with Alice and the restaurant and the Group W bench and the twenty-seven 8 by 10 color glossy pictures with the circles and arrows and a paragraph on the back of each one. Something along those lines. (Hey, anybody with a dad named Woody can't be all bad.)

Back then, PrintFonts wouldn't work for love nor money. I must've hit ten bugs before finally giving up with a partial solution. Well, I'm very happy to say that PrintFonts works just fine in WinWord 6.0, at least as far as I can tell. It's a simple macro that prints samples of all your fonts and looks something like this:

```
Sub MAIN
Caps$="A B C D E F G H I J K L M N O P Q R S T U V W X Y Z "
Lower$="a b c d e f h i j k l m n o p q r s t u v w x y z"
Points$ = InputBox$("Print fonts at which point size?")
FileNew
Insert Str$(CountFonts())+" fonts at " + Points$ + " points."
InsertPara
For i = 1 To CountFonts()
  NormalStyle
  Insert Font$(i) + ": "
  Font Font$(i), Val(Points$)
  Insert Caps$ + Lower$
  InsertPara
Next i
FilePrint
DocClose 2
End Sub
```

Try typing that into your machine and playing with it a bit until it does what *you* want it to. If you need a tip about what a certain command does — for example, if the DocClose 2 command baffles you, as well it should! — just stick your cursor inside the command and hit F1. WordBasic Help springs to your rescue. Pretty good stuff.

FALL BACK ON THE RECORDER

Every man is his own doctor of divinity, in the last resort.

Robert Louis Stevenson
An Inland Voyage, 1878

In general, I recommend that folks not use the macro recorder. It often produces garbage, a sequence of commands that neither makes sense nor replicates the actions you've performed. There's a reason for that. The macro recorder is faced with an impossible task. It has to turn old-fashioned keystrokes into Basic commands, and the translation can be elusive at times.

Yeah, there comes a time, sooner or later, when you need to break down and use the macro recorder. Usually that happens when you just can't think of what a certain command might be called, and all your hunting and pecking and F1-Help runs come to naught. If you can do something in WinWord, you can use the macro recorder to find out, more or less, how to do it in WordBasic. Here's how.

The recorder can come in handy.

Bring up the WordBasic editor by clicking on Tools, then Macro, making sure that Macros Available In shows NORMAL.DOT, typing in a name, and clicking either Create or Edit. You'll get the editor shown in Figure 7.1.

See that blue button with a 1 after it, the second button on the macro Toolbar? That's the one you want. Click it. Now go do whatever it was you needed to do in your macro. Click on something or hit a key. Not only will the action be performed, but WordBasic will put the command that did it right there in your macro. Once you have the command handy, you can hit F1 and learn much more about it.

Record one macro command.

ROLL YOUR OWN

It is common sense to take a method and try it. If it fails, admit it frankly and try another. But above all, try something.

F. D. Roosevelt
1932

I hope you find this little introduction to WordBasic useful. Nope, I didn't show you even a teensy-tiny fraction of WordBasic's 800-plus commands. Nor did I drone on about control structures or variable types, nesting or calling parameters, or naming conventions or structured design.

If you were learning Latin, I wouldn't start you with the subjunctive mood, either.

Rather, I hope you've seen how WordBasic fits into the grand scheme and, having seen its power, you've come to the conclusion that this is something you need to learn. It is, it is.

If you're the self-starting type—particularly if you already know a bit about Basic, any Basic—you have everything you need to get going. Don't wait; dive in now. WinWord ships with dozens of macros, ready for you to take apart. Combined with the smattering of rather eclectic macros you'll find in this book, WordBasic's extensive F1 help, and the brief introduction to the mechanics of WordBasic that's included in the WinWord User's Manual, you have an excellent base on which to build. Just remember to save often and save well, keep hitting F1, and experiment!

If you don't have any exposure to computer programming, I'd recommend that you try a quick course at your local community college or adult education center. A simple programming course will do; you don't need anything fancy. Intro to Programming or Intro to Basic—any kind of Basic—is ideal.

Word for Windows Companion

If you'd like a thorough introduction to the why's and wherefore's of WordBasic, once again, I'd like to point you to *Word for Windows Companion* by Stone, Poor, and Crane (MS Press). It's as thorough an introduction to the mechanics as you'll find. And I think you'll find this current chapter on macros invaluable in seeing the forest through *Companion's* trees.

Hacker's Guide

Should you find yourself spending more than a few hours a week slogging through macros—or if you discover that the official documentation, like the *Word Developer's Kit* (MS Press), speaks with forked tongue—you ought to look at the *Hacker's Guide to Word for Windows,* which is being updated by Scott Krueger even as I write this. Check and make sure you get the *Hacker's Guide* for WinWord 6.0; the earlier version, which Vince Chen and I wrote, has much that applies to WinWord 6.0, but it is specific to version 2.0a. Between *Companion* and *Hacker,* you'll have it down in no time.

8 The Underground Template

Good deeds are better than wise sayings.

Talmud
Pirke Avot

Let's put your knowledge to work. We're going to build the Underground Letterhead, a well-connected sucker that you can modify to print your own letters, memos, or whatever. Once you see how it works, you'll be able to tweak it to your heart's content.

No, this isn't a Microsoft Wizard. It's a down-home, built from the ground up, nitty-gritty, get yer hands dirty Woody Wizard. It's not a pretty face that purports to do the work for you, and then leaves you in the lurch. It's a workin' stiff that you can bang on until you get it right.

If you aren't yet happy with the letter templates you've seen floating around—and if you think the WinWord 6.0 Wizards are a distinct step back from the capabilities of the old WinWord 2.0 templates—welcome to the family. This is the place to start.

I'm going to show you how to make a template that prints a pretty fancy letter on your existing, preprinted letterhead. (If you don't have a letterhead, not to worry; I'll show you how to do that, too.) It'll take the whole chapter to do this one template justice.

What's in the Underground Letterhead.

If you hired a consultant to put together a template this fancy, you'd spend many hundreds of dollars. I know. I've charged that much and more. (Besides, if you hired somebody else to do it, you probably wouldn't get what you really wanted anyway.)

Oh. Be sure to smile as you work. A happy template is a good template; joy in the work shows through in the product.

TERMINOLOGY

There are technical terms for all this stuff, but I don't want to bog you down in printer's gobbledygook. So here are the terms I'm going to use in this chapter.

The first page   The first page of your letter is usually different from all the other pages. It may have a preprinted logo, or you may want to devise and have the computer print your own logo. It usually has some information at the top, like your name or address—which you may or may not want to print with the computer—and it may have other text preprinted elsewhere. I'll call the first page the ... uh ... "first page."

The second page   Everything other than the first page I'll call the "second page." If your letter extends beyond one page, chances are very good that the second and all subsequent pages have nothing preprinted on them, that you have an empty playing field. That's the situation I'll talk about here. If you have something preprinted on pages 2, *et seq.*, you'll have to take them into account when drawing margins.

LAYOUT

> Things are seldom what they seem.
> Skim milk masquerades as cream.
>
> W. S. Gilbert
> *H.M.S. Pinafore*, 1878

First we need to block out the letter. If you have preprinted letterhead, get a sheet. (If you don't have preprinted letterhead, start with a plain piece of paper.) Grab a pencil and a good eraser, and—for those of you using a nonmetric version of WinWord—a ruler that measures in tenths of an inch. You're going to draw all sorts of stuff on that piece of preprinted letterhead.

Margins

> In getting my books, I have been always solicitous of an ample margin; this is not so much through any love of the thing itself, however agreeable, as for the facility it affords me of penciling suggested thoughts.
>
> Edgar Allen Poe
> *Marginalia*, 1844

Establish margins   Start by blocking out your *second page* margins. The margins will affect every page in your letter, so if you want to think of this as "the margins for every page but the first one," you'll be fine. Ignore any preprinted stuff on the paper; we'll set aside space for the preprinted regions momentarily. If you find yourself distracted by preprinted stuff on the page, go find the kind of paper that you'll be using for page 2 and all subsequent pages and work with it, or flip the first page sheet of paper over and work with the blank side. Again, these are margins for page 2, *et seq.*

Just draw lines on the paper that correspond to where you want your margins.

The U.S. version of WinWord ships with 1-inch top and bottom margins and 1.25-inch side margins. I tend to gab a lot, so I like wider margins: 1 inch on top, 0.5 inch on the bottom, and 1 inch left and right. (See Figure 8.1.)

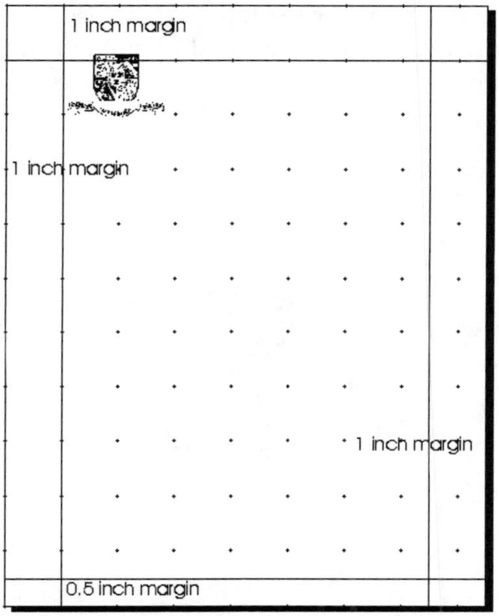

Give yourself lots of room.

Figure 8.1 Margins on My Page 1

Don't do anything on the computer yet. Simply draw in the lines, and make sure you can live with them.

Logos

> Logos *n* : reason that in ancient Greek philosophy
> is the controlling principle of the universe.
>
> Webster's *New Collegiate Dictionary*, 1979

Once the margins are set, you need to reserve space for anything that's preprinted on the *first page*. I tend to think of these things as "logos," but you may have a list of names on the left-hand side or a preprinted address on the bottom.

No need to do anything on the computer. Just take your pencil and draw rectangles around the preprinted places that you want left alone. Typically, you'll probably block off room at the upper left corner or the entire top of the page. When you have the rectangles situated just right, use the ruler and measure the distance that each box extends beyond the margins. Jot down the distances.

For example, my letterhead consists of a logo preprinted in the upper left corner of the sheet. When I draw a box around the logo, it extends 2 inches beyond the left margin and 1.5 inches below the top margin. (See Figure 8.2.) So I know I need to reserve an extra 2 × 1.5 inch area, in addition to the margins, in the upper left corner of my first page.

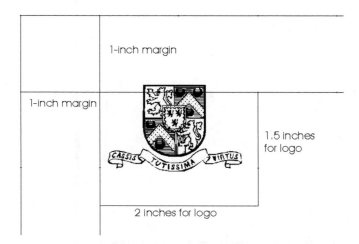

Figure 8.2 Logo Space on My Page 1

You still haven't done anything on the computer, right? Good. You'll find it much easier to figure out what you want and get the details nailed down before you go monkeying around in WinWord.

DIY Logos

L'art pour l'art.*

Victor Cousin
Lecture at the Sorbonne, 1818

If you have a preprinted first page, skip down to the next section on creating the template. Okay. You're here because you don't have a logo and you want to use WinWord to print one on your first page. Good.

*Art for art's sake.

The whole topic of computer-printed (and, usually, computer-generated) logos is a complex one. All too often folks get bogged down in designing logos when they're making a letterhead template, as we are right now. That isn't a good idea. There's plenty of confusion floating around already without tossing logo design into the fray.

At this point, you only need to know how big your logo graphic will be and where you want it. Using a pencil, draw a box on your letterhead to allocate space for the logo. Don't get bogged down in trying to design a logo right now. You can come back to it later.

If you're going to do a logo, it's better to get a graphic design tool like CorelDRAW! (if you're drawing your own) or Picture Publisher (if you're scanning in an existing logo), and use the right tool for the job.

General logo advice

Although WinWord can create a logo—and WordArt might even produce a decent-looking one—if you're picky and want anything beyond a simple picture, you won't be happy with what WinWord can do.

CREATING THE TEMPLATE

> All things return eternally, and ourselves with them: We have already existed times without number, and all things with us.
>
> F.W. Nietzsche
> *Thus spoke Zarathustra*, 1885

You have your margins staked out and boxes drawn on the first page to cover everything that's preprinted on the page. Now it's time to start making the template. Click on File, then New, click the Template button, and then click OK. You should be staring at something called Template1.

Right now, before you do anything else, give your new template a name. Click on File, then Save (or click on the FileSave button on the Toolbar), and type in a name. I used _UNDERGD—the underscore character at the beginning assures that this template will appear at the top of my lengthy list of templates whenever I create a new file—but you can use whatever you like. Click OK, type in the Summary Info, and click OK again. Now your Underground Letterhead template has a name.

Underground Template is born.

Applying Margins

Click on File, then Page Setup. Bring up the Margins filecard. Make sure that the Apply To: box reads Whole Document. Then type in your margins (see Figure 8.3). Remember that these are the margins for the *second* (and all subsequent) *pages*. Click OK.

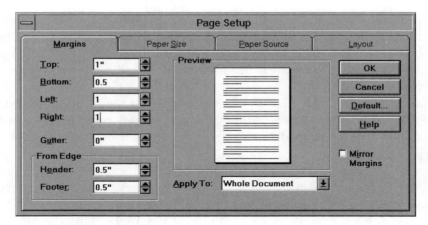

Figure 8.3 Underground Margins

Show All

Hit Enter a few times to stick a handful of paragraph marks in the document. You'll need them shortly. (You *do* have WinWord set up to show paragraph marks, right? If not, click the Show All button on the Toolbar, and reread Chapter 1!)

Adding Frames

> For all that nature by her mother wit
> Could frame in earth.
>
> Edmund Spenser
> *The Faerie Queene*, 1590

Time to block out the preprinted areas on the first page. If you're having WinWord bring in an electronic logo, you should set aside space for the logo. If your first page has nothing preprinted (ah, lucky you!), skip down to the next section on Fixed Text.

We're going to set aside these rectangles by drawing frames on the template, anchoring them in place, and allowing WinWord to wrap text around the frames. As long as you don't type anything in the frame, nothing will print there and WinWord will automagically work its way around the preprinted areas on your first page.

Show the margins

Make sure you're in Page View. Click Tools, then Options. Bring up the View filecard. Click on the box that says Text Boundaries. (The Text Boundaries check box controls whether WinWord shows margins and a bunch of other things. It'll be very handy for this exercise.) You should have something that looks like Figure 8.4.

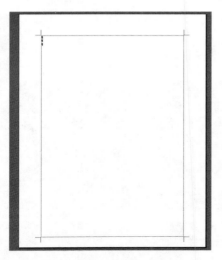

Figure 8.4 Underground Letterhead Text Boundaries

You'll probably want to flip-flop back and forth between looking at the page as a whole and looking at a specific, tiny part. Use the magnifying glass View Zoom button on the Toolbar to zoom in and out. Start out with the whole page visible.

View Zoom

Click on Insert, then Frame. Your cursor will turn into a crosshair (+). Locate a block you want to carve out of your first page. Click and drag it to create a box about the right size, in roughly the correct location, of that first set-aside box. You won't get it exactly right. Don't worry about it; just get it close.

Insert the frame.

As soon as you have the box roughed out, click Format, then Frame. This is where you get to twiddle and fine-tune the box so that it falls at precisely the correct place on the page.

Size it precisely.

On my first page, I need a 2 × 1.5-inch frame situated in the far upper left corner of the page, inside the margins. So my frame looks like Figure 8.5. Note how you need to wrap text Around the frame. Also note that the Size is set at Exactly, the Horizontal and Vertical Position are probably easiest to specify in terms of distance from the margin, you don't want the frame to Move with Text, and you must Lock Anchor.

When you think you have the frame lined up right, with the size and location just the way you want it, click the Print button on the Toolbar. WinWord prints the page with a border around the frame, which is just perfect for holding up to a strong light and verifying that the frame covers whatever needs to be covered.

True confessions time: It took me a while to jimmy and jigger these settings around so I liked them. Don't get frustrated if you don't get it right the first time. Just keep at it until you've finally assembled something you can live with.

Hey, nobody gets this right the first time.

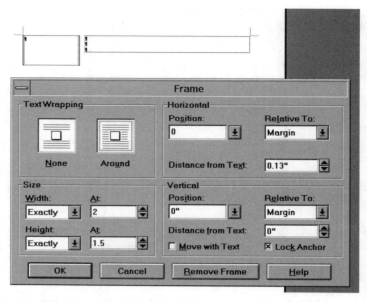

Figure 8.5 Formatting My Frame

Repeat the process if you need to block out more than one rectangular section on the first page. When you're done, you'll have a template that looks something like Figure 8.6, possibly with several frames on the page.

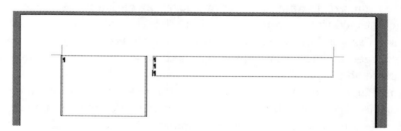

Figure 8.6 Final Frame

Paper Feed

> Feed by measure and defy the physician.
>
> John Heywood
> *Proverbs*, 1546

Now's as good a time as any to tell WinWord which paper tray it should use to pull in your letterhead. Every printer is different, and every user has his or her own idea of how to load first and second pages. Click on File, then Page Setup, bring up the Paper Source filecard, and make sure that the Apply To: box shows WHOLE DOCUMENT. Personally, I load letterhead manually. That's why I set Figure 8.7 the way you see it.

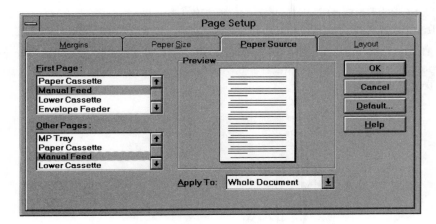

Figure 8.7 Page Setup

Fixed Text and Date

Now that we've told WinWord which areas of the page to avoid, it's time we start putting in the components that make a letter. Precisely what appears next, and where, is completely up to you.

When I had my letterhead printed by Ye Olde Local Print Shoppe, I intentionally designed the letterhead so I could use the same letterhead for many different purposes. My letterhead works for business stationery. In my business template, I print "Pinecliffe International" across the top, with an address immediately beneath. It also works for personal stationery. I create a second template that puts "Woody Leonhard" on the top and my home phone number beneath. I've made similar templates for everybody in the family, plus a couple of small businesses I run on the side.

Versatile preprinted stationery

Do you ever wish that you could make a small change to your company's stationery without spending megabucks at the local print shop? Does your company have several divisions, or do business under several different names? Such alterations are easy to do with a laser printer. Just make sure that you have the print shop put on only the stuff that will never, ever change, and you can print the rest on your printer. You can save hundreds—even thousands! —of dollars by thinking through the best division of labor between the print shop and your laser printer.

To put this kind of fixed text in your template, just type! There's nothing particularly fancy or complicated about it. Format away. Change fonts. Move the paragraphs around. Do whatever you like. There are just two tricks:

- When you hit the place where you want today's date, click on Insert, then Date and Time, and pick a format you like, but be absolutely sure you check the Insert As Field box. (See Figure 8.8.)

- At the very end, put the last paragraph mark wherever you want the main part of the letter to begin. We'll work from that point in the Underground Template's macros.

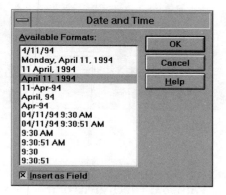

Figure 8.8 Make Sure You Insert As Field

One approach   I put my company name up at the top and made it pretty big. With the cursor still in the company name, I stuck a line under it by clicking on Format, then Borders and Shading…, and picking a 2¼-point bottom border. Then comes my address in a script font, with a couple of Wingding graphics (using Insert/Symbol). Finally, there's the date, inserted as a field, natch. All of these paragraphs are centered.

My fixed text, with all its boundaries, looks like Figure 8.9. See how the final paragraph mark is right where I want the letter to begin?

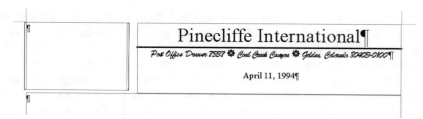

Figure 8.9 The Top of My First Page

Keep printing test samples as you're working, holding them up to the light against your preprinted letterhead. Make sure you keep saving your work as you go along.

When you're happy with what you see, it's time to get rid of the boxes around the frames. Click inside each frame, one at a time. Click Format, then Borders and Shading..., click the None box in the upper left corner, and click OK.

Get rid of the frame borders.

Attaching DIY Logos

If all of your logos are preprinted, and you don't want WinWord to stick a logo on each page, skip on down to the next section, the Moral of the Story. You need to stick a picture or two in your letters, right? And you have a frame blocked out for each one. Good.

If you can live with WinWord's drawing capabilities—including WordArt, which can do some pretty cool stuff—go ahead and stick your cursor in a frame, and do your drawing thing. Insert/Object will get you into the WordArt applet or the Equation Editor (which can make pretty righteous logos!).

If you're bringing in a graphic from a file, though, you should consider how much that graphic may swell the size of your file. You'll find that there's a lot of overhead in sticking a graphic in every document you create.

Logos can really put a lot of bytes on your template.

Although it takes longer and it's potentially more troublesome, I strongly recommend that you consider linking graphics into your Underground Letterhead template, instead of putting the graphic in the file. To do that, stick your cursor in the frame that's going to hold the graphic, click Insert, then Picture, and make sure that the Link To File box is checked and that the Save Picture In Document box is *not* checked.

Moral of the Story

> An expert is one who knows more and more about less and less.
>
> Nicholas Murray Butler
> President, Columbia University

Don't be intimidated by "professional" this and that. You needn't be a professional graphic artist to do a bang-up job with a letterhead template. It's mostly a question of finding a combination that looks good to you.

I'm a lousy graphic artist, can't hardly draw a straight line with a pencil and ruler, and damn near flunked art in grade school, much less high school. But when I took my printed letterhead back to Ye Olde Local Print Shoppe, to show them how a laser can work with nice embossed letterhead, they asked for several copies. They're using the Pinecliffe International letterhead to show their commercial customers how to strike a balance between preprinted stuff and Ye Olde

You're working with incredibly powerful tools.

Local Laser. Believe me, if ol' artistically challenged Woody can put it together, so can you.

Now let's put a little intelligence behind the Underground Letterhead's pretty face.

AUTONEW MACRO

> Everyone agreed that Clevinger was certain to go far in the academic world. In short, Clevinger was one of those people with lots of intelligence and no brains, and everyone knew it except those who soon found out. In short, he was a dope.
>
> Joseph Heller
> *Catch-22*, 1961

Every time WinWord creates a new document based on a template, it looks inside that template to see if it contains a macro called AutoNew. We're going to build our own AutoNew macro for the Underground Letterhead. WinWord will obligingly run it every time we create a new doc based on the Underground Letterhead template.

 I'm not going to put you on. When you start doing fancy stuff like this, you're going to bump into bugs. I hit so many bugs in WordBasic and the Dialog Editor that I damn near threw my copy of the *Word Developer's Kit* through my monitor (if you're in the mood for bugs, try to create a drop-down list box that extends outside the dialog!). But if you follow along closely, I'll try to show you where the stones are so you can walk through this quagmire without getting your shoes too dirty. Lucky you. By the time you read this, you'll be able to learn all about these bugs in the *Hacker's Guide*.

Custom Dialogs

Dialog editor   To build the AutoNew macro, we'll want to plug into WinWord's dialog editor. The dialog editor makes creating and maintaining dialog boxes much simpler than in the not-so-good old days, when all dialog boxes were created by hand.

Creating AutoNew   You need to find out if the WinWord dialog editor is installed on your system. The simplest way to do that is to open up your Underground Letterhead template. Let's call it `_UNDERGD.DOT`. Click on Tools, then Macro, make sure that the Macros Available In box shows `_UNDERGD.DOT` (or whatever your Underground Letterhead template is called), type in AutoNew (no spaces), and click Create. (See Figure 8.10.)

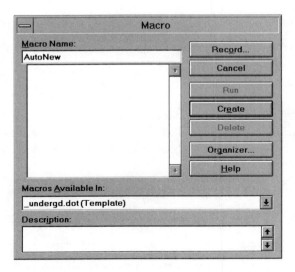

Figure 8.10 The Underground Letterhead's AutoNew

You should be looking at the WordBasic program editor, which we first encountered in the previous chapter, Figure 7.1. If you click the button all the way over on the right on the macro Toolbar—the one that looks like an ATM machine —you may be greeted by WordBasic's Dialog Editor. (See Figure 8.11). **Back to the macro pane**

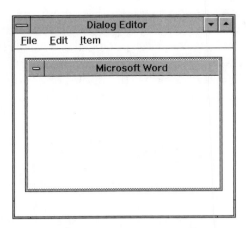

Figure 8.11 MACRODE.EXE in Action

If you get some sort of obscure error message about "Can't find MACRODE.EXE or one of its components," though, you'll have to dig out your WinWord installation disks. Go through the Custom/Complete setup and pull in the Macro Dialog Editor. Then go back and click the ATM button. **May have to go get MACRODE.EXE**

AutoNew Dialog

> Write with the learned, but speak with the vulgar.
>
> Thomas Fuller
> *Gnomologia*, 1732

Let's start by building a dialog for AutoNew. Double-click on the box you see in the dialog editor. You'll find a dialog title box like that in Figure 8.12. Type in a good title for your custom dialog box. I used Underground Letterhead. Click OK.

Figure showing Dialog Information box:

Dialog Information

Position — X: [ ] ☒ Auto   Y: [ ] ☒ Auto
Size — Width: [320] ☐ Auto   Height: [144] ☐ Auto

Text$: [Underground Letterhead]   ☒ Auto Quote
Field: [ ]
Comment: [ ]
OptGroup: [ ]

[OK]   [Cancel]

Figure 8.12 Title Box

We're going to build this custom dialog so you have plenty of room to type in the recipient's name and address. We'll also put together a list of common notes: Urgent, Confidential, FAX, Via Overnight, and on and on. You get to type in your own list.

Text, Text Box   Click on Item, then Text. Type To: (no quotes or anything, just To:). Click on Item again, then Text Box. Move things around a bit and you'll have something like Figure 8.13.

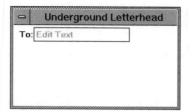

Figure 8.13 Edit Text Unfolds

Multiple line text box   This is a strange one. We want to make a big text box there where it says Edit Text, that'll hold a multiple line Address. After going back and forth through the official documentation, I found that the only way to do that is to double-click on the gray Edit Text, and clear the check box beside the Auto that follows Height. (Intuitive, eh?) See Figure 8.14. While you're at it, change the Field box so it says `.ADDRESS`, with a period at the beginning.

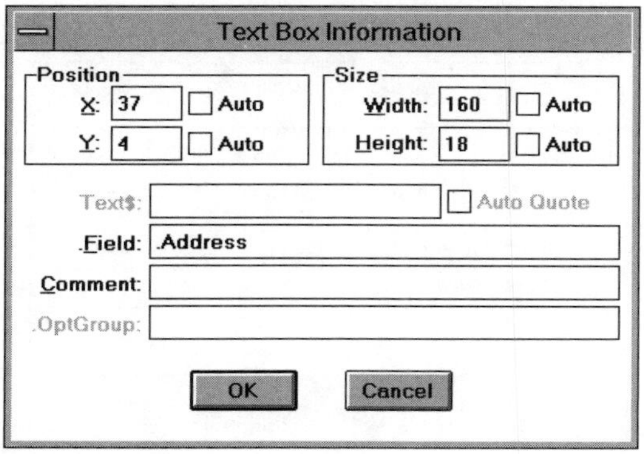

Figure 8.14 Set Up the .Address Field

Now click OK, pop back into the dialog box itself, and click and drag the Edit Text box so it looks big enough to hold a typical name and address. You should get something that looks like Figure 8.15.

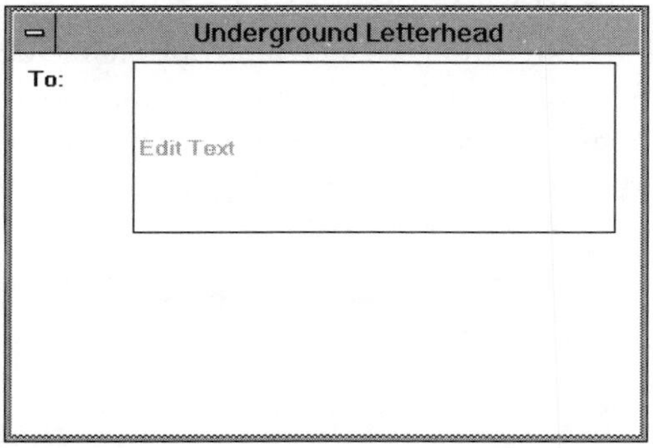

Figure 8.15 Addressee Covered

Next, we need a place to stick notes, like Confidential, Urgent, Via FedEx, and so on. That takes a drop-down list box. Click on Item, then List Box. Pick Drop-Down and click OK. Then stretch and drag the list box into place. Double-click on the list box and give it a decent Text, like Notes$(), and a good Field name, like, say, .Note. See Figure 8.16.

Notes

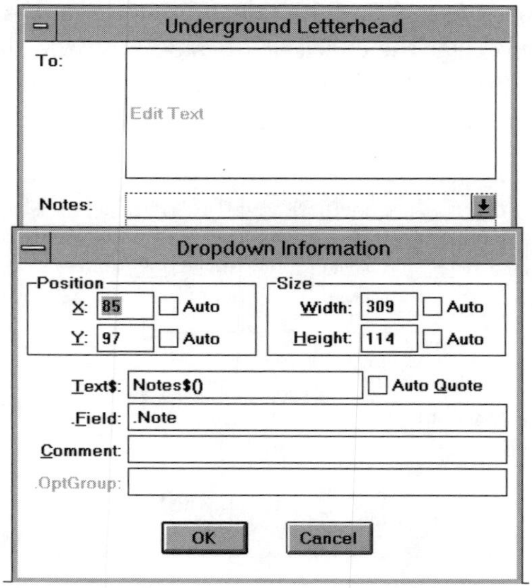

Figure 8.16 Notes Covered

Summary Info   WinWord documents can contain five kinds of summary information: Title, Subject, Author, Keyword, and Comments. Let's put lines in for each of those. In each case, click on Item, then Text, and type in the label (for example, Title:). Then click on Item, then TextBox, stretch and drag the box to the proper location, double-click on the TextBox, and give it an appropriate Field (for example, .Title).

Experiment with the Edit/Duplicate menu item, and you'll see how it can speed this kind of mass duplication. When you're done you should have five more TextBoxes and labels, arranged like Figure 8.17. Don't worry too much

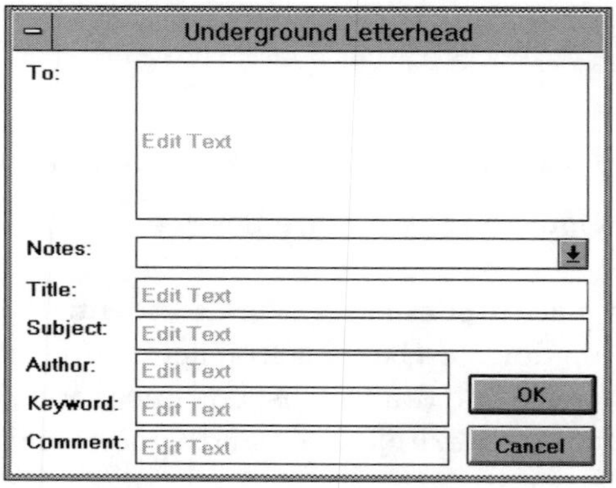

Figure 8.17 The Final Underground Letterhead Dialog

about the details at this point. You'll have a chance to come in and clean it all up shortly.

Finish off the dialog by clicking on Item, then Button, picking OK, and clicking OK. Drag your OK button to wherever feels right. Then hit Enter (that's a nifty trick!), and a Cancel button will appear immediately below.

Notes
OK, Cancel
Buttons

Running the Dialog

> Try not to become a man of success, but rather a man of value.
>
> Albert Einstein

With your fancy new custom dialog box in front of you, click on Edit, then Select Dialog. Then click Edit, and Copy. There. The whole dialog is now on the clipboard.

Flip over to the AutoNew macro (remember the AutoNew macro?), stick your cursor between Sub MAIN and End Sub, and click Edit/Paste. You should have something that looks more or less like this:

Copy dialog to
macro

```
Sub MAIN
Begin Dialog UserDialog 406, 224, "Underground Letterhead"
    Text 10, 5, 24, 13, "To:", .Text1
    TextBox 85, 5, 310, 84, .Address, 1
    Text 10, 98, 46, 13, "Notes:", .Text7
    DropListBox 85, 98, 310, 114, Notes$(), .Note
    Text 10, 120, 36, 13, "Title:", .Text2
    TextBox 85, 120, 310, 18, .Title
    Text 10, 140, 57, 13, "Subject:", .Text3
    TextBox 85, 140, 310, 18, .Subject
    Text 10, 160, 49, 13, "Author:", .Text4
    TextBox 85, 160, 215, 18, .Author
    Text 11, 180, 64, 13, "Keyword:", .Text5
    TextBox 85, 180, 215, 18, .Keywords
    Text 10, 200, 69, 13, "Comment:", .Text6
    TextBox 85, 200, 215, 18, .Comments
    OKButton 313, 170, 88, 21
    CancelButton 312, 197, 88, 21
End Dialog
End Sub
```

If your dialog looks a little different from what I have, you can go ahead and type in the stuff you see here. It's a difficult, error-prone method for creating a dialog box, but it can be done. (You can close the dialog editor now. We're done with it.)

Notes$()   Before you can test your new dialog, you'll have to patch in a few lines of code. First come the Notes. Figure out which notes—things to type at the top of a letter—you might want and write them down. Then set up the Notes$() array with those values, or you can crib from my list if you prefer. The list can go right after Sub MAIN. Remember to change the number in the Dim statement to correspond to how many notes you have, where the first note is Notes$(0). For example, if you have 11 notes, you need a Dim Notes$(10), and the first Note to appear on the screen is the one you stick in Notes$(0).

On Error Goto   Finally, some technocrap has to go after the End Dialog to tell WinWord that it should present the dialog to the user and wait for an answer. I also set the macro up so, should the user click Cancel inside the dialog, WinWord just exits gracefully. Your AutoNew macro might look something like this:

```
Sub MAIN
Dim Notes$(10)
Notes$(0) = "(no note)"
Notes$(1) = "Via FAX"
Notes$(2) = "Confidential"
Notes$(3) = "Via FedEx"
Notes$(4) = "Express Mail"
Notes$(5) = "Priority Mail"
Notes$(6) = "UPS Blue"
Notes$(7) = "UPS Red"
Notes$(8) = "Overseas Air"
Notes$(9) = "Registered"
Notes$(10) = "Certified"
Begin Dialog UserDialog 406, 224, "Underground Letterhead"
   Text 10, 5, 24, 13, "To:", .Text1
   TextBox 85, 5, 310, 84, .Address, 1
   Text 10, 98, 46, 13, "Notes:", .Text7
   DropListBox 85, 98, 310, 114, Notes$(), .Note
   Text 10, 120, 36, 13, "Title:", .Text2
   TextBox 85, 120, 310, 18, .Title
   Text 10, 140, 57, 13, "Subject:", .Text3
   TextBox 85, 140, 310, 18, .Subject
   Text 10, 160, 49, 13, "Author:", .Text4
   TextBox 85, 160, 215, 18, .Author
   Text 11, 180, 64, 13, "Keyword:", .Text5
   TextBox 85, 180, 215, 18, .Keywords
   Text 10, 200, 69, 13, "Comment:", .Text6
   TextBox 85, 200, 215, 18, .Comments
   OKButton 313, 170, 88, 21
   CancelButton 312, 197, 88, 21
End Dialog
```

```
Dim dlg As UserDialog
On Error Goto UserClickedCancel
Dialog dlg
On Error Goto 0

UserClickedCancel:
End Sub
```

Go ahead and click the right wedgie-button to "play" the macro. See how it behaves? Neat.

Take a test drive.

From Dialog to Doc

> A man with his belly full of the classics is an enemy
> of the human race.
>
> Henry Miller
> *Tropic of Cancer*, 1930

Finally, we need to pull the information out of the dialog and stick it in the new document. That isn't too tough. All of the code that follows goes after the On Error Goto 0 line and before UserClickedCancel:. You'll find the final code listed in Appendix E.

First, I'm going to freeze the date, by selecting the {date} field (actually, I'll just select the whole document), updating the field so it shows today's date, unlinking it — that is, converting the field to text, throwing the field away entirely — and then I'll move to the end of the document.

Freeze the date.

```
EditSelectAll
UpdateFields
UnlinkFields
EndOfDocument
```

By updating and then unlinking the field, the document will always contain the date on which it was created, the date on which this AutoNew macro was run. A little subtlety is lurking here that might interest you. It all has to do with {date}, and how and when it can be changed:

But which date?

- If you put a {date} field in a document, it changes every time the field is updated. If you put a {date} field in a document today and then print it, you get today's date. Great. But if you come back a week later and print the same document again, you may or may not get the original date — depending on whether the field is updated, which, in turn, is controlled by an obscure check box on the Tools/Options/Print filecard.

- That's why Microsoft invented the {createdate} field—except it doesn't work right either! {createdate} is supposed to produce the day the document was created. Which is great. But if you put a {createdate} field in a template, start a new document based on that template, and don't update the field, it shows the date the *template* was created.

It's so confusing that I always recommend that folks use the {date} field in their templates, coupled with AutoNew macros that select the field, update it, and then unlink it so that it turns into "plain" text. That also makes it simpler for a typist who may not understand fields and what they do. (As if I did!)

So much for the date.

Stick in a note, if one was chosen. Next, I'll check to see if the user selected a note. The drop-down list box returns the index number of the selected item in its Field. In this case, `DLG.NOTE` contains the index in Notes$() that corresponds to the item the user picked. In other words, if the user picked Notes$(3) from the list, `DLG.NOTE` comes back 3. Makes sense, eh?

If that number is zero—we set up Notes$(0) to be synonomous with no note —the user doesn't want anything stuck in the document, so I can skip on down to the next task. If it's not zero, I'll put the appropriate Notes$() entry in the document and then add a couple of paragraph marks to separate the note from the name and address:

```
If dlg.Note <> 0 Then
   Insert Notes$(dlg.Note)
   InsertPara
   InsertPara
End If
```

So far so good? This is going by pretty fast, but if you learn best by playing with something that works, it's a good starting point. This macro is pretty straight-forward—you won't find a lot of convoluted logic or programming spaghetti code in it—and it's not hard to understand if you take it in small chunks, as we're doing here. Remember that the final macro code is in Appendix E.

Bookmarks over the name and address Next, I need to put the address into the letter. This would be quite straightforward, except that some envelope printing programs run much faster if you put a bookmark over the name and address. No, it isn't necessary. Yes, it is the kind of forward thinking you should try to build into your macros when you can. We'll go with the Rolls Royce version.

WOPR's Enveloper and PrintEnvelope The shareware add-on WOPR (see Chapter 10) has an envelope printer (Enveloper) that quickly "grabs" the name and address covered by the bookmark called "NameAddress," if it finds one. Not to be outdone, WinWord's envelope printer looks for the bookmark "EnvelopeAddress" and does the same thing.

Of course WOPR's smart grab predates WinWord's by years, and WOPR's method came from a macro called PrintEnvelope, by Guy Gallo and James Gleick, a year before that—yet another example of how shareware sets the standard that Redmond eventually mimics—but I digress…

I've written the Underground Template in such a way that it puts *both* bookmarks over the name and address so that you can use it with either WOPR's Enveloper or WinWord's ToolsCreateEnvelope envelope printer. Here's the WordBasic code that'll do it:

```
InsertPara
CharLeft 1, 1
EditBookmark "NameAddress"
EditBookmark "EnvelopeAddress"
SelType 1
Insert dlg.Address
On Error Resume Next
AutoText
On Error Goto 0
CharRight
```

This snippet puts a paragraph mark in the document, then backs up and selects that paragraph mark. It then plants two different bookmarks on the selected paragraph mark. Finally, it turns the cursor into a single point, tossing off the selected paragraph mark, and puts the address from the dialog box into the document. The bookmark expands to cover all the inserted stuff (bookmarks work a little funny—see Chapter 4—but that's what they do).

Stuff the name and address into the letter.

Then I "click" the F3 AutoText button, disabling error trapping just before the "click" and restoring it immediately after. If the user has set up an AutoText entry in this template, this will expand the shortcut keys to bring in the full name and address. For example, if the user creates an AutoText entry that defines "js" as:

Yes, you can use AutoText for a name and address.

John Smith
123 Anyplace
Hometown, USA 12345

typing "js" in the To: box puts js in the new document, and the AutoText "click" then expands it to John Smith/123 Anyplace/Hometown, USA 12345. That's a capability of the old WinWord 2.0 letter templates that didn't make it into the fancy-schmancy WinWord 6.0 wizards.

WinWord insists on generating an obnoxious beep if the AutoText "click" fails to find a matching AutoText entry. I could program around it, but it would add a handful of obfuscating lines that really wouldn't demonstrate much. So I live with the beep. (Think of the Roadrunner with Wile E. Coyote at his tail. Meep meep.)

Finally, I move the cursor to the right so that it's at the end of the document once again, completely outside the bookmarked areas.

The five summary info's

Next I need to put the Title, Subject, Author, Keywords, and Comments from the dialog box into the file's summary information. That's easy.

```
If dlg.Title<>"" Then FileSummaryInfo .Title = dlg.Title
If dlg.Subject<>"" Then FileSummaryInfo .Subject = dlg.Subject
If dlg.Author<>"" Then FileSummaryInfo .Author = dlg.Author
If dlg.Keywords<>"" Then FileSummaryInfo .Keywords = dlg.Keywords
If dlg.Comments<>"" Then FileSummaryInfo .Comments = dlg.Comments
```

Don't blindly update the summary info.

WinWord automatically fills in the title and author unless you do something to change them. So I go through each of the five Summary Info entries, see if the user typed anything in the dialog box, and then only if they typed something into the box do I update the FileSummaryInfo.

Next, I want to put a simple header in the document, should it extend to a second page. The header is just the first line of the address (typically, a company or person's name), followed by the page number. It goes like this:

```
N$ = GetBookmark$("NameAddress")
InsertBreak
FilePageSetup .DifferentFirstPage = 1
ViewHeader
eol = InStr(N$, Chr$(13))
Insert Left$(N$, eol - 1) + " - Page "
InsertField "Page"
CloseViewHeaderFooter
CharLeft 1, 1
EditClear
ViewPage
```

In English, I retrieve the name and address (which may have been expanded by the AutoText "click"), put it in a variable called N$, stick a page break in the doc (to move to the second page), set up headers so they are Different First Page, pop into the second page's header, and stick the first line of the name and address in the header, followed by a hyphen and the page number. Then I move out of the header, delete the page break, and switch into Page View.

The salutation comes last.

Finally, I want to put "Dear " in the document and leave the cursor ready for the salutation. That's easy:

```
InsertPara
Insert "Dear "
```

That's the end of the macro.

Bug Redux

You might be curious as to why I did things this way. Truth be told, I *had* to do it more or less this way because of four bugs in WordBasic:

- I had to put the drop-down Notes list box at the top of the dialog. The official docs say that you can create a drop-down list box that drops below the level of the dialog box itself. The official docs lie; the *Word Developer's Kit* and the F1 help are wrong. The dialog editor lets you create a drop-down list box like that, but you can't use it. If you try it, WinWord dies with an Error 512, parameter out of range.

- You can't retrieve the contents of a bookmark when the cursor is in a header or footer. This isn't documented anywhere in the official docs, either. It's a plain-and-simple bug.

- There's no way to set up a second page header in a single-page document (though it was easy in WinWord 2.0). If you read between the lines in the official docs, you'll see that it isn't possible, but it took a couple of Microsoft Consulting Partners—nonpareil WinWord experts—several hours to figure out what was wrong and how to work around it (thanks, Jim and Lee!).

- Closing the header pane always flips you into Normal View, so I had to manually switch to Page View. That isn't documented anywhere. It doesn't make any sense, but that's how WinWord works.

Now you know why you need the *Hacker's Guide*. I won't say that the official docs are useless. I *will* say that they will drive you nuts. I lost several hours working around those bugs—on Christmas Eve, no less!—because the *Hacker's Guide* wasn't ready when I wrote the macro. If you write macros, you need it.

Don't let the bugs put you off! If you have a reliable, honest reference book in front of you, working around the problems really isn't that difficult. Just be sure to look things up when your macros behave strangely.

Oh. If you tend to type the name and address in text boxes using CTRL+ENTER to skip between lines, you might want to check for a Chr$(11) end-of-line marker instead of a Chr$(13) paragraph mark in the InStr() command. **Newline vs. paragraph mark**

If you have your documents set up so they skip an extra line at the end of each paragraph, you'll want to replace all paragraph marks in the address with Chr$(11) newlines.

There you have it. The complete macro is in Appendix E.

FINISHDOCUMENT MACRO

> May Allah make our end better than our beginning.
>
> Arab saying

Now for the flip side. I've set up the Underground Letterhead to get you going, to pull information from you and get it slapped into the document. What about the tail end, when it's time to print? After several years of battering this problem around, I've hit upon a solution that works for me, and I hope it works for you. I won't claim it's perfect, but it does pretty well.

I take care of the tail end by creating a kitchen sink macro I call FinishDocument. It takes care of just about everything I need to do when a document is done. If you print a lot of letters, you might want to make this a *global* macro.

FinishDocument Dialog

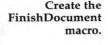 **Create the FinishDocument macro.**

Open up your Underground Letterhead template (probably _UNDERGD.DOT). Click on Tools, then Macro. Make sure that the name of your template appears in the Macros Available In box, type FinishDocument (all one word, no space), and click Create. You'll see the standard Sub MAIN/End Sub pair.

 Dialog Editor

Now click the Dialog Editor button on the Toolbar, the one on the far right that looks like an ATM machine. Once again you'll be propelled into the WinWord dialog editor. Double-click on the dialog box in the middle and type something astute like, oh, Underground Letterhead. (See Figure 8.18.)

Figure 8.18 The FilePrint Dialog Begins

Next, I put in a drop-down list for Signatures, so I can stick things like "Sincerely, / / / / Woody" or "Love and kisses, / / / / Igor" at the end of a document automatically. If you always use the same signature block and set this up so that it uses your most common signature block automatically, you could save a little time. But be cautious about slavishly using an automatic signature block. If the typist is pretty quick, he or she may actually take more time to hunt and find the correct signature block than to simply type the signature block. **Signature block**

Click on Item, then Text, and type in Signature:. Then click on Item, then ListBox, then Drop-Down, then OK. Double-click on the drop-down list box, and give it a Text$ of Signatures$() and a Field of .Signature (note the period). (See Figure 8.19.) Click OK. Finally, arrange things so they look like Figure 8.19. **Drop-down list settings**

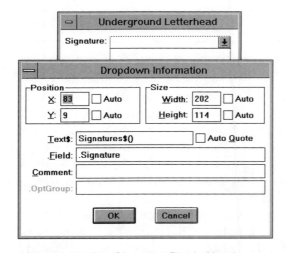

Figure 8.19 The Signature Block. Head.

Next I set up something for the typist's initials. Since I type my own letters, I don't use it. Well, that isn't entirely true. Sheeesh. May as well come clean. I've been honest with ya so far. Just promise you won't tell anybody, okay? If I want to impress somebody with a terribly official looking letter I use WL:pc for typist's initials; you can draw your own conclusions. **Typist's Initials**

Now click once on the thing (it's called a Text Control, but "thing" will do) on the dialog box that says Signature:. Click Edit, then Duplicate. See how you get a clone, just below the original? Neat. Type Initials:. Click once on the drop-down list, click Edit, then Duplicate. Ah, ain't automation wunnerful? Double-click on the new drop-down list box and give it a Text$ of Initials$() and a Field of .Initial. (See Figure 8.20.) Click OK, and rearrange things so that they look like Figure 8.20. **Paint the text and drop-down box on the dialog.**

Figure 8.20 Typist's Initials

Spell Check box Next, I put a box on the dialog to make it easy to check spelling. I've learned, over the years, that if I don't bang myself over the head about doing a spell check, I forget. So it goes right here at the top—and you'll see shortly how I set this macro up so WinWord does a spell check unless I specifically turn it off. You may not be so forgetful; you may spell everything correctly the first time; you may have a perfectly clean desk and a well-manicured lawn. If so, I envy you. And you won't want this check box. So be it.

To put a check box in the dialog, click Item, then Button (nope, not one of the "Box"es!), then Check Box, then OK. Double-click on the check box, give it a Text$ of Check Spelling and a Field of .Spell. (See Figure 8.21.) Rearrange things so that they look more or less like Figure 8.21.

It's fascinating how Microsoft's terminology flip-flops, eh? In the menu, you click on Item, then Button. The dialog you then get says Check Box, and that's what you want: a check box. The WordBasic command is CheckBox. But the dialog you get when you double-click on a check box in the dialog editor says Check Button Information. Lemme tell ya, Windows has lots of check boxes. This is the only place I've ever seen a check box called a "Button." It isn't a button, doesn't act like a button, doesn't look like a button. Oy.

Anyway, I load up the dialog box with the following check boxes:

Purpose	Field Entry
hyphenation	.Hyphenate
cc: list	.CCList

Enclosures list	.Enc
"Squish" option	.Squish
Envelope printing	.Envelope

You can see how the check boxes are arranged in Figure 8.22.

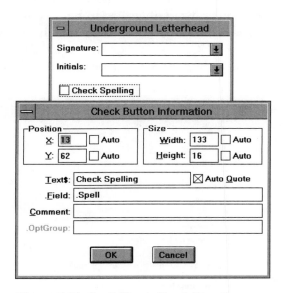

Figure 8.21 Spell Check Check Box. Box

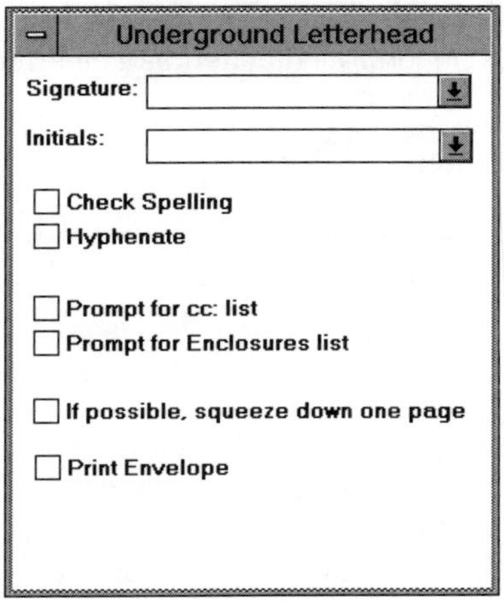

Figure 8.22 More Check Boxes

You may want to add a couple of check boxes of your own. In particular, I automatically do a File/Save when I hit the point in this routine where the formatting is done. You may want to make that an option and only save if the Save The (Whale?) File button is checked. They're really easy; you just follow this Item/Button/Check Box routine.

Print "X" Copies. Finally, I set up the Print "X" Copies by clicking on Insert, then Text to put in the Print, clicking on another Insert, then Text to put in the Copies, and clicking yet again on Insert, then Text Box to let the user type in the number of copies. The Copies text box has a Field of .Copies. And, of course, the OK and Cancel buttons, inserted the same way as in the AutoNew dialog. The final FilePrint dialog box is in Figure 8.23.

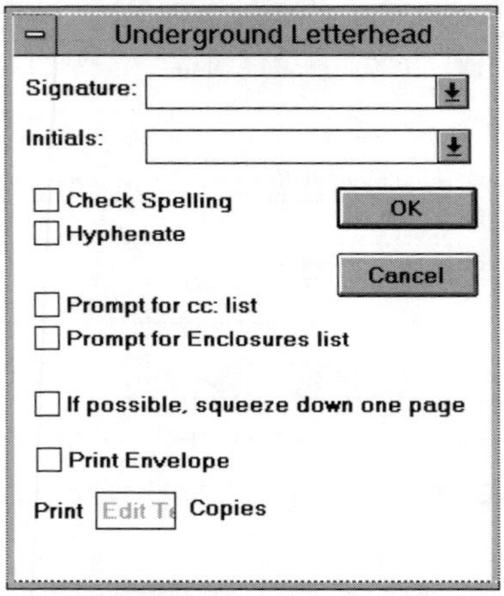

Figure 8.23 Underground Letterhead FilePrint Dialog

Running the FinishDocument Dialog

Now click on Edit, Select Dialog, then Edit, Copy. Flip over to the FinishDocument macro and Edit Paste. You should have something that looks more or less like this:

```
Sub MAIN
Begin Dialog UserDialog 298, 256, "Underground Letterhead"
  Text 8, 9, 71, 13, "Signature:", .Text1
  DropListBox 83, 9, 202, 114, Signatures$(), .Signature
  Text 8, 33, 50, 13, "Initials:", .Text2
  DropListBox 83, 35, 203, 114, Initials$(), .Initial
  CheckBox 13, 62, 133, 16, "Check Spelling", .Spell
  CheckBox 13, 79, 104, 16, "Hyphenate", .Hyphenate
```

```
    CheckBox 13, 113, 148, 16, "Prompt for cc: list", .CCList
    CheckBox 13, 130, 205, 16, "Prompt for Enclosures list", .Enc
    CheckBox 13, 162, 278, 16, "If possible, squeeze down one page",\
      .Squish
    CheckBox 14, 189, 278, 16, "Print Envelope", .Envelope
    Text 12, 215, 32, 13, "Print", .Text3
    TextBox 51, 212, 50, 18, .Copies
    Text 109, 214, 50, 13, "Copies", .Text4
    OKButton 202, 63, 88, 21
    CancelButton 202, 96, 88, 21
End Dialog
End Sub
```

Just as with the AutoNew dialog, you should look at your dialog code and see how close it comes to this code, changing yours to look like this, if you like.

Folks look at custom dialog box code listings like this, with the Begin Dialog/ End Dialog pair, and the hundreds of inscrutable numbers, and get weak in the knees. There's no reason to be intimidated. You can do a good first cut with the dialog editor, then do your final tweaks—if you ever care about final tweaks!— by hand.

Up at the top of the macro, just after Sub MAIN, you should stick in your choices for signatures. Make sure you Dim the Signatures$() array properly and fill in the array from Signatures$(0) onward. (See how you just slipped into using the term "array"? That's what Signatures$() is.) Personally, I use these Signatures$():

Signatures$()

```
Dim Signatures$(4)
Signatures$(0) = "(none)"
Signatures$(1) = "Sincerely," + String$(4, 13) + "Woody Leonhard"
Signatures$(2) = "Thank you!" + String$(4, 13) + "Woody Leonhard"
Signatures$(3) = "Sincerely," + String$(4, 13) + "Linda Sharp"
Signatures$(4) = "Sincerely," + String$(4, 13) + "Justin Leonhard"
```

The String$(4,13) function you see there tells WinWord to create a string of four Chr$(13)s—four paragraph marks. If you want five paragraph marks for a signature block, use String$(5,13); for three, use String$(3,13). You get the idea. You can monkey around with the numbers after the macro is up and running.

Next, you'll want to define all the available Initials$(). Here's what I use:

```
Dim Initials$(3)
Initials$(0) = "(none)"
Initials$(1) = "WL:pc"
Initials$(2) = "LKS-L:pc"
Initials$(3) = "JML:pc"
```

Down below the End Dialog line you have to start wallowing in the techno gobbledygook that gets the dialog started. The line after End Dialog should look like this:

```
Dim fpdlg As UserDialog
```

You can actually use any name you like in place of "fpdlg." Some day WinWord will be smart enough that you won't have to play these silly naming games or put up with inscrutable commands like Dim … As UserDialog.

Predefined "default" values

WordBasic makes it easy for you to establish initial, "default" values in custom dialog boxes. In this case, I want to pick Signatures$(1) as the default value—I want the dialog box to come up with "Sincerely, / / / / Woody Leonhard" showing in the Signatures: drop-down list. All I need to do is set the index for the drop-down list box to 1. Like this:

```
fpdlg.Signature = 1
```

That line tells WordBasic to show Signatures$(1) when the dialog box pops up. If you don't tell WordBasic anything at all, it uses index number zero. That's why Notes$(0) showed up in the AutoNew dialog.

Similarly, setting a check box field to 1 "checks" the box. If you don't do anything, the check box comes up unchecked. Here's how I set the initial values:

```
fpdlg.Spell = 1
fpdlg.Hyphenate = 1
fpdlg.Squish = 1
fpdlg.Envelope = 1
fpdlg.Copies = "1"
```

Who starts out checked?

Since there's no entry for Initials, the dialog comes up with Initials$(0). The Spell box is checked, as are the Hyphenate, Squish, and Envelope check boxes. The Prompt for cc: List and Enclosure List boxes are not checked. You can set them any way you like, of course.

Finally, I set the number of Copies to 1, but WinWord insists on treating any Text Box as text—it won't work with a number. So the line FPDLG.COPIES = "1" assigns a *character* one, not a *number* one, to the Copies box. That's why the number one is surrounded by quotes. Funny how WordBasic can be so smart, but so dumb, if ya know what I mean.

Then there's the rest of the gobbledygook that's necessary to splash a dialog up on the screen and bring the user-entered values back. (See the preceding discussion about the AutoNew macro; it works similarly.) Again, I made a safe bailout so the macro ends without burping should the user click the Cancel button. This part of the macro looks like this:

```
Dim fpdlg As UserDialog
fpdlg.Signature = 1
fpdlg.Spell = 1
fpdlg.Hyphenate = 1
fpdlg.Squish = 1
fpdlg.Envelope = 1
fpdlg.Copies = "1"
On Error Goto UserClickedCancel
Dialog fpdlg
On Error Goto 0

UserClickedCancel:
End Sub
```

The entire text of the macro is in Appendix E, so if you get lost, look there.

First, save everything. Then click the right-wedgie "Play" button, and ... uh ... play with the dialog box. See how it works? Good.

Play

From Dialog to Doc Again

> You've got the brain of a four-year-old boy,
> and I bet he was glad to get rid of it.
>
> Groucho Marx
> *Horsefeathers*, 1932

So much for the pretty face. Now let's polish off the program. I intentionally avoided using a couple of WinWord capabilities that would make the macro much simpler. In particular, I decided to avoid using styles, and I decided to implement the cc: and Enc: lists as tables, instead of paragraphs with hanging indents. I call that "idiot proofing," and I don't mean that as an insult. Let me explain.

You see, when it comes to WinWord, *I'm* the world's worst idiot! No, you didn't read through 231 pages of this book to be dumped, duped, and disillusioned by a fraud. Usually I know what's going on, more or less. But when I start banging out letters, and doing day-to-day meat and taters stuff, the last thing I want to do is *think*. I discovered long ago that if I made this stuff fancy, it would work fine for a week or a month, then something would go *bump!* and it'd take forever to figure out what the hell was going wrong.

I don't want to remember that a certain part of a letter is in a funny double-spaced style. It hurts to remember that, at certain times, in certain places, I have to type a CTRL+ENTER instead of just hitting Enter to get a new line. I hate that. And

The problems with styles

I get all turned around when I try to play with hanging indent stuff, especially cc: lists or Enc: lists. It's just too bloody confusing and not worth the effort.

So you won't find any styles tied to this macro. In fact, you won't find any styles in the template! By doing the end-of-doc stuff in the Normal style and implementing the lists as tables, you can go in and change the letter — add a new item to a cc: list, say, or delete one of the Enclosures — without futzing around with weird formatting problems. In my humble opinion, that's the biggest shortcoming with the WinWord 6.0 Wizards; it's also one of the things they did right with the old WinWord 2.0 templates.

The price I pay is a slightly more complex macro. But, hey, that's what macros are for. Do 'em once, do 'em right, and forget about 'em, I say.

Keep With Next As soon as I run this macro, I need to jump to the bottom of the document, and set things up so that the tail-end stuff, from the signature block to the end of the document, appears on the same page. That's pretty standard practice. It's easy to do in the macro:

```
EndOfDocument
InsertPara
FormatParagraph .KeepWithNext = 1
```

and as long as we add stuff to the very end of the document, it'll all be formatted as Keep With Next.

Signature block Next comes the signature block. If the returned subscript, the Field, is zero, there's nothing to add — presumably, the user doesn't want a signature block inserted in there because either the signature block is already there or the user doesn't normally put a signature block on his or her letters. If the user asks for a signature block, I'll stick a paragraph mark before and after it and keep the cursor at the end of the document.

```
If fpdlg.Signature <> 0 Then
   InsertPara
   Insert Signatures$(fpdlg.Signature)
   InsertPara
End If
```

Initials Then come the initials, which behave in the same way as the signature block.

```
If fpdlg.Initial <> 0 Then
   InsertPara
   Insert Initials$(fpdlg.Initial)
   InsertPara
End If
```

Next comes the cc: list, which I put in a 2-column, 1-row table, with the first column half an inch wide:

cc: list

```
If fpdlg.CCList <> 0 Then
  On Error Resume Next
  CCItem$ = InputBox$("Items for the cc: list.",\
    "Underground Letterhead")
  On Error Goto 0
  If CCItem$ <> "" Then
    InsertPara
    TableInsertTable .NumColumns = 2, .NumRows = 1
    TableColumnWidth "0.5 in", .RulerStyle = 1
    Insert "cc:"
    NextCell
    Insert CleanString$(CCItem$)
    EndOfDocument
  End If
End If
```

Let me step through that slowly. The On Error Resume Next statement tells WinWord to ignore any errors—it shuts off error trapping. I do that because, if the user clicks Cancel, I want to continue with the rest of the macro. On Error Goto 0 simply reinstates error trapping.

On Error Resume Next

The InputBox$ puts a dialog box on the screen, asking the user to type in something. Whatever is typed, in this case, comes back in the variable called CCItem$. If the user typed in anything, CCItem$ is not empty (that is, not equal to an empty string), and I want to:

Insert the cc: list.

- Put a paragraph mark in the doc, to get a little breathing room from what precedes the cc: list.

- Stick a table in the doc, with two columns and one row.

- Then I want to adjust the first column so that it's half an inch wide and let the other column expand to cover the rest of the document (that's what .RULERSTYLE = 1 does; don't ask me why it's called RulerStyle!).

- Put the characters cc: in the first cell, jump to the next cell, and put the stuff that came in from the InputBox$() into the document.

Unfortunately this incarnation of WordBasic has a weird bug in it that screws up the InputBox$ text. It's a little hard to explain. It has to do with how InputBox$ treats paragraph marks (they come out as Chr$(11) + Chr$(10) despite what the official docs say), and how that differs from how documents treat paragraph marks (put a Chr$(11) + Chr$(10) in a doc and you get, effectively, *two* paragraph marks). The general solution is to run the output

from an InputBox\$ through the CleanString\$() function in order to keep WordBasic from sticking garbage in your documents. Finally, the macro jumps to the end of the document.

The Enclosures list

The Enc: list goes the same way as the cc: list:

```
If fpdlg.Enc <> 0 Then
  On Error Resume Next
  EncItem$ = InputBox$("Items for the Enc: list.",\
    "Underground Letterhead")
  On Error Goto 0
  If EncItem$ <> "" Then
    InsertPara
    TableInsertTable .NumColumns = 2, .NumRows = 1
    TableColumnWidth "0.5 in", .RulerStyle = 1
    Insert "Enc:"
    NextCell
    Insert CleanString$(EncItem$)
  End If
End If
```

Spell check

Spell checking is really easy. If you make sure that the cursor is at the beginning of the document and nothing is selected and then call ToolsSpelling, WinWord handles the rest.

```
If fpdlg.Spell <> 0 Then
  StartOfDocument
  ToolsSpelling
End If
```

Hyphenation

Hyphenation isn't quite so easy. WinWord has two very different methods of hyphenating. You can force WinWord to ask you if each, individual hyphenation is OK, or you can just let WinWord go do its thing in an automatic hyphenation.

Personally, I always do an automatic hyphenation. I imagine that if you're very picky about your letters, you may want to do it manually, so I've allowed for that, too, but only by changing the macro. Here's how it looks:

```
If fpdlg.Hyphenate <> 0 Then
  StartOfDocument
REM To force manual hyphenation, set .AutoHyphenation = 0
  ToolsHyphenation .AutoHyphenation = 1
End If
```

If you want manual hyphenation, you should change the ToolsHyphenation line to look like this:

```
ToolsHyphenation .AutoHyphenation = 0
```

Of course you could put this auto vs. manual choice in the dialog box, too, but I'd be willing to bet that, once you've chosen manual or auto hyphenation, you probably won't change your mind. So why clutter the dialog box?

ShrinkToFit is such a nice capability that I couldn't let it go. But it has a few quirks that I had to program around.

ShrinkToFit

I started out building a big macro that did all sorts of things until I realized that page counts can be squirrelly. WinWord won't produce an accurate page count unless you explicitly force a repagination. (Indeed, I'm not sure you'll always get an accurate page count, even then!).

I've had enough headaches with *un*intended repagination that the last thing I need is a couple of rounds of intended repagination. So I punted. This is what I came up with:

```
If fpdlg.Squish <> 0 Then
   ToolsRepaginate
   If SelInfo(4) > 1 Then
     ToolsShrinkToFit
     StartOfDocument
     Msg$ = "Can you live with your letter shrunk this much?"
     Title$ = "Underground Letterhead"
     If MsgBox(Msg$, Title$, 256 + 32 + 4) = 0 Then EditUndo
   End If
End If
```

I start out by repaginating. Hate to do that, but if I don't, SelInfo(4)—which is supposed to return the total number of pages in a document—may come up with a bad number. I saw it happen a dozen times.

If the document has more than one page, I shrink the document. As far as I can tell, WinWord always reduces the point size enough to reduce the page count by one, if it's at all humanly possible. Unfortunately sometimes when it reduces the size in Page View, WinWord tosses the visible page way off the screen, scrolling down below the last page in a document.

That's why I had to use a StartOfDocument to bring the doc back into view. I figured that, at the very least, the Formatting Toolbar would show the point size of the first character in the document. In fact, I wanted to Goto the NameAddress bookmark, but that scrolled off too, whether I went there before or after doing the ShrinkToFit.

But the Formatting Toolbar is screwy, too. It doesn't show the point size of the currently selected text immediately after a ShrinkToFit. I finally threw my hands up and punted once again with what you see. This macro has a bug: after the ShrinkToFit, WinWord doesn't show the correct point size in the Formatting Toolbar. For the life of me, I couldn't figure out how to make it right. So I figure folks will have to judge by looking at the text whether it's too tiny. Not a pretty solution.

The numbers in the MsgBox() command are rather interesting. A 256 shows a picture of a question mark. A 32 says the second button should be the highlighted "default" button, the one that "clicks" if the user hits Enter. A 4 says you want a message box with a Yes and a No box. That's what we got. For more info on MsgBox numbers, just type MsgBox in the WordBasic editor and hit F1.

MsgBox() returns a zero if the second button—in this case the No button—is clicked. If the user can't live with the shrink, it'd best be Undone.

Print! At Last!   Ah, we're finally ready to print the letter! Funny. I'd forgotten all about that, we were having so much fun.

The big problem with printing is that you have to check and make sure that the number that the user typed in is valid. Unfortunately WinWord's FilePrint command isn't smart enough to produce reasonable error messages if the user should type in something like a zero or a letter.

```
c = Val(fpdlg.Copies)
If c > 0 And c < 32768 Then
   FilePrint .NumCopies = fpdlg.Copies
Else
   Msg$ = "Invalid Number of Copies: " + fpdlg.Copies
   Title$ = "Underground Letterhead"
   MsgBox Msg$, Title$, 16
End If
```

FilePrint must be well fed.   In fact, FilePrint requires the number fed to it to be in the range from 1 through 32767. That's why I bumped out an error message if the number should be off. The number in the MsgBox there—number 16—sticks a Stop sign on the dialog and only leaves the user with an OK button. (See Figure 8.24.)

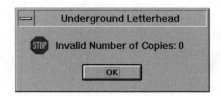

Figure 8.24 Ya Cain't Print Zero Copies

Next, I move the cursor up near the top of the letter, but not all the way to the very first paragraph because that is often in a framed-out section of the document. I then Save. If the document doesn't yet have a name, the user is prompted for one in the usual way.

```
EditGoTo "NameAddress"
CharRight 2
Print "Click cancel to bypass the Save"
On Error Resume Next
FileSave
```

The envelope printing part is easy if you use Enveloper, tough if you don't. The straight WinWord envelope printer requires you to wade through all the gobbledygook that usually goes with built-in WordBasic dialogs. The first 8 lines here are pure WordBasic technobabble.

Envelope

```
If fpdlg.Envelope <> 0 Then
   Dim tce As ToolsCreateEnvelope
   GetCurValues tce
   On Error Goto DoneWithEnvelopes
   Dialog tce
   ToolsCreateEnvelope tce
End If
DoneWithEnvelopes:
REM If you use WOPR, delete the above 8 lines and use this:
REM If fpdlg.Envelope <> 0 Then Enveloper
```

That's it. Be sure to save it! The whole macro is in Appendix E.

Put It on the Toolbar!

> I always keep a stimulant handy in case I see a snake—
> which I also keep handy.
>
> W.C. Fields

Hey, you didn't go through all that trouble to keep this macro buried! Better get it up on the Toolbar quickly. I have the perfect place for it—I use it to replace the AutoFormat, ShrinkToFit, and Spell Check buttons on my standard Toolbar.

Open up the Underground Letterhead template, probably `_UNDERGD.DOT`. Click on Tools, then Customize, and bring up the Toolbar filecard. *This is important:* Make sure that Save Changes In shows `_UNDERGD.DOT`.

Bring up the Customizer.

You need to decide if you can get rid of some of your standard Toolbar buttons when you're working with documents based on this template, thereby freeing up room on the Toolbar. One by one, select those buttons, click and drag them off the Toolbar. Poof! They're gone.

Drag it to the Toolbar.   In the Categories box, scroll down and click on Macros. In the Macros box, click and drag FinishDocument over to the Toolbar. Pick a picture—I use the smiley face, but I'll certainly understand if you defer to something a little less … garish—click OK and you're done.

I hope you enjoy this little sucker and can put it to use, modified to your heart's content. In many ways it's the distillation of several years of work with WinWord. Live Long and Prosper.

9 Power User Bag o' Tricks

Every new idea has something of the pain and peril of childbirth about it;
ideas are just as mortal and just as immortal as organized beings are.

Samuel Butler
Note-Books, 1890

Here's a hodge-podge of really cool, useful tricks. You probably won't need all of them — in fact, I'll feel good if you use anywhere near half of them. In addition to being useful all by themselves, you may find the spark of an idea floating around here that'll solve a problem that's been dogging you.

FILEOPEN DEFAULT TO *.*

FileOpen doesn't do the DOC-Extension shtick.

WinWord's File Open is okay if you always want to open .DOC files. But some folks want to see files that end in .WFW, or all the files that start with the letter a, or who-knows-what-all. I like to see all *.DOC and *.DOT files when I do a FileOpen. WinWord 2.0 respected the DOC-EXTENSION= entry in the [MICROSOFT WORD 2.0] section of WIN.INI, but WinWord 6.0 turns a blind eye. The DOC-EXTENSION= entry in WINWORD6.INI is only used for FileSave, which is pretty strange. Fortunately, fixing FileOpen is quite simple.

Click on Tools, then Macro, make sure NORMAL.DOT is showing in the Macros Available In box, type FileOpen (all one word), and click Create. WinWord pops up with the built-in FileOpen macro:

```
Sub MAIN
Dim dlg As FileOpen
GetCurValues dlg
Dialog dlg
FileOpen dlg
End Sub
```

You need to add three lines, in the correct places.

```
Sub MAIN
Dim dlg As FileOpen
GetCurValues dlg
dlg.Name = "*.doc;*.dot"
On Error Goto UserClickedCancel
Dialog dlg
FileOpen dlg
UserClickedCancel:
End Sub
```

On the DLG.NAME = line, specify which files you want to see. The example here shows all *.DOC and *.DOT files. WinWord uses the standard Windows naming conventions, that is, DOS wildcards with multiple choice separated by semicolons. Click File, then Close, and Yes, you want to save changes. It's that easy.

Oh. If you want to make WinWord pick up the DOC-EXTENSION = setting in the [MICROSOFT WORD 2.0] section of WIN.INI, use this line to pick up the dlg.Name:

```
dlg.Name = "*." + GetProfileString$(,"DOC-extension")
```

However, be very sure that you have a DOC-EXTENSION = entry in WIN.INI before you use that line! Not everybody has one.

COMMAND LINE SWITCHES

> There is great force hidden in a sweet command.
>
> George Herbert
> *Outlandish Proverbs*, 1640

You can set up WinWord to start in various ways, by adding so-called **command line switches** to the line that invokes WinWord. In Windows' Program Manager, you can click on File, then Run, type in

```
c:\winword\winword.exe /n
```

for example, and WinWord starts with the /n switch activated. (If WinWord is in a directory other than C:\WINWORD, you'll have to use that directory, natch.)

If you find yourself starting WinWord at various times with different command line switches, you might want to set up several different WinWord icons in Program Manager, each connected to a different switch. For example, if you want to set up an icon in Program Manager to start WinWord without a "Document1" document open (that's what the /n switch does), it's a simple three-step process:

1. In Program Manager, hold down the Control key and drag the WinWord icon — the one you usually click to start WinWord — to some other point on the desktop. You'll get a copy of the first icon.

2. With that new icon still highlighted, click on File, then Properties. You'll get a dialog box that looks like Figure 9.1.

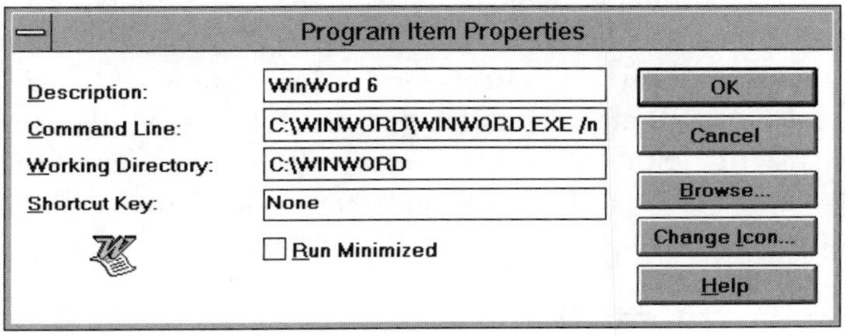

	Program Item Properties	
Description:	WinWord 6	OK
Command Line:	C:\WINWORD\WINWORD.EXE /n	Cancel
Working Directory:	C:\WINWORD	
Shortcut Key:	None	Browse...
	☐ Run Minimized	Change Icon...
		Help

Figure 9.1 A New ProgMan Icon

3. Put the command line switch of your choice on the command line. In Figure 9.1, I've put the /n switch on the command line. You'll probably want to change the Description, too. When you're done, click OK.

That's all it takes to put command line parameters to work.

You can always stick the name of a file on the command line, and WinWord will start with that file showing. A line like this:

File name on the command line.

```
c:\winword\winword.exe c:\winword\mydocs\foobar.doc
```

always starts WinWord with the indicated file loaded (providing the file exists). That isn't exactly a command line switch, but it works. The command line switches I know about are covered in the next sections.

/a To Clean Boot

/a starts WinWord clean, bypassing the customary start-up sequence. With the /a switch on the command line, WinWord does not load NORMAL.DOT. It doesn't run the autoexec macro. Nothing in the \STARTUP directory gets attached.

If your add-ons are giving you problems, try this one.

This is a WinWord "clean boot," if you will. It's a debugging setting. You'll use this command line switch if WinWord won't start right or if it triggers an error immediately on starting.

/m To Run a Macro ... Sometimes

Use /m to start WinWord with a macro or a command.

The /m switch starts WinWord, and in the middle of the customary start-up sequence (after NORMAL.DOT is brought in, but before the contents of the \STARTUP directory are loaded) /m runs the macro or built-in command you have specified. You designate the macro or built-in command like this:

```
c:\winword\winword.exe /mMyMacro
```

Note in particular that there is no space after the "m." It looks a little strange, but that's how things are done.

Bypass autoexec.

This switch has many side effects, and I don't think anybody knows all of them just yet. Running a macro with the /m switch keeps WinWord from running the autoexec macro in NORMAL.DOT, *but it does not prevent any other autoexec macro (in any template in the \STARTUP directory) from running.* To start WinWord without its global autoexec macro, just use this command line:

```
c:\winword\winword.exe /m
```

No tip

The presence of an /m on the command line also keeps the Tip of the Day from appearing. Frankly, that makes me wonder if there aren't some other, more subtle, oddities waiting in the wings.

The only valid entries for the /m switch are names of macros in NORMAL.DOT **and built-in WinWord commands. In particular, you can't use the name of a macro in any of the templates in your** \STARTUP **directory as an /m parameter. That's pretty strange; it's hard to imagine why that kind of restriction is placed on the /m parameter. I think it's a bug.**

One of the most-often-used WinWord alternative startup lines is

```
c:\winword\winword.exe /mFile1
```

It starts WinWord with the most recently used file (the file listed as number 1 on the File menu) and it works because the built-in command File1 opens the first file on that list.

/n Start With Nothing

The /n switch starts WinWord without a blank doc, without a "Document1." Instead of starting with a fresh new document, you're greeted by WinWord's "short menus," the electronic equivalent of a blank stare.

If you do use the /n switch, be aware of the fatal bug that's described in Chapter 6 (under "/n and FileFind"). At least in WinWord 6.0 (it might be fixed in the version you're using), starting with the /n switch and then using FileFind is a sure way to crash your machine, triggering a General Protection Fault. That bug is so strange it, too, has me wondering if there is something lurking behind the scenes with the /n switch that we just haven't discovered yet.

/w Start Without Tip

The /w switch starts WinWord without Tip of the Day. Programmers may find it useful because the Tip of the Day locks up WinWord. WinWord won't respond to much of anything until you hit OK.

HOT-SWITCHING PRINTERS

> The old order changeth, yielding place to new.
>
> Alfred Tennyson
> *The Passing of Arthur*, 1869

Some folks need to switch printers all the time. This is often necessary when you have a fax modem that works like a standard printer driver. You might also have dedicated envelope-printing or label-printing printers.

Here's a real quick and dirty macro you can use to switch printers on the fly, print the current doc, and then switch the printer back. You'll need to know the name of the printer as it appears in the [PRINTERPORTS] **section of** WIN.INI, **so dive into** WIN.INI **and take a look.**

In this example, I'll use "HP LaserJet III"; your name will vary, and you must be sure you spell it precisely as it appears in the [PRINTERPORTS] section.

```
Sub MAIN
NewPrinter$ = "HP LaserJet III"
Dim fps As FilePrintSetup
GetCurValues fps
OldPrinter$ = fps.Printer
WinIni$ = GetProfileString$("PrinterPorts", NewPrinter$)
Port$ = Mid$(WinIni$, InStr(WinIni$, ",") + 1, 5)
NewSetup$ = NewPrinter$ + " on " + Port$
FilePrintSetup NewSetup$
FilePrint
FilePrintSetup OldPrinter$
End Sub
```

Installing
SwapPrinters

To get the macro working, click on Tools, then Macro, and make sure that NORMAL.DOT is showing in the Macros Available In box. Type in a name like SwapPrinters, and click Create. Type in the macro, click File, then Close. Yes, you want to save changes. To make it most useful, put SwapPrinters on the Toolbar by clicking Tools, then Customize, and make sure that NORMAL.DOT is in the Save Change In box. Click on Macros, and then drag SwapPrinters over to the Toolbar. That's it.

PERMANENTLY UNCURLING QUOTES

By necessity, by proclivity, and by delight, we all quote.

Ralph Waldo Emerson
Letters, 1875

Thanks to Peter Deegan, the WinWord Wizard of Oz, for this bit of enlightenment.

WinWord 6 automagically turns your boring old "straight" quotes into pretty smart, "curly," or typesetter quotes, and curls them in the correct direction, beginning and ending. Microsoft calls them smart. I reserve judgment.

Eliminating Curly Quotes in New Text

The automatic curling capability is part of *both* AutoCorrect and AutoFormat. As explained in Chapter 1, AutoCorrect sees a quotation mark being typed and corrects it to a curly quote. But what's not so obvious is that AutoFormat, too, will take it upon itself to produce curly quotes for the WinWord beast.

Sometimes you don't want curly quotes. Either they don't suit your personal style or the boss doesn't like them. Sometimes they're extremely problematic when exporting a document to some other program; even some otherwise smart page mark-up packages have a hard time treating curly quotes properly. Also you may have noticed that WinWord's Text Only export (Save As) filters don't switch curly quotes back to straight quotes. It's a real jungle.

It ends up that you have to change two parts of WinWord to get rid of the curlies. Whoever thought this through was out to lunch when the design decision was made.

So, how do you turn OFF smart quotes? Ah, an easy question, with a not-so-easy answer! To well and thoroughly eliminate curly quotes from all your future typing, you must click on Tools, then AutoCorrect, and uncheck the box marked Change Straight Quotes to Smart Quotes. Then, you must click on Tools, Options, bring up the AutoFormat filecard, and uncheck the box marked Replace Straight Quotes with Smart Quotes.

Eliminating Curly Quotes in Existing Text

We've won only half the battle, however. If you want to really and truly get rid of curly quotes, you'll have to go back into any existing documents and zap them out. That ain't so easy. WinWord provides no direct method of changing curly quotes back into straight quotes. You would think that AutoFormat could do it, but nooooooo.

Want to see how that works? Take a document with a few straight quotes and a few curly quotes. Click on Tools, Options, bring the AutoFormat filecard up, and clear out the Replace Straight Quotes with Smart Quotes box. Now let WinWord AutoFormat the doc. See that? It doesn't change the curly quotes back to straight ones. Bummer.

The only way I've found to turn curly quotes back to straight ones is with WinWord's Replace command. You need to run it four times, once each for " , " , ' , and '.

Doing it manually can be a real drag and messy, but you can use a short macro to change all curlies to straights throughout an entire document. To run the macro, click on Tools, then Macro, type in a name, and click Create. Type in the lines:

```
Sub MAIN
EditReplace Chr$(145), Chr$(39), .ReplaceAll, .Wrap=1
EditReplace Chr$(146), Chr$(39), .ReplaceAll, .Wrap=1
EditReplace Chr$(147), Chr$(34), .ReplaceAll, .Wrap=1
EditReplace Chr$(148), Chr$(34), .ReplaceAll, .Wrap=1
End Sub
```

Then bring up the document you want to change and click the right-wedgie "Play" button. You can also save the macro and use Tools/Macro/Run it whenever you need to zap out the curlies.

UNCURLING CURLY QUOTES AS YOU TYPE

Thanks to Herb Tyson for this and the next tip, two fine bits of hacking.

Curly quotes are cool, and I recommend them several places in this book. Sometimes, though, you really want a straight double quote (") as you type; nothing else will do. It's a real pain to click and clack your way through the menus to turn everything off just to get one lousy straight quote.

Well, there's another trick. Again, I have no idea why it works. If you type either an open double quote (") or a close double quote (") and immediately hit Edit/ Undo (with the Edit menu, the Toolbar button, CTRL+Z, or ALT+BACKSPACE), WinWord uncurls the quote.

It doesn't work on single curly quotes (or apostrophes). Only on double quotes. And it doesn't appear to be documented anywhere. Go figger.

MACRO ASSIGNMENT SHORTCUT

WinWord makes it infuriatingly difficult to figure out what macro or command is assigned to a specific Toolbar button, menu entry, or key combination. If you need to figure this out very often, you'll find yourself bouncing through many layers of obscure dialog boxes.

Well, there's a trick, and I don't think it's documented anywhere. Push CTRL+ALT and the plus key over on the number pad. The cursor turns into a cloverleaf. Now push the key combination in question, or click on the Toolbar button or menu item. (For example, if you want to know what SHIFT+F1 does, just push SHIFT+F1.) Presto-chango. The answer is before your very eyes.

The trick is in the ToolsCustomizeKeyboardShortcut command, which is not documented in the WordBasic references.

PAGE NUMBERING ON FOLDED SHEETS

Ever want to print two "pages" side-by-side on a sheet of paper? Something like Figure 9.2.

Page 1	Page 2

Figure 9.2 Two Pages On One Sheet

If you format your document to be landscape (in File/Page Setup), arrange for two snaking columns. It's pretty easy, by and large, except for the page numbers!

Actually, the page numbers aren't too bad, either. Make sure that you tell WinWord to show field codes, not results. If you're printing two "pages" on a single sheet of paper, stick your cursor wherever you want the page number on the left side (probably in a header or footer), click Insert, Field, and double-click the equal sign (=). Then stick your cursor to the right of the equal sign, click Insert, Field, and double-click Page. Get rid of those lousy *MERGEFORMAT options, and rearrange the field so that it looks like this:

Two pages on a sheet

```
{ = 2* ({page} - 1) + 1 }
```

That will give you the correct page number on the left-hand side. (For example, on the first sheet of paper, you'll get a 1; on the second sheet of paper, you'll get a 3; then a 5; and so on.)

Now pop over to the right side of the page, Insert, Field twice, and change the field to look like this:

```
{ = 2* ({page} - 1) + 2 }
```

That's all it takes. Make WinWord show field results and you'll see that all the pages are numbered properly. If you're working with three "pages" on a single sheet of paper, the first "page" is { = 3* ({page} - 1) + 1 }, the second is { = 3* ({page} - 1) + 2 }, and the third is { = 3* ({page} - 1) + 3 }. For four pages, it's { = 4* ({page} - 1) + 1 }, and so on.

Three pages on a sheet

CROP MARKS

Liberals feel unworthy of their possesions.
Conservatives feel they deserve everything they've stolen.

Mort Sahl

WinWord has Hobbes' Time with crop marks. They really should be a built-in part of the program, but somehow they're still a bit of manual malarkey that will frustrate you time and again.

The idea is pretty simple. You're printing on $8^{1}/_{2} \times 11$-inch (or A4) paper. The pages you're printing will be sent off to be duplicated and trimmed to a smaller size—perhaps to the size of this book, 7.375×9.125 inches, or maybe to 6×9, or 7×10.

What's a crop mark?

The folks at the print shop really appreciate it if you can draw little marks on your printed pages to show them precisely where the final, trimmed pages begin and end. With those little marks they can (presumably) line up their equipment to get margins printed the way you want them. In practice, it doesn't always work so well, but it's a good theory anyway.

Oh. The official documentation on this (including the *MS Knowledge Base* article on the topic) is a starting point, but it won't get you very far. Several book chapters and macros have been published, but they all seem to forget important points. If you've been struggling with those instructions, or trying and failing with those macros, forget everything you've "learned" before proceeding with the instructions I'm going to give you in the following sections.

The Easy Way

Fake it if you can.

You can print crop marks in two easy ways:

- Buy a product (like the LaserMaster WinJet) that puts crop marks on the paper automatically.

- Print a bunch of crop-marked pages using a draw program (like CorelDRAW!). When the draw program is done, feed the same paper through the printer a second time and print your document on the premarked sheets. Most laser printers have extremely good registration; your local print shop will never know the difference.

Unfortunately there are times when you can't punt. For those times, it's best to buckle down, strap on your hip waders, and jump into the crop kludge.

The Hard Way

First, a handful of tips for working with crop marks, borne of far too much experience with this problem:

Leave Page Size alone.

1. *Don't* change the paper size in the File/Page Setup/Page Size filecard. You'll be tempted to do it over and over again, but you'll ultimately find yourself adding and subtracting fudge numbers; a gutter will really make your head spin. *Keep it simple*, and stick to your "real" page size, the size of the piece of paper on which you're going to print.

Do the work in the margins.

2. *Do* change the margins in the File/Page Setup/Margins filecard, and when you do, make sure that WHOLE DOCUMENT is showing in the Apply To: box. You'll probably find it easiest to figure out the margin sizes if you have two pieces of paper at hand—one the size of the paper you're printing on, the other the size of the finished pages—plus a sharp pencil with a big eraser, a calculator, and a very accurate ruler, with markings in tenths of an inch. (The paper may come in eighths of an inch, but WinWord only works in hundredths! Ah, metrication won't come a moment too soon.)

Paragraph indents can get complicated.

3. *Don't* change the indents in Format/Paragraph unless it's absolutely necessary. Try to put all the sizing worms in one can. Isolate them to the File/Page Setup/Margins filecard, and you'll only have one set of calculations to juggle, instead of three.

With those precautions out of the way, here's how I set up crop marks. I'll step you through an example for a 6 × 9-inch document with 1-inch margins all around (4 × 7-inch printed area) printed on 8½ × 11-inch paper.

I could give you a bunch of fancy mathematical formulae, but the process gets very complicated, very quickly, especially if you're working with a gutter or with mirror margins. Instead of an analytical approach, I'll show you how to get started, and then let you fudge the measurements so they line up the way you want them.

This method may trigger ugly "outside of printable area" errors with some printer drivers when you try to print, but they're harmless. Ignore them and your documents will print fine. At least the crop marks will be in place, and you'll have the greatest fighting chance of making some sense of all this.

"Outside of printable area" errors

Crop Marks Step by Step

> A sure sign of an amateur is too much detail
> to compensate for too little life.
>
> Anthony Burgess
> *Times Literary Supplement,* 1971

Figure out what size margins you'll need by subtracting the finished page size from the size of the paper you're using, dividing by two, and making allowances for gutters or mirror margins, if necessary. In this case, we want 2-inch top and bottom margins, and 2.25-inch left and right margins. On my 8½ × 11-inch page, that leaves a 4 × 7-inch working area, with 1-inch borders all the way around and a finished page size of 6 × 9 inches. Great.

Calculate Margins

Click on File, then Page Setup, bring up the Margins filecard, and enter the left, right, top, and bottom margins. Then, down in the box marked From Edge, type in a zero in both the Header: and Footer: boxes. We're going to get rid of one additional source of complication right here at the get-go. Click OK. Type an X in the document so you can tell where the left margin begins when you start printing and measuring.

Make sure that you can see paragraph marks; click the ShowAll button if you have to. Now flip into Page View, and zoom out so you can see the whole page. You should have something like Figure 9.3.

ShowAll

We're going to stick crop marks on this document by putting tables in the header and footer, adding "border" lines to the table cells where appropriate to simulate crop marks. We'll start with the crop mark in the upper left-hand corner.

If your margins are different on odd- and even-numbered pages (that is, if you have gutters or mirror margins), you'll have to set up your document with Different Odd and Even Headers, and then repeat these instructions twice, once working on an odd-numbered page and again working on an even-numbered page.

Figure 9.3 Ready to Crop

The upper left crop mark

Click View, then Header and Footer. Make sure your cursor is in the header, click Table, then Insert Table, and put a 3-column, 1-row table in the header. In the first cell, select the end-of-cell marker, the thing that looks like a light bulb, so that the entire first cell is highlighted.

Click on Format, then Borders and Shading, and, by clicking on the bottom and rightmost edges of the dummy text in the Borders box, put the thinnest line possible on the bottom and right sides of the cell. Click OK. See how the borders of the cell are going to make good crop marks? Well, usable ones, anyway.

Space between columns

Click Table, then Cell Height and Width. In the Column filecard, set Width of Column 1 to 0.25 inch, and—*this is important!*—set the Space Between Columns to 0. All the reference material you'll find leaves out that crucial point: if you don't set Space Between Columns to 0, you'll have to futz around with yet another variable. Bleccch.

Indent from left

In the Row filecard, set the Height to Exactly 1 inch (so that the bottom of the crop mark will print at 1 inch, which is where I want it for the example), and the Indent From Left to –1.25 inches. (Yeah, negative one and a quarter inches; if I start this cell at –1.25 inches and let it run a quarter of an inch, it'll end up 1 inch to the left of the text, which is right where we want it for this 6 × 9 document.) Your document should look something like Figure 9.4.

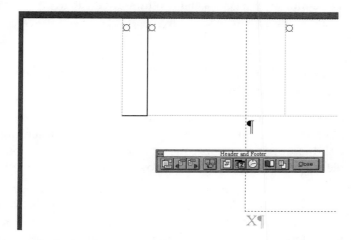

Figure 9.4 Upper Left Crop Mark

Now stick your cursor in the second cell. Click on Table, then Cell Height and Width, flip to the Column filecard, and set Column 2 Width to the width of the finished page—in this case, 6 inches. **The finished page's width**

Finally, select the end-of-cell marker in the third cell, click on Format, then Borders and Shading, and, by clicking on the bottom and leftmost edges of the dummy text in the Borders box, put the thinnest line possible on the bottom and left of the final cell. That's the crop mark in the upper right corner of the page. **The upper right crop mark**

See what we're doing here? There's a table cell in the middle with no border. That cell is the same width as the finished page. Immediately to its left and right are vertical lines, the crop marks that delineate the beginning and end of the finished page. Then we tried to jockey the height of the table so that the bottom of the table—the place where we put the horizontal line—corresponds to the top of the finished page.

The table itself is just a bit of jury-rigged hocus pocus; we're only using it as a framework, something handy to hang lines on. Although WinWord has myriad ways to draw lines, making horizontal and vertical lines intersect at a precise location is not simple. The table eases matters a bit.

Now *save everything!* Do it now, while you're thinking about it. Good. You'd be surprised how many times I GPF right about now. Hit the printer icon and print the page. Break out your ruler, and see how the crop marks are lining up, compared to the big X in the upper left corner of the doc.

Adjusting Ex Post Facto

There comes Poe, with his raven, Like Barnaby Rudge,
Three-fifths of him genius and two-fifths sheer fudge.

James Russell Lowell
Fable for Critics, 1848

Fudge   If the crop marks aren't in the right place—and they rarely are, on the first try, believe me—here's what you can do:

- If the distance between the crop marks is off, you've really screwed something up. The width of the second cell controls the distance between the marks. If you bollixed that up, you probably messed up something else, too. Your best bet is to delete the whole header and start over again. Don't worry. It happens.

- If you need to move the crop marks to the left, stick your cursor somewhere in the table, click Table, then Cell Height and Width, bring up the Row filecard, and adjust the Indent From Left number. It's a negative number, so to move the crop marks left, you have to make the number more negative. If it's –1.25 inches and you want to move your crop marks left a quarter inch, make it –1.5 inches.

- If you need to move the crop marks to the right, do the Table/Cell Height and Width/Row/Indent From Left thing, and make the number less negative. If it's –1.25 inches and you need to move the marks right a quarter inch, make it –1.0 inches.

- If you need to move the crop marks up or down, stick your cursor in the table, click Table, then Cell Height and Width, bring up the Row filecard, keep it at Exactly (so it doesn't start flip-flopping around on you), and either increase or decrease the distance.

- If you need to put something in the header (like, uh, a header!), stick your cursor in front of the paragraph mark that follows the table, and do whatever you would normally do.

That's the whole game, right there. As long as the distance between the crop marks is correct, you just need to move them *as a group* up, down, left, or right. Since the marks are attached to cells in a table, you need only move the whole table up, down, left, or right.

It's easy when you see what's happening. It just took me, oh, four *years* to figure out what was really going on behind the scenes. *Duhhhh.*

Crop Marks in the Footer

I was born below par
to th' extent of two whiskies.

Charles Edward Montague
Fiery Particles, 1923

Once the crop marks in the header are looking good, it's easy to put the two crop marks on the bottom of the page. Zoom out so you can see the whole page. Click View, then Header and Footer. Go into the header and copy the table—select the whole table and nothing but the table, and copy it to the clipboard.

Just copy them down.

Then click the first button in the Header and Footer Toolbar, the one that looks like a sheet of paper with a jaundiced floppy disk drive above and below. You'll be propelled into the footer.

Hit Enter once to put an extra, usable paragraph mark in the footer, above the crop marks. That's the paragraph mark you'll use for footers on the finished page. Then paste the table into the footer.

Important: Get an extra para mark in there.

Stick your cursor in the first cell of the table. Click Format, then Borders, and switch the border around:

Change the sides of the cell with lines.

- Click on the bottom edge of the dummy text in the Borders box. That gets rid of the line at the bottom of the cell.

- Click the top edge of the dummy text in the Borders box. That puts a line at the top of the cell.

Hop over to the last cell, and, *mutatis mutandis*, change it to have a line at the top of the cell instead of the bottom. You should have something that looks suspiciously like Figure 9.5.

Figure 9.5 Bottom Crop Marks

There's a paragraph mark at the bottom of the footer, below the table, that you can't delete; WinWord won't let you zap it out, for love nor money. The best kludge I've found is to select that paragraph mark, click Format, then Font, and set it to be 1 point tall.

Rogue paragraph mark

Get the real footer in there.

Now type in whatever footer you're going to want on the finished page. Eyeball it so it sits far enough above the bottom crop marks. Then, *and only then*, after you've stuck your finished pages' footers into the doc, print out a sample copy.

Chances are good that the bottom crop marks will either be too high or too low. Simply stick your cursor in the table there, click Table, then Cell Height and Width, and adjust the Height of Row 1 setting, leaving it on Exactly, until you get the crop mark precisely where you want it. Save everything. In fact, save several copies. Congratulations. You've just accomplished one of the most difficult tasks in WinWordDum.

10 On Beyond the Underground

People think that all I have to do is stand up and tell a few jokes.
Well, that's not as easy as it looks.
Every year it gets to be more of an effort to stand up.

George Burns

I hope you've found the tips and explanations in this book to be interesting, even entertaining. But don't imagine, even for a moment, that we've done anything more than scratch the surface.

WinWord 6.0 is among the most complex, most powerful, most useful computer programs ever written. There are so many nooks and crannies that you could spend weeks—months!—exploring nuances of just one small part of it. *Nobody* knows all of it. True fact.

In this final chapter, I hope to give you an idea of what's out there, other products you can use to make WinWord work better. I also want to give you my best take on where WinWord is heading, what's comin' down the pike.

ADD-INS AND SIDE CARS

Plato having defined man to be a two-legged animal without feathers, Diogenes plucked a cock and brought it to the Academy and said, "This is Plato's man." On which account this addition was made to the definition: "With broad flat nails."

Diogenes the Cynic
ca. 350 BC

One of the most exciting capabilities WinWord brings to the table is its amazing ability to accommodate new things. You've seen how you can write a macro and weave it into the very fabric of WinWord. How an industrial strength template can save hours of work. How a well-placed {field} or a cleverly designed

255

style can expand WinWord's horizons, adding functions not even WinWord's creators imagined possible.

WinWord's extensibility has kick-started an entire industry, a market for specialized products that either solve a specific problem or extend WinWord's capabilities in often-amazing ways.

The myriad products available to make WinWord work better go by many different names: add-ins, add-ons, sidecars, and plug-ins; macros, libraries, and developer's helpers; converters, crackers, translators, and mailers; templates, fonts, organizers; and on and on.

What they all have in common is this: WinWord's phenomenal design and macro language make it possible to meld those add-ins into WinWord itself, so they work with WinWord, not against it. Any software house with a bit of motivation can shoe-horn its products into WinWord and make them behave as if they're part of WinWord.

I've tried to assemble here a list of WinWord add-ons and helpers that are specific to WinWord itself. Not that I'm giving short shrift to other products that can tie into WinWord! Heavens, no. Just about anything can tie into WinWord. What I'm searching for here, though, are those products that are integral to WinWord, tied to WinWord at the wrists and ankles.

What's a Shareware?

Several of the products listed here are shareware. If you're unfamiliar with shareware, let me bend your ear for a minute. The topic is near and dear to my heart because my background is in shareware, and I'm very proud of it!

Try it; if you keep using it, pay for it.

Shareware has been described as the last bastion of the 1960s. The fundamental concept is pretty straightforward: somebody with a program to sell *gives* a copy to you. You try it out. If you keep using it, you're asked to pay for it.

Yeah, that flies in the face of every good business principle; I can see the MBAs out there sputtering, "But! But! But!" I mean, can you imagine the salesman at Tricky Dicky's Computer Emporium handing you a 486/66, helping you haul it to the car, and oh-by-the-way asking you to send him a check if you use the machine? Well, that's how shareware works. And it *does* work. I'm living proof. I've made a living at shareware for several years now, put food on the table, put gas in the car, and kept the Coal Creek Canyon wolves from the door.

Where do you get it?

Shareware is typically distributed via bulletin boards, including the big ones like CompuServe. There are also companies that specialize in selling diskettes filled with shareware. You may have a "shareware disk vendor" in your local mall, or you may get catalogs from one of hundreds of companies that sell disks by phone. Shareware has also sprung up in grocery stores, swap markets, user group meetings, on books' companion disks, and in myriad other channels.

All of these sources of shareware have one thing in common. If you pay to get the shareware, you're paying the distributor for their time, effort, and material. You are *not* paying the author for the product itself.

Shareware revolves around trust. First, the "author" (who may be an individual or a company) trusts the users to pay for a product if they continue to use it. Second—and every bit as important—the users trust the author to put together something that's worthy of evaluation. Downloading shareware from bulletin boards can be expensive; disk vendors don't operate as nonprofit organizations (at least not intentionally!); and it takes time and effort to give a shareware package a good workout. The best shareware packages honor both sides of the equation. They're complete, well-documented, fully functional, and at least relatively bug-free—even to the point of circumventing bugs in the underlying product. I won't mention WinWord by name. **Trust works both ways**

Why would an author choose to distribute his or her product as shareware? Aside from the legitimate claim of temporary insanity—crafting top-notch shareware is both difficult and financially risky—most authors market their products as shareware because they're more interested in creating cool solutions to real problems than in adding to the advertising cacophony. Launching a "commercial" product can cost hundreds of thousands of dollars, and almost all of that money goes into stuff that doesn't mean squat in the product itself: packaging, distribution, and advertising.

Besides, it's an ego thing. Most shareware authors and shareware companies are built on a vision of how things should be done, and done right. It's very rare that shareware companies get caught up in the conspicuous consumption that's rampant in the industry; you'll find few shareware companies with fancy offices or large staffs. The money tends to go straight back into producing more good stuff.

So why would anybody in their right mind pay for something they already have? That's a tough question! **Why should I pay?**

First and foremost, it's the right thing to do. Go ahead and laugh if you like, but most companies and individuals pay for ("register") their shareware because they know that their money is going to a good cause. It helps build better products and provides an incentive to keep doing excellent work. I don't think it's an exaggeration to say that many of the most important improvements in WinWord over the years have been "borrowed" from other products, lifted from companies that have braved the waters to bring important new ideas and approaches to market.

An active WinWord shareware market provides a rich gene pool for the next version of WinWord. If you want to see the future of WinWord, you need to look at its shareware!

Second, most shareware has "negative incentives." For example, nag screens —pesky dialog boxes that pop up and say "you haven't registered yet"—are a common (and effective!) registration inducement. Many folks simply forget to register: I've done it myself. The nag screens force the user to think about registering, even if it's only for a fraction of a second.

Finally, almost all shareware has some sort of registration incentive. Details vary, but many shareware authors send a care package to folks who register, with the latest version of the software, maybe a manual or Getting Started booklet, or a different "bonus" program that might be of interest. Registration also entitles you to technical support. Sometimes it will also bestow a discount on new versions of the software or on other products the author may have available. Goodies and incentives abound; check each product's documentation for details.

The Association of Shareware Professionals is the granddaddy of all shareware organizations. Shareware authors who are ASP members are bound by a set of rules, and you have recourse to ASP should you feel that an ASP author isn't treating you right.

By Design

Streetwise Software's By Design adds a hundred professionally designed templates, intelligent docs with hooks straight into an address book, 25 fonts, 150 pieces of clip art, and a whole bunch more. Retails for $99, but you can probably find it cheaper on your neighborhood software retailer's shelf. Streetwise Software, 2210 Wilshire Blve, Suite 836, Santa Monica, CA 90403; voice 800-743-6765.

DocsDB

Jorge Vismara has put together an extensive collection of routines that let you organize and maintain documents, including long file names, search criteria, virtual cabinets, folders and subjects, and other useful touches. Lists for $129.95. JV Consultants, 3013 Yale Ave., Marina del Rey, CA 90292; orders: 800-362-7329 or 310-827-8786; fax 310-827-8786.

DocStudio

ALKI Software, the folks who wrote WinWord 6.0's Wizards, bring you a greatly enlarged selection of templates, indeed, a template generator. You get dozens of different document types, with 19 family "looks." Includes 35 Bitstream fonts. List $139.95, but if you can find the ALKI brochure in your WinWord box and use the order form, it's just $69.95. ALKI Software, 300 Queen Anne Ave. N, Suite 410, Seattle, WA 98109; voice 800-NOW-WORD (800-669-9673) or 206-286-2600; fax 206-286-2785.

DocuPower, Fileware

Dan Goodman's Fileware adds all the file management routines Microsoft forgot: make directories, delete, rename, copy, move. Long file names, directory jump, and more. It has its own custom color Toolbar, and ships with a quick, handy telephone book. Shareware from Total System Solutions, $39.95.

DocuPower Pro™, also from Total System Solutions, lets you put descriptive names—up to 60 characters long—on all of your files, and group them in folders. Open, insert, print or fax documents, file find and text search, file management, and a bunch of additional utilities. $39.95, shareware.

Both award-winning programs are available from Total System Solutions, Inc., 1530 East 18th Street, Suite 6H, Brooklyn NY 11230; voice 800-814-2300 or 718-375-2997; bulletin board 718-375-6261.

FileBox6

An add-on file manager from Bud Brown that works on the file folder metaphor: long file names, folders within folders, click and drag, point and shoot, all the good stuff a long file name manager needs. $20 Shareware from Bud Brown, CompuServe 73277,3615.

gScript, gTools

WinWord gadfly and long-time WordBasic maven Guy Gallo is assembling another outstanding collection of WinWord extensions, including a routine that keeps track of the last status of your desktop—so you can pick right up where you left off—a way to print "watermarks" on laser printers, and many others. Guy's gScript, regarded by many as the ultimate script writing tool, is also being adapted to WinWord 6.0. I didn't have precise ordering details as we went to press, but urge you to download the gTools and gScript files on CompuServe's MSWORD forum, or to contact Guy on CompuServe at 71171,3555.

Hacker's Guide to Word for Windows, **Second Edition**

Hacker's Guide to Word for Windows, Second Edition by Woody Leonhard, Vincent Chen, and Scott Krueger, Addison-Wesley, 1994. 800 pages + 2 disks, $39.95.

No, it isn't shareware. Yes, it is a *vital* reference for anyone who tackles WordBasic and wishes to maintain some semblance of sanity. Vince Chen and I wrote the original version, for WinWord 2.0. Scott Krueger—one of the world's foremost authorities on the topic—brought it up to date for WinWord 6.0. (Check for availability; the 6.0 version may not quite be on the stands by the time you read this.) Accept no substitutes! This is the naked, unvarnished truth about WinWord and WordBasic.

And it's just as snarly and opinionated as the 2.0 version.

MasterWord

ALKI software continues its string of top-notch WinWord add-ons with the latest incarnation of MasterWord. This one gives you an "Easy" menu, to help with fonts, wizards, and more. There's a "Command Central" to help you locate commands that might otherwise be buried deep in an obscure menu. And much more. MasterWord lists for $99.95, but the ALKI brochure that may have come in your WinWord box has an order form for $59.95. ALKI Software, 300 Queen Anne Ave. N, Suite 410, Seattle, WA 98109; voice 800-NOW-WORD (800-669-9673) or 206-286-2600; fax 206-286-2785.

MegaWord

Romke Soldaat, virtuoso WordBasic expert, has assembled a nonpareil collection of ultra-cool stuff you should see. Everything from novice user assists to fancy, fancy macros. Megaword is $49 from Merlot International, 1, chemin des Moulines, 34230 St. Bauzille de la Sylve, France; voice 800-2424-PSL; fax 713-524-6398; CompuServe 100273,32.

Microsoft Word 6.0 Legal Resource Kit

If you're of the legal persuasion, you should pick up the phone and order this kit. It contains new macros for Lexis and Nexis, and a handful of other useful things. Contact your local Microsoft office; in the U.S., 800-426-9400. It's free.

Microsoft Word Assistant

Yes, even Microsoft is getting into the add-on business! This package includes 25 more TrueType fonts, including a variant on the Font Assistant that Microsoft includes with its TrueType Fonts 2 package. A bunch of templates, including dozens of forms. And 100 clip-art images from 3G Graphics.

You can pick up Word Assistant just about anywhere for $49.95 or less. There's also a card in the WinWord box.... although the card *does* say you can "brighten up your docs" by "applying a style sheet." *Sheeeesh*. Word hasn't had style sheets since the days of DOS. Oh, well.

Microsoft Word Developer's Kit

Microsoft Word Developer's Kit, Microsoft Press, 1994. 944 pages + disk, $39.95.

This is the party line. It explains how WordBasic and .WLLs *should* work. Still in all, it's a crucial reference book. As Microsoft says, "It includes a complete discussion on using WordBasic to customize Word 6.0 ... also includes the WordBasic function reference, sample macros on a disk, as well as advanced programming topics on using the Word API, Microsoft Messaging API (MAPI), and Open Database Connectivity (ODBC) with Word 6.0." It's available at many bookstores.

PRIME 6.0

The WinWord savants at PRIME Consulting Group offer the latest incarnation of their add-on, dubbed PRIME 6.0. New capabilities include a "batch" spell checker that lets you break free and do something else while WinWord checks spelling in the background; a complete AutoText manager; a set of routines that bring some sanity to the bookmark madness, and much more. PRIME 6.0 is $39.95. To order call Advanced Support Group at 800-659-4696 or 314-965-5630.

Quicture 2.0

Tired of WinWord's sluggish handling of graphics? If you have large documents with lots of pictures, Quicture will save you hours of frustration as you wait for the hourglass to come back. Quicture automatically strips the graphics out of WinWord docs, replacing them with full-size boxes that include the graphic files' names. The replacement boxes scroll like wildfire, and the pictures get squished down to a fraction of their original size. One click restores the doc to its original self for printing or moving to a different machine. $49 from WexTech Systems, Inc., 310 Madison Ave, Suite 905, New York 10164-2414. Call 212-949-9595 or fax 212-949-4007.

WOPR

This is my baby, so apologies in advance for tooting my own horn. WOPR (Woody's Office POWER Pack™) was assembled by ten of the world's top WinWord experts, including five Microsoft Consulting Partners. It's the number one WinWord add-on, with innovations that advance the state of the art in Windows word processing. Toolbar customizing. Fast, easy, flexible envelopes. Booklets, 2-up and 4-up printing. Toner saver. Quick right-click spell check and thesaurus lookup. A file manager that's the best in the business, even better than WordPerfect's. A file new that finally lets *you* control your templates—instead of the other way around. A clip-art viewer/inserter that's fast and bullet-proof. And on and on. If you're a novice or a guru, you'll find tons of goodies that will help you work faster and smarter, all day, every day. I guaran-damn-tee it.

Yo! Look here!

WOPR has won numerous awards; it's been praised in every computer magazine you've ever read, all around the world. (Well, OK, we missed the *Mongolian Mathematical Monthly*, but we're trying.) It comes with a 100% no-questions-asked lifetime money-back guarantee, and it's just $49.95 + s/h. Here's the clincher: If you call and order now, and say *The Underground Guide* to the person on the phone, you'll get $10 off the usual price; that's my way of saying "thanks" for picking up this book.

There's a reason why they call it "Whopper."

WOPR 6.0 is ASP shareware from Pinecliffe International. Order from our distributor, Advanced Support Group, 11900 Grant Place, Des Peres, MO 63131; voice 800-OK-WINWORD (800-659-4696) or 314-965-5630; fax 314-966-1833;

CompuServe 70304,3642. Registered users get unlimited free phone support, big discounts on (autographed!) books and other goodies, and advance notice on Very Important WinWordStuff.

WordCab

Frank Ramos' free file management front end for WinWord. Shows title, date/time of last modification and filename of all .DOC files in a directory. Allows searching by title or file name, and filtering so only files matching a specified string in the title or filename will be shown. Pick up the `WORDCA.ZIP` file on the CompuServe MSWORD forum.

WHERE TO TURN FOR HAAAAAAALP!

> When fame and success
> Come to you, then retire.
> This is the ordained Way.
>
> Lao-tzu
> *Tao Te Ching*, ca. 250 BC

Wei wu wei.*   Yes, you can call Microsoft on the phone. And wait. And wait. And pay more money to Ma Bell and wait some more.

Far and away the best solution to the Microsoft Product Support blues is to hop on CompuServe. You post a message, come back in a few hours (or sometimes —if the boards are really going crazy—a day), and there's your answer, well researched and complete, from a handful of really top-notch WinWord experts.

WinCIM   Drop by your local software store and pick up a copy of the CompuServe sign-up package, preferably with a copy of WinCIM, the CompuServe access software for Windows. Get on-line, GO MSWORD, and you'll be in the middle of the most knowledgeable WinWord Groupies on the planet. There's not just 'Softies, either, by the way. As often as not you'll hear from somebody else who either is looking for the same thing you seek or possibly has solved the problem and is willing to share a solution.

If you have a WordBasic question or something of a more advanced nature, GO PROGMSA and talk to the folks who support Programming Microsoft Applications.

The most important tip in this book:

Get on CompuServe.

*Doing not-doing.

Appendix

A The Cast of Characters

In the WinWord world, each character has a number; the character number sits behind the scenes. The letter you see on the screen or printed on a page is created by looking up that character in whichever font you have applied.

TIMES NEW ROMAN CHARACTERS

Chapter 2 got into some detail on this topic. Table A.1 lists the characters from number 32 (space) through number 255 (ÿ) in the Times New Roman font.

Table A.1 Characters in New Times Roman

32		54	6	76	L	98	b	120	x
33	!	55	7	77	M	99	c	121	y
34	"	56	8	78	N	100	d	122	z
35	#	57	9	79	O	101	e	123	{
36	$	58	:	80	P	102	f	124		
37	%	59	;	81	Q	103	g	125	}
38	&	60	<	82	R	104	h	126	~
39	'	61	=	83	S	105	i	127	
40	(	62	>	84	T	106	j	128	
41	)	63	?	85	U	107	k	129	
42	*	64	@	86	V	108	l	130	,
43	+	65	A	87	W	109	m	131	ƒ
44	,	66	B	88	X	110	n	132	„
45	-	67	C	89	Y	111	o	133	…
46	.	68	D	90	Z	112	p	134	†
47	/	69	E	91	[	113	q	135	‡
48	0	70	F	92	\	114	r	136	^
49	1	71	G	93	]	115	s	137	‰
50	2	72	H	94	^	116	t	138	Š
51	3	73	I	95	_	117	u	139	‹
52	4	74	J	96	`	118	v	140	Œ
53	5	75	K	97	a	119	w	141	

Table A.1 Characters in New Times Roman (Continued)

142		165	¥	188	¼	211	Ó	234	ê
143		166	|	189	½	212	Ô	235	ë
144		167	§	190	¾	213	Õ	236	ì
145	'	168	¨	191	¿	214	Ö	237	í
146	'	169	©	192	À	215	×	238	î
147	"	170	ª	193	Á	216	Ø	239	ï
148	"	171	«	194	Â	217	Ù	240	ð
149	•	172	¬	195	Ã	218	Ú	241	ñ
150	–	173	–	196	Ä	219	Û	242	ò
151	—	174	®	197	Å	220	Ü	243	ó
152	˜	175	¯	198	Æ	221	Ý	244	ô
153	™	176	°	199	Ç	222	Þ	245	õ
154	š	177	±	200	È	223	ß	246	ö
155	›	178	²	201	É	224	à	247	÷
156	œ	179	³	202	Ê	225	á	248	ø
157		180	´	203	Ë	226	â	249	ù
158		181	µ	204	Ì	227	ã	250	ú
159	Ÿ	182	¶	205	Í	228	ä	251	û
160		183	·	206	Î	229	å	252	ü
161	¡	184	,	207	Ï	230	æ	253	ý
162	¢	185	¹	208	Ð	231	ç	254	þ
163	£	186	º	209	Ñ	232	è	255	ÿ
164	¤	187	»	210	Ò	233	é		

WINGDING CHARACTERS

Table A.2 lists the characters from number 32 (space) through number 255 (ÿ) in the Wingdings font. Chapter 2 explains how these characters can be different from the ones in Table A.1.

Table A.2 Characters in Wingdings

32		39		46		53		60	
33		40		47		54		61	
34		41		48		55		62	
35		42		49		56		63	
36		43		50		57		64	
37		44		51		58		65	
38		45		52		59		66	

Table A.2 Characters in Wingdings (Continued)

67	✎	105	♓	143	❹	181	✿	219	⊂
68	✏	106	ℓ	144	❺	182	☆	220	⊃
69	✐	107	&	145	❻	183	◷	221	∩
70	☞	108	●	146	❼	184	◔	222	∪
71	✑	109	○	147	❽	185	◕	223	←
72	✒	110	■	148	❾	186	◷	224	→
73	✋	111	□	149	❿	187	◔	225	↑
74	☺	112	❑	150	☙	188	◑	226	↓
75	😐	113	❒	151	฿	189	◕	227	↖
76	☹	114	❐	152	๊	190	◒	228	↗
77	✺	115	◆	153	๛	191	◷	229	↙
78	☠	116	◆	154	❧	192	◔	230	↘
79	⚑	117	◆	155	❦	193	◕	231	←
80	⚐	118	❖	156	❧	194	◔	232	→
81	✈	119	◆	157	❧	195	❧	233	↑
82	☼	120	⊠	158	·	196	✍	234	↓
83	⬤	121	◿	159	•	197	✎	235	↖
84	❄	122	⌘	160	·	198	✐	236	↗
85	✞	123	✾	161	○	199	✏	237	↙
86	✝	124	✹	162	○	200	✑	238	↘
87	✠	125	"	163	●	201	✒	239	⇐
88	✵	126	"	164	⊙	202	✎	240	⇒
89	✿	127		165	◎	203	✾	241	⇑
90	☾	128	⓪	166	○	204	✠	242	⇓
91	☽	129	①	167	▪	205	ß	243	⇔
92	ॐ	130	②	168	□	206	☝	244	⇕
93	✲	131	③	169	⟁	207	☟	245	⬂
94	♈	132	④	170	✦	208	✍	246	⬀
95	♉	133	⑤	171	★	209	✎	247	⬁
96	♊	134	⑥	172	✳	210	✏	248	⬃
97	♋	135	⑦	173	✴	211	✑	249	▫
98	♌	136	⑧	174	✵	212	✒	250	▫
99	♍	137	⑨	175	✺	213	⊗	251	✘
100	♎	138	⑩	176	⊕	214	⊠	252	✓
101	♏	139	❶	177	⊕	215	◁	253	☒
102	♐	140	❷	178	✧	216	▷	254	☑
103	♑	141	❸	179	⌗	217	◄	255	▦
104	♒	142	❸	180	◈	218	▼		

B Built-In Styles

WinWord ships with 74 built-in styles, ready for you to use.

Style	Description/Definition
Annotation Reference	Default Paragraph Font + Font: 8 pt
Annotation Text	Normal + Font: 10 pt
Body Text	Normal + Space After 6 pt
Body Text Indent	Normal + Indent: Left 0.25", Space After 6 pt
Caption	Normal + Bold, Space Before 6 pt After 6 pt
Closing	Normal + Indent: Left 3"
Default Paragraph Font	The font of the underlying paragraph style +
Endnote Reference	Default Paragraph Font + Superscript
Endnote Text	Normal + Font: 10 pt
Envelope Address	Normal + Font: 12 pt, Indent: Left 2", Position: Center Horiz. Relative To Page, 0.13" From Text, Bottom Vert. Relative To Margin, Width: 5.5", Height: Exactly 1.38"
Envelope Return	Normal + Font: 10 pt
Footer	Normal + Tab stops: 3" Centered, 6" Right Flush
Footnote Reference	Default Paragraph Font + Superscript
Footnote Text	Normal + Font: 10 pt
Header	Normal + Tab stops: 3" Centered, 6" Right Flush
Heading 1	Normal + Font: Arial, 14 pt, Bold, Kern at 14 pt, Space Before 12 pt After 3 pt, Keep With Next
Heading 2	Normal + Font: Arial, 12 pt, Bold, Italic, Space Before 12 pt After 3 pt, Keep With Next
Heading 3	Normal + Font: Times New Roman, 12 pt, Bold, Space Before 12 pt After 3 pt, Keep With Next
Heading 4	Normal + Font: Times New Roman, 12 pt, Bold, Italic, Space Before 12 pt After 3 pt, Keep With Next
Heading 5	Normal + Font: Arial, Space Before 12 pt After 3 pt
Heading 6	Normal + Font: Arial, Italic, Space Before 12 pt After 3 pt
Heading 7	Normal + Font: Arial, 10 pt, Space Before 12 pt After 3 pt
Heading 8	Normal + Font: Arial, 10 pt, Italic, Space Before 12 pt After 3 pt
Heading 9	Normal + Font: Arial, 9 pt, Italic, Space Before 12 pt After 3 pt
Index 1	Normal + Indent: Hanging 0.15", Tab stops: 6" Right Flush …

Style	Description/Definition
Index 2	Normal + Indent: Left 0.15" Hanging 0.15", Tab stops: 6" Right Flush …
Index 3	Normal + Indent: Left 0.31" Hanging 0.15", Tab stops: 6" Right Flush …
Index 4	Normal + Indent: Left 0.46" Hanging 0.15", Tab stops: 6" Right Flush …
Index 5	Normal + Indent: Left 0.61" Hanging 0.15", Tab stops: 6" Right Flush …
Index 6	Normal + Indent: Left 0.76" Hanging 0.15", Tab stops: 6" Right Flush …
Index 7	Normal + Indent: Left 0.92" Hanging 0.15", Tab stops: 6" Right Flush …
Index 8	Normal + Indent: Left 1.07" Hanging 0.15", Tab stops: 6" Right Flush …
Index 9	Normal + Indent: Left 1.22" Hanging 0.15", Tab stops: 6" Right Flush …
Index Heading	Normal +
Line Number	Default Paragraph Font +
List	Normal + Indent: Hanging 0.25"
List 2	Normal + Indent: Left 0.25" Hanging 0.25"
List 3	Normal + Indent: Left 0.5" Hanging 0.25"
List 4	Normal + Indent: Left 0.75" Hanging 0.25"
List 5	Normal + Indent: Left 1" Hanging 0.25"
List Bullet	Normal + Indent: Hanging 0.25", Bullet
List Bullet 2	Normal + Indent: Left 0.25" Hanging 0.25", Bullet
List Bullet 3	Normal + Indent: Left 0.5" Hanging 0.25", Bullet
List Bullet 4	Normal + Indent: Left 0.75" Hanging 0.25", Bullet
List Bullet 5	Normal + Indent: Left 1" Hanging 0.25", Bullet
List Continue	Normal + Indent: Left 0.25", Space After 6 pt
List Continue 2	Normal + Indent: Left 0.5", Space After 6 pt
List Continue 3	Normal + Indent: Left 0.75", Space After 6 pt
List Continue 4	Normal + Indent: Left 1", Space After 6 pt
List Continue 5	Normal + Indent: Left 1.25", Space After 6 pt
List Number	Normal + Indent: Hanging 0.25", Auto Numbering
List Number 2	Normal + Indent: Left 0.25" Hanging 0.25", Auto Numbering
List Number 3	Normal + Indent: Left 0.5" Hanging 0.25", Auto Numbering
List Number 4	Normal + Indent: Left 0.75" Hanging 0.25", Auto Numbering
List Number 5	Normal + Indent: Left 1" Hanging 0.25", Auto Numbering
Message Header	Normal + Font: Arial, 12 pt, Indent: Hanging 0.75"

Normal	Font: Garmond (W1), 11 pt, English (US), Flush left, Line Spacing Single, Space After 12 pt, Widow/Orphan Control
Normal Indent	Normal + Indent: Left 0.5"
Page Number	Default Paragraph Font +
Signature	Normal + Indent: Left 3"
Subtitle	Normal + Font: Arial, 12 pt, Italic, Centered, Space After 3 pt
Table of Authorities	Normal + Indent: Hanging 0.15", Tab stops: 6" Right Flush …
Table of Figures	Normal + Indent: Hanging 0.31", Tab stops: 6" Right Flush …
Title	Normal + Font: Arial, 16 pt, Bold, Kern at 14 pt, Centered, Space Before 12 pt After 3 pt
TOA Heading	Normal + Font: Arial, 12 pt, Bold, Space Before 6 pt
TOC 1	Normal + Tab stops: 6" Right Flush …
TOC 2	Normal + Indent: Left 0.15", Tab stops: 6" Right Flush …
TOC 3	Normal + Indent: Left 0.31", Tab stops: 6" Right Flush …
TOC 4	Normal + Indent: Left 0.46", Tab stops: 6" Right Flush …
TOC 5	Normal + Indent: Left 0.61", Tab stops: 6" Right Flush …
TOC 6	Normal + Indent: Left 0.76", Tab stops: 6" Right Flush …
TOC 7	Normal + Indent: Left 0.92", Tab stops: 6" Right Flush …
TOC 8	Normal + Indent: Left 1.07", Tab stops: 6" Right Flush …
TOC 9	Normal + Indent: Left 1.22", Tab stops: 6" Right Flush …

Appendix
C Standard Key Assignments

WinWord 6.0 ships with these standard key assignments. Of course, you can change key assignments any time by clicking on Tools, then Customize, and bringing up the Keyboard filecard.

You can print your custom key assignments by clicking on File, then Print, and choosing Key Assignments from the drop-down list.

FORMATTING

Changing font and font size

Change font	CTRL+SHIFT+F
Change font size	CTRL+SHIFT+P
Increase font size to next available size	CTRL+SHIFT+>
Decrease font size to previous available size	CTRL+SHIFT+<
Increase font size by 1 point	CTRL+]
Decrease font size by 1 point	CTRL+[

Changing text formatting

Change case of letters	SHIFT+F3
Create all capital letters	CTRL+SHIFT+A
Make text bold	CTRL+B
Underline text	CTRL+U
Underline single words	CTRL+SHIFT+W
Double underline words	CTRL+SHIFT+D
Apply hidden text format	CTRL+SHIFT+H
Italicize text	CTRL+I
Create small capital letters	CTRL+SHIFT+K
Apply subscripts (auto spacing)	CTRL+=
Apply superscripts (auto spacing)	CTRL+SHIFT+=
Remove formatting applied by using shortcut keys or menu commands (plain text)	CTRL+SHIFT+Z
Create Symbol font	CTRL+SHIFT+Q
Display nonprinting characters	CTRL+SHIFT+*

Line spacing

Create single-spaced lines	CTRL+1
Create double-spaced lines	CTRL+2
Create one-and-a-half-spaced lines	CTRL+5
Add one line of space preceding text	CTRL+0 (zero)
Remove space preceding text	CTRL+0 (zero)

Paragraph alignment

Center paragraph	CTRL+E
Justify paragraph	CTRL+J
Left-align paragraph	CTRL+L
Right-align paragraph	CTRL+R
Indent paragraph from left	CTRL+M
Remove paragraph indent from left	CTRL+SHIFT+M
Create hanging indent	CTRL+T
Reduce hanging indent	CTRL+SHIFT+T

Styles

Apply style name (Formatting toolbar displayed)	CTRL+SHIFT+S
Open Format Style dialog box	CTRL+SHIFT+S
Remove paragraph formatting	CTRL+Q
Start AutoFormat	CTRL+K
Apply Normal style	CTRL+SHIFT+N
Apply Heading 1 style	ALT+CTRL+1
Apply Heading 2 style	ALT+CTRL+2
Apply Heading 3 style	ALT+CTRL+3
Apply List style	CTRL+SHIFT+L

DELETING

Delete one character to left of insertion point	BACKSPACE
Delete one word to left of insertion point	CTRL+BACKSPACE
Delete one character to right of insertion point	DELETE
Delete one word to right of insertion point	CTRL+DEL
Cut (delete) selected text	CTRL+X
Undo last action	CTRL+Z
Cut to Spike	CTRL+F3

COPYING AND PASTING

Copy text or graphics	CTRL+C
Copy formats	CTRL+SHIFT+C

Move text or graphics	F2
Paste text or graphics	CTRL+V
Paste formats	CTRL+SHIFT+V

INSERTING

Field	CTRL+F9
Spike contents	CTRL+SHIFT+F3
AutoText entry	AutoText entry name+CTRL+ALT+V
Line break	SHIFT+ENTER
Page break	CTRL+ENTER
Column break	CTRL+SHIFT+ENTER
Optional hyphen	CTRL+HYPHEN
Nonbreaking hyphen	CTRL+SHIFT+HYPHEN
Nonbreaking space	CTRL+SHIFT+SPACEBAR
Copyright symbol	ALT+CTRL+C
Registered trademark symbol	ALT+CTRL+R
Trademark symbol	ALT+CTRL+T
Ellipsis	ALT+CTRL+period
Single opening quotation mark	CTRL+`,`
Single closing quotation mark	CTRL+','
Double opening quotation mark	CTRL+`,"
Double closing quotation mark	CTRL+',"

EXTENDING A SELECTION

Use the following shortcut keys to select text and graphics when you're in Extend mode. When you use Extend mode to extend a selection, Word is in a continuous selection mode until you turn off extend mode. Select text and graphics in the same direction as the arrow keys you press.

Select nearest character	F8+character
Extend selection	F8
Reduce the size of selection	SHIFT+F8

SELECTING

Outside a table

One character to right	SHIFT+RIGHT ARROW
One character to left	SHIFT+LEFT ARROW
To end of word	CTRL+SHIFT+RIGHT ARROW

To beginning of word	CTRL+SHIFT+LEFT ARROW
To end of line	SHIFT+END
To beginning of line	SHIFT+HOME
One line down	SHIFT + DOWN ARROW
One line up	SHIFT+UP ARROW
To end of paragraph	CTRL+SHIFT+DOWN ARROW
To beginning of paragraph	CTRL+SHIFT+UP ARROW
One screen down	SHIFT+PAGE DOWN
One screen up	SHIFT+PAGEUP
To end of document	CTRL+SHIFT+END
To beginning of document	CTRL+SHIFT+HOME
To include entire document	CTRL+A
To vertical block of text	CTRL+SHIFT+F8, then use the arrow keys
To a specific location in a document	F8+arrow keys

Inside a table

A column	Hold down ALT and click the left mouse button
A column (or block)	CTRL+SHIFT+F8
An entire table	ALT+5 on the numeric keypad

MOVING

To a character, word, para, column, or object

One character to left	LEFT ARROW
One character to right	RIGHT ARROW
One word to left	CTRL+LEFT ARROW
One word to right	CTRL+RIGHT ARROW
One paragraph up	CTRL+UP ARROW
One paragraph down	CTRL+DOWN ARROW
To previous frame or object	ALT+UP ARROW
To next frame or object	ALT+DOWN ARROW
One column to left	CTRL+UP ARROW
One column to right	CTRL+DOWN ARROW

To a line, page, screen, top or bottom of doc

Up one line	UP ARROW
Down one line	DOWN ARROW
To end of line	END
To beginning of line	HOME
Up one page	ALT+CTRL+PAGE UP
Down one page	ALT+CTRL+PAGE DOWN
Up one screen	PAGE UP

Down one screen	PAGE DOWN
To bottom of screen	CTRL+PAGE DOWN
To top of screen	CTRL+PAGE UP
To end of document	CTRL+END
To beginning of document	CTRL+HOME
To previous revision	SHIFT+F5

Repeat

Repeat Find or Go To command	SHIFT+F4

In a table

Next cell in row	TAB
Previous cell in row	SHIFT+TAB
First cell in row	ALT+HOME
Top cell in column	ALT+PAGE UP
Last cell in row	ALT+END
Last cell in column	ALT+PAGE DOWN
Previous row	UP ARROW
Next row	DOWN ARROW
Insert new paragraphs into cell	ENTER
Insert a tab character into cell	CTRL+TAB

OUTLINE VIEW

Promoting, demoting

Promote paragraph	ALT+SHIFT+LEFT ARROW
Demote paragraph	ALT+SHIFT+RIGHT ARROW
Demote to body text	CTRL+SHIFT+N
Move selected paragraphs up	ALT+SHIFT+ UP ARROW
Move selected paragraphs down	ALT+SHIFT+ DOWN ARROW

Changing display

Expand text under heading	ALT+SHIFT+PLUS SIGN
Collapse text under heading	ALT+SHIFT+MINUS SIGN
Show all text or headings	ALT+SHIFT+A
Display all text	Asterisk (*) key on numeric keypad
Display character formatting	Forward slash (/) key on numeric keypad
Show first line or all of body text	ALT+SHIFT+L
Show all headings with Heading 1 style	ALT+SHIFT+1
Show all headings up to Heading n	ALT+SHIFT+n

FIELDS

Inserting

Insert DATE field	ALT+SHIFT+D
Insert PAGE field	ALT+SHIFT+P
Insert TIME field	ALT+SHIFT+T
Insert blank field	CTRL+F9

Manipulating

Update linked information in source document	CTRL+SHIFT+F7
Update selected fields	F9
Unlink field	CTRL+SHIFT+F9
Switch between field codes or results	SHIFT+F9
View field codes	ALT+F9
Perform action in field	ALT+SHIFT+F9
Go to next field	F11
Go to previous field	SHIFT+F11
Lock field	CTRL+F11
Unlock field	CTRL+SHIFT+F11

MERGING DOCUMENTS

Preview a mail merge	ALT+SHIFT+K
Merge a document	ALT+SHIFT+N
Print the merged document	ALT+SHIFT+M
Edit a mail merge data document	ALT+SHIFT+E

WINDOWS, MENUS, AND COMMANDS

Moving around

Go to next pane	F6
Go to previous pane	SHIFT+F6
Go to next document window	CTRL+F6
Go to previous document window	CTRL+SHIFT+F6
Move document window	CTRL+F7, arrow keys, ENTER

Changing size

Maximize application window	ALT+F10
Maximize document window	CTRL+F10
Change size of document window	CTRL+F8
Restore document window to its previous size	CTRL+F5
Restore application window to its previous size	ALT+F5
Split window	ALT+SHIFT+C

Menus

Make menu bar active	F10
Cancel menu	ESC
Display shortcut menu	SHIFT+F10
Add command to menu	CTRL+ALT+EQUAL SIGN
Remove command from menu	CTRL+ALT+MINUS SIGN
Assign action to shortcut key	CTRL+ALT+ PLUS SIGN on the numeric keypad
Remove shortcut key assignment	CTRL+ALT+ MINUS SIGN on the numeric keypad

MENU COMMANDS

File

New	CTRL+N
Open	CTRL+O
Close	CTRL+W
Save	CTRL+S
Save As	F12
Print Preview	CTRL+F2
Print	CTRL+P
Exit	ALT+F4

Edit

Undo	CTRL+Z
Repeat	CTRL+Y
Clear	DELETE
Cut	CTRL+X
Copy	CTRL+C
Paste	CTRL+V
Select All	CTRL+A
Find	CTRL+F
Replace	CTRL+H
Go To	CTRL+G
Bookmark	CTRL+SHIFT+F5
Update Link	CTR+SHIFT+F7

View

Normal	ALT+CTRL+N
Outline	ALT+CTRL+O
Page Layout	ALT+CTRL+P

Insert

Page Numbers	ALT+SHIFT+P
Annotation	ALT+CTRL+A
Date And Time	ALT+SHIFT+D
Footnote	ALT+CTRL+F
Endnote	ALT+CTRL+E
Mark Index Entry	ALT+SHIFT+X
Mark Citation Entry	ALT+SHIFT+I
Mark TOC Entry	ALT+SHIFT+O

Format

Font	CTRL+D
Change Case	SHIFT+F3
AutoFormat	CTRL+K
Style	CTRL+SHIFT+S

Tools

Spelling	F7
Thesaurus	SHIFT+F7

Table

Select Table	ALT+5 on the numeric keypad

Window

Split	ALT+CTRL+S

Help

Contents	F1
Context-sensitive Help	SHIFT+F1

Appendix

D WinWord's Files

When WinWord 6.0 installs itself, it puts files all over the place. This is a list of those files, with locations and descriptions where appropriate.

Many software manufacturers take great care to time and date-stamp their distribution files. Not so WinWord 6.0. Dates on the files range all over the place, from September to October, 1993. You'll know that you're running WinWord 6.0 if your WINWORD.EXE is 348,316 bytes long, and is dated 10/27/93.

I have not double-checked this list; it's one of the few things in *The Underground Guide* that I've accepted at face value, taken directly from "official" Microsoft sources.

Table D.1 Program Files

File	Location	Description
WINWORD.EXE	WINWORD	
WINWORD6.REG	WINWORD	WinWord 6.0 registration file
WWINTL.DLL	WINWORD	The language DLL contains all the interface-related information of WINWORD.EXE.
MAPIVIM.DLL	WINDOWS\SYSTEM	DLL allowing WORD 6.0 FOR WINDOWS to use MAPI calls on a VIM (Lotus CC Mail's competing API to MAPI) mail
SDM.DLL	WINDOWS\SYSTEM	Standard Dialog
TTEMBED.DLL	WINDOWS\SYSTEM	TrueType embedding stuff
TTEMBED.INI	WINDOWS	Typeface exclusion list
COMPOBJ.DLL	WINDOWS\SYSTEM	Memory allocator for OLE
OLE2.DLL	WINDOWS\SYSTEM	Version 2.01
OLE2.REG	WINDOWS\SYSTEM	OLE2 registration file
OLE2CONV.DLL	WINDOWS\SYSTEM	Converts Mac PICT to WMF.
OLE2DISP.DLL	WINDOWS\SYSTEM	For IDispatch support. Provides support for OLE automation; required for WORD 6.0 FOR WINDOWS.
OLE2NLS.DLL	WINDOWS\SYSTEM	Provides national language support routine that allows apps to interpret & compare strings, dates, etc. in any language.
OLE2PROX.DLL	WINDOWS\SYSTEM	Proxy manager; used when object doesn't have server hooked into object.
STORAGE.DLL	WINDOWS\SYSTEM	Docfile support library

Table D.1 Program Files (Continued)

File	Location	Description
DIALOG.FON	WINWORD	For dialog improvements
MSFNTMAP.INI	WINDOWS	Lists TT fonts and equivalent Windows, Mac and Adobe fonts.

Table D.2 Setup Files

File	Location	Description
ACMSETUP.EXE	WINWORD\SETUP	
ACMSETUP.HLP	WINWORD\SETUP	
_MSSETUP.EXE	WINWORD\SETUP	
ADMIN.INF	WINWORD\SETUP	Equivalent of WINWORD6.INF for network install
CTL3DV2.DLL		
CTL3D.DLL	WINDOWS\SYSTEM	Shared DLL used to give the dlgs of GRAM.DLL, setup, EE, WordArt, MSinfo, Button Editor, ODBC, WORDHELP.DLL a 3d look
DECOMP.EXE	WINWORD\SETUP	
MSCPYDIS.DLL	WINWORD\SETUP	
MSSETUP.DLL	WINWORD\SETUP	
SETUP.STF	WINWORD\SETUP	Logic of setup + most text strings
WORD_BB.DLL	WINWORD\SETUP	Contains billboards, graphics & any custom actions (= sampapp.dll).
WINWORD6.INF	WINWORD\SETUP	Setup information file (disk layout)
WWSETUP.TTF	WINWORD\SETUP	TT font

Table D.3 Help and Tutorial Files

File	Location	Description
WDREADME.HLP	WINWORD	Combines the info previously located in README.DOC + PRINTERS.DOC + CONVINFO.DOC + MACROCNV.DOC + GRAPHICS.DOC.
WINWORD.HLP	WINWORD	WINWORD.HLP contains all the procedures and other WinWord stuff.
WRDBASIC.HLP	WINWORD	WRDBASIC.HLP contains the WordBASIC and Fields topics.
SHARERES.DLL	WINDOWS\SYSTEM	Shared code for help and cbt

Table D.3 Help and Tutorial Files (Continued)

File	Location	Description
WORDCBT.DLL	WINDOWS\SYSTEM	Allows Help to find the CBT, regardless of where the CBT is located.
WORDHELP.DLL	WINWORD	Must be installed at all times; used by help and WINWORD.EXE. Version 1.12.002
WORDPSS.HLP	WINWORD	
WORDRES.DLL	WINWORD	Shared resources (toolbar buttons) for help and cbt
WPHELP.HLP	WINWORD	WordPerfect Help
CBTLIB4.DLL	WINWORD\WORDCBT	CBT concurrency DLL
CBTNORM.DOT	WINWORD\WORDCBT	CBTNORM.DOT = normal.dot file with CBT defaults
FX.DLL	WINWORD\WORDCBT	Special effects resource
MOUSEMV.DEX	WINWORD\WORDCBT	MOUSEMV.DEX = used in CBT to make the mouse cursor move as if someone were moving it with the mouse
PAUSE.DEX	WINWORD\WORDCBT	
SAMPLE1.DOC	WINWORD\WORDCBT	
SAMPLE2.DOT	WINWORD\WORDCBT	
SAMPLE3.DOC	WINWORD\WORDCBT	
SAMPLE4.DOC	WINWORD\WORDCBT	
SAMPLE5.DOC	WINWORD\WORDCBT	
SAMPLE6.DOC	WINWORD\WORDCBT	
SAMPLE7.DOC	WINWORD\WORDCBT	
SAMPLE8.DOC	WINWORD\WORDCBT	
SAMPLE8A.DOT	WINWORD\WORDCBT	
SAMPLE9.DOC	WINWORD\WORDCBT	
SAMPLE10.DOC	WINWORD\WORDCBT	
SAMPLE11.DOC	WINWORD\WORDCBT	
SAMPLE12.DOC	WINWORD\WORDCBT	
TUTFX.DEX	WINWORD\WORDCBT	Allows CBT runtime to use special effects; Version 1.01.
WDCBT.DEX	WINWORD\WORDCBT	For CBT to find WINWORD.EXE
WINNERS.DOC	WINWORD\WORDCBT	Used by the MailMerge Ex. & Demos
WORDCBT.CBT	WINWORD\WORDCBT	CBT runtime. Replaces WINWORD.CBT
WNFISH3.WMF	WINWORD\WORDCBT	
WNFISH4.WMF	WINWORD\WORDCBT	
WORDCBT.LES	WINWORD\WORDCBT	CBT data file
PREVIEW.LES	WINWORD\WORDCBT	Change from 3 to 1 file; saves disk space + will improve compression ratio

Table D.3 Help and Tutorial Files (Continued)

File	Location	Description
NEW_LILS.DOC	WINWORD\WORDCBT	
NEWDEMO.DOC	WINWORD\WORDCBT	
NEWS1.DOC	WINWORD\WORDCBT	
NEWS2.DOC	WINWORD\WORDCBT	

Table D.4 System Files

File	Location	Description
ODBC.DLL	\WINDOWS\SYSTEM	
ODBCADM.EXE	\WINDOWS\SYSTEM	
ODBCINST.DLL	\WINDOWS\SYSTEM	
ODBCINST.HLP	\WINDOWS\SYSTEM	
SIMBA.DLL	\WINDOWS\SYSTEM	
SIMADMIN.DLL	\WINDOWS\SYSTEM	
MSJETDSP.DLL	\WINDOWS\SYSTEM	Shared for dBase, Paradox, and Access.
XBS110.DLL	\WINDOWS\SYSTEM	dBase IISAM (might include Fox)
DRVDBASE.HLP	\WINDOWS\SYSTEM	
DRVFOX.HLP	\WINDOWS\SYSTEM	
PDX110.DLL	\WINDOWS\SYSTEM	
DRVPARDX.HLP	\WINDOWS\SYSTEM	
RED110.DLL	\WINDOWS\SYSTEM	
DRVACCSS.HLP	\WINDOWS\SYSTEM	
PSCRIPT.DRV	\WINDOWS\SYSTEM	Golden version from WFW 3.11; Version 3.10 - installed on setup
UNIDRV.DLL	\WINDOWS\SYSTEM	Golden version from WFW 3.11; Version 3.10 - not installed on setup

Table D.5 Proofing Tools

File	Location
MSSPEL2.DLL	WINDOWS\MSAPPS\PROOF
MSSP2_EN.LEX	WINDOWS\MSAPPS\PROOF
HYPH.DLL	WINWORD
HY_EN.LEX	WINWORD
MSTHES.DLL	WINDOWS\MSAPPS\PROOF
MSTH_AM.LEX	WINDOWS\MSAPPS\PROOF
GRAM.DLL	WINWORD
GR_AM.LEX	WINWORD

Table D.6 Mini Applications ("Applets")

File	Location	Description
MACRODE.EXE	WINWORD	
GRAPH.EXE	WINDOWS\MSAPPS\MSGRAPH	
MSGRAPH.HLP	WINDOWS\MSAPPS\MSGRAPH	
MSGRAPH3.REG	WINDOWS\MSAPPS\MSGRAPH	
WORDART2.EXE	WINDOWS\MSAPPS\WORDART	
WORDART2.HLP	WINDOWS\MSAPPS\WORDART	
WORDART2.REG	WINDOWS\MSAPPS\WORDART	
PUBOLE.DLL	WINDOWS\SYSTEM	Used by Word Art
EQNEDIT.EXE	WINDOWS\MSAPPS\EQUATION	
EQNEDIT.HLP	WINDOWS\MSAPPS\EQUATION	
EQNEDIT2.REG	WINDOWS\MSAPPS\EQUATION	
MTEXTRA.TTF	WINDOWS\SYSTEM	Equation Editor TrueType font
COMMTB.DLL	WINDOWS\SYSTEM	Lets users edit their own buttons or icons
MSTOOLBR.DLL	WINDOWS\SYSTEM	Routines for Microsoft Toolbar

Table D.7 Fonts

File	Location
ALGER.TTF	WINDOWS\SYSTEM
ARLRDBD.TTF	WINDOWS\SYSTEM
BOOKOSB.TTF	WINDOWS\SYSTEM
BRAGGA.TTF	WINDOWS\SYSTEM
BRITANIC.TTF	WINDOWS\SYSTEM
BRUSHSCI.TTF	WINDOWS\SYSTEM
COLONNA.TTF	WINDOWS\SYSTEM
DESDEMON.TTF	WINDOWS\SYSTEM
FTLTLT.TTF	WINDOWS\SYSTEM
GOTHIC.TTF	WINDOWS\SYSTEM
IMPACT.TTF	WINDOWS\SYSTEM
KINO.TTF	WINDOWS\SYSTEM
LATINWD.TTF	WINDOWS\SYSTEM
MATURASC.TTF	WINDOWS\SYSTEM
PLAYBILL.TTF	WINDOWS\SYSTEM
LINEDRAW.TTF	WINDOWS\SYSTEM

Table D.8 Clip Art

File	Location	Description
`*.WMF`	`WINWORD\CLIPART`	Clipart files. You can move them.

For the following table of templates and macros, the numbers on the end of the file names correspond to design families: 1 = Classic (TmsRmn), 2 = Contemporary (Arial Narrow), 3 = Typewriter (Courier), and 4 = TBD (Special 3rd look for Resume rather than Typewriter)

Table D.9 Templates, Macros

File	Location	Description
`BROCHUR1.DOT`	`WINWORD\TEMPLATE`	Stylesheets for autoformatting
`DIRECTR1.DOT`	`WINWORD\TEMPLATE`	
`FAXCOVR1.DOT`	`WINWORD\TEMPLATE`	
`FAXCOVR2.DOT`	`WINWORD\TEMPLATE`	
`LETTER1.DOT`	`WINWORD\TEMPLATE`	
`LETTER2.DOT`	`WINWORD\TEMPLATE`	
`LETTER3.DOT`	`WINWORD\TEMPLATE`	
`MANUAL1.DOT`	`WINWORD\TEMPLATE`	
`MANUSCR1.DOT`	`WINWORD\TEMPLATE`	
`MANUSCR3.DOT`	`WINWORD\TEMPLATE`	
`MEMO1.DOT`	`WINWORD\TEMPLATE`	
`MEMO2.DOT`	`WINWORD\TEMPLATE`	
`MEMO3.DOT`	`WINWORD\TEMPLATE`	
`PRESENT1.DOT`	`WINWORD\TEMPLATE`	
`PRESREL1.DOT`	`WINWORD\TEMPLATE`	
`PRESREL2.DOT`	`WINWORD\TEMPLATE`	
`PRESREL3.DOT`	`WINWORD\TEMPLATE`	
`REPORT1.DOT`	`WINWORD\TEMPLATE`	
`REPORT2.DOT`	`WINWORD\TEMPLATE`	
`REPORT3.DOT`	`WINWORD\TEMPLATE`	
`RESUME1.DOT`	`WINWORD\TEMPLATE`	
`RESUME2.DOT`	`WINWORD\TEMPLATE`	
`RESUME4.DOT`	`WINWORD\TEMPLATE`	
`THESIS1.DOT`	`WINWORD\TEMPLATE`	
`MACRO60.DOT`	`WINWORD\MACROS`	Sample macros

Table D.9 Templates, Macros (Continued)

File	Location	Description
CONVERT.DOT	WINWORD\MACROS	1 batch converter + macro EditConversion Options; opens mstxtcnv.ini
LAYOUT.DOT	WINWORD\MACROS	Sample layout macros
TABLES.DOT	WINWORD\MACROS	Sample table macros
INVOICE.DOT	WINWORD\TEMPLATE	Invoice form
PURCHORD.DOT	WINWORD\TEMPLATE	Purchase order form
WEEKTIME.DOT	WINWORD\TEMPLATE	Weekly Time Sheet form

Table D.10 Wizards (These Are Templates)

File	Location	Description
AGENDA.WIZ	WINWORD\TEMPLATE	
AWARD.WIZ	WINWORD\TEMPLATE	
CALENDAR.WIZ	WINWORD\TEMPLATE	
FAX.WIZ	WINWORD\TEMPLATE	
LETTER.WIZ	WINWORD\TEMPLATE	
MEMO.WIZ	WINWORD\TEMPLATE	
MSINFO.EXE	WINDOWS\MSAPPS\MSINFO	Microsoft System Information
NEWSLTTR.WIZ	WINWORD\TEMPLATE	
PLEADING.WIZ	WINWORD\TEMPLATE	
RESUME.WIZ	WINWORD\TEMPLATE	
TABLE.WIZ	WINWORD\TEMPLATE	
CLASSIC1.WZS		
CLASSIC2.WZS		
CLASSIC3.WZS		
CLASSIC4.WZS		
MODERN1.WZS		
MODERN2.WZS		
MODERN3.WZS		
MODERN4.WZS		

Table D.11 Sample Letters (Which Are Also Templates)

File	Location	Description
ADPR01.DOT	WINWORD\LETTERS	Press release for new product
CRED01.DOT	WINWORD\LETTERS	Collection letter (30 days past due)
CRED05.DOT	WINWORD\LETTERS	Returned check (polite request for payment)
CRED11.DOT	WINWORD\LETTERS	Credit report: request
CSTMRC01.DOT	WINWORD\LETTERS	Complaint under investigation
CSTMRC03.DOT	WINWORD\LETTERS	Apology: delayed delivery
CSTMRR03.DOT	WINWORD\LETTERS	Announcement: price increase
CSTMRR05.DOT	WINWORD\LETTERS	Thank you: for suggestion
EMPRL02.DOT	WINWORD\LETTERS	Resume cover letter
EMPRL03.DOT	WINWORD\LETTERS	Thank you: for applying
MKTG02.DOT	WINWORD\LETTERS	Thank you: for inquiry (information enclosed)
MKTG07.DOT	WINWORD\LETTERS	Direct mail offer: product upgrade
OTHER10.DOT	WINWORD\LETTERS	Letter to Mom
SPACE03.DOT	WINWORD\LETTERS	Landlord: lease expiring; price increase
SUPPL14.DOT	WINWORD\LETTERS	Return for credit

Table D.12 Text Filters (Converters)

File	Location	Description
MSWORD6.CNV	WINDOWS\MSAPPS\TEXTCONV	
RFTDCA.CNV	WINDOWS\MSAPPS\TEXTCONV	
RTF_DCA.TXT	WINDOWS\MSAPPS\TEXTCONV	
TXTWLYT.CNV	WINWORD	
WORDDOS.CNV	WINDOWS\MSAPPS\TEXTCONV	
RTF_PCW.TXT	WINDOWS\MSAPPS\TEXTCONV	
WORDMAC.CNV	WINDOWS\MSAPPS\TEXTCONV	
RTF_MW5.TXT	WINDOWS\MSAPPS\TEXTCONV	
WORDWIN2.CNV	WINDOWS\MSAPPS\TEXTCONV	
WPFT5.CNV	WINDOWS\MSAPPS\TEXTCONV	
WPFT5.EQU	WINDOWS\MSAPPS\TEXTCONV	WordPerfect Equation Editor
RTF_WP5.TXT	WINDOWS\MSAPPS\TEXTCONV	
WRITWIN.CNV	WINDOWS\MSAPPS\TEXTCONV	
XLBIFF.CNV	WINDOWS\MSAPPS\TEXTCONV	
MSTXTCNV.INI	WINDOWS	All conv. options read by the conv. from MSTXTCNV.INI

Table D.13 Graphics Filters

File	Location
CGMIMP.FLT	WINDOWS\MSAPPS\GRPHFLT
DRWIMP.FLT	WINDOWS\MSAPPS\GRPHFLT
EPSIMP.FLT	WINDOWS\MSAPPS\GRPHFLT
GIFIMP.FLT	WINDOWS\MSAPPS\GRPHFLT
IFFGIF.DLL	WINDOWS\MSAPPS\GRPHFLT
IFFPCX.DLL	WINDOWS\MSAPPS\GRPHFLT
PCXIMP.FLT	WINDOWS\MSAPPS\GRPHFLT
IFFTIFF.DLL	WINDOWS\MSAPPS\GRPHFLT
TIFFIMP.FLT	WINDOWS\MSAPPS\GRPHFLT
PICTIMP.FLT	WINDOWS\MSAPPS\GRPHFLT
WPGEXP.FLT	WINDOWS\MSAPPS\GRPHFLT
WPGIMP.FLT	WINDOWS\MSAPPS\GRPHFLT
MS.CGM	WINDOWS\MSAPPS\GRPHFLT
MS.DRW	WINDOWS\MSAPPS\GRPHFLT
MS.EPS	WINDOWS\MSAPPS\GRPHFLT
MS.GIF	WINDOWS\MSAPPS\GRPHFLT
MS.PCT	WINDOWS\MSAPPS\GRPHFLT
MS.PCX	WINDOWS\MSAPPS\GRPHFLT
MS.TIF	WINDOWS\MSAPPS\GRPHFLT
MS.WPG	WINDOWS\MSAPPS\GRPHFLT

Appendix

E Underground Letterhead Macro

This is the final version of the Underground Letterhead's AutoNew macro, as described in Chapter 8.

```
Sub MAIN
REM The Underground Letterhead AutoNew macro
REM Copyright © 1991-1994 by Pinecliffe International
REM For details, see "The Underground Guide to Word for Windows"
REM by Woody Leonhard (Addison-Wesley, 1994)
Dim Notes$(10)
Notes$(0) = "(no note)"
Notes$(1) = "Via FAX"
Notes$(2) = "Confidential"
Notes$(3) = "Via FedEx"
Notes$(4) = "Express Mail"
Notes$(5) = "Priority Mail"
Notes$(6) = "UPS Blue"
Notes$(7) = "UPS Red"
Notes$(8) = "Overseas Air"
Notes$(9) = "Registered"
Notes$(10) = "Certified"
Begin Dialog UserDialog 406, 224, "Underground Letterhead"
  Text 10, 5, 24, 13, "To:", .Text1
  TextBox 85, 5, 310, 84, .Address, 1
  Text 10, 98, 46, 13, "Notes:", .Text7
  DropListBox 85, 98, 310, 114, Notes$(), .Note
  Text 10, 120, 36, 13, "Title:", .Text2
  TextBox 85, 120, 310, 18, .Title
  Text 10, 140, 57, 13, "Subject:", .Text3
  TextBox 85, 140, 310, 18, .Subject
  Text 10, 160, 49, 13, "Author:", .Text4
  TextBox 85, 160, 215, 18, .Author
  Text 11, 180, 64, 13, "Keyword:", .Text5
  TextBox 85, 180, 215, 18, .Keywords
  Text 10, 200, 69, 13, "Comment:", .Text6
  TextBox 85, 200, 215, 18, .Comments
  OKButton 313, 170, 88, 21
```

```
    CancelButton 312, 197, 88, 21
End Dialog
Dim dlg As UserDialog
On Error Goto UserClickedCancel
Dialog dlg
On Error Goto 0
EditSelectAll
UpdateFields
UnlinkFields
EndOfDocument
If dlg.Note <> 0 Then
    Insert Notes$(dlg.Note)
    InsertPara
    InsertPara
End If
InsertPara
CharLeft 1, 1
EditBookmark "NameAddress"
EditBookmark "EnvelopeAddress"
SelType 1
Insert dlg.Address
On Error Resume Next
AutoText
On Error Goto 0
CharRight
If dlg.Title <> "" Then FileSummaryInfo .Title = dlg.Title
If dlg.Subject <> "" Then FileSummaryInfo .Subject = dlg.Subject
If dlg.Author <> "" Then FileSummaryInfo .Author = dlg.Author
If dlg.Keywords <> "" Then FileSummaryInfo .Keywords = dlg.Keywords
If dlg.Comments <> "" Then FileSummaryInfo .Comments = dlg.Comments
N$ = GetBookmark$("NameAddress")
InsertBreak
FilePageSetup .DifferentFirstPage = 1
ViewHeader
eol = InStr(N$, Chr$(13))
Insert Left$(N$, eol - 1) + " - Page "
InsertField "Page"
CloseViewHeaderFooter
CharLeft 1, 1
EditClear
ViewPage
InsertPara
Insert "Dear "
UserClickedCancel:
End Sub
```

And here is the final version of the FinishDocument macro, also from Chapter 8.

```
Sub MAIN
Dim Signatures$(4)
Signatures$(0) = "(none)"
Signatures$(1) = "Sincerely," + String$(4, 13) + "Woody Leonhard"
Signatures$(2) = "Thank you!" + String$(4, 13) + "Woody Leonhard"
Signatures$(3) = "Sincerely," + String$(4, 13) + "Linda Sharp"
Signatures$(4) = "Sincerely," + String$(4, 13) + "Justin Leonhard"
Dim Initials$(3)
Initials$(0) = "(none)"
Initials$(1) = "WL:pc"
Initials$(2) = "LKS-L:pc"
Initials$(3) = "JML:pc"
Begin Dialog UserDialog 298, 256, "Underground Letterhead"
  Text 8, 9, 71, 13, "Signature:", .Text1
  DropListBox 83, 9, 202, 114, Signatures$(), .Signature
  Text 8, 33, 50, 13, "Initials:", .Text2
  DropListBox 83, 35, 203, 114, Initials$(), .Initial
  CheckBox 13, 62, 133, 16, "Check Spelling", .Spell
  CheckBox 13, 79, 104, 16, "Hyphenate", .Hyphenate
  CheckBox 13, 113, 148, 16, "Prompt for cc: list", .CCList
  CheckBox 13, 130, 205, 16, "Prompt for Enclosures list", .Enc
  CheckBox 13, 162, 278, 16, "If possible, squeeze down one page", .Squish
  CheckBox 14, 189, 278, 16, "Print Envelope", .Envelope
  Text 12, 215, 32, 13, "Print", .Text3
  TextBox 51, 212, 50, 18, .Copies
  Text 109, 214, 50, 13, "Copies", .Text4
  OKButton 202, 63, 88, 21
  CancelButton 202, 96, 88, 21
End Dialog
Dim fpdlg As UserDialog
fpdlg.Signature = 1
fpdlg.Spell = 1
fpdlg.Hyphenate = 1
fpdlg.Squish = 1
fpdlg.Envelope = 1
fpdlg.Copies = "1"
On Error Goto UserClickedCancel
Dialog fpdlg
On Error Goto 0
EndOfDocument
InsertPara
FormatParagraph .KeepWithNext = 1
```

```
If fpdlg.Signature <> 0 Then
  InsertPara
  Insert Signatures$(fpdlg.Signature)
  InsertPara
End If
If fpdlg.Initial <> 0 Then
  InsertPara
  Insert Initials$(fpdlg.Initial)
  InsertPara
End If
If fpdlg.CCList <> 0 Then
  On Error Resume Next
  CCItem$ = InputBox$("Items for the cc: list.", "Underground Letterhead")
  On Error Goto 0
  If CCItem$ <> "" Then
    InsertPara
    TableInsertTable .NumColumns = 2, .NumRows = 1
    TableColumnWidth "0.5 in", .RulerStyle = 1
    Insert "cc:"
    NextCell
    Insert CleanString$(CCItem$)
    EndOfDocument
  End If
End If
If fpdlg.Enc <> 0 Then
  On Error Resume Next
  EncItem$ = InputBox$("Items for the Enc: list.", "Underground Letterhead")
  On Error Goto 0
  If EncItem$ <> "" Then
    InsertPara
    TableInsertTable .NumColumns = 2, .NumRows = 1
    TableColumnWidth "0.5 in", .RulerStyle = 1
    Insert "Enc:"
    NextCell
    Insert CleanString$(EncItem$)
  End If
End If
If fpdlg.Spell <> 0 Then
  StartOfDocument
  ToolsSpelling
End If
If fpdlg.Hyphenate <> 0 Then
  StartOfDocument
REM To force manual hyphenation, set .AutoHyphenation = 0
  ToolsHyphenation .AutoHyphenation = 1
```

```
End If
If fpdlg.Squish <> 0 Then
  ToolsRepaginate
  If SelInfo(4) > 1 Then
    ToolsShrinkToFit
    StartOfDocument
    Msg$ = "Can you live with your letter shrunk this much?"
    Title$ = "Underground Letterhead"
    If MsgBox(Msg$, Title$, 256 + 32 + 4) = 0 Then EditUndo
  End If
End If
c = Val(fpdlg.Copies)
If c > 0 And c < 32768 Then
  FilePrint .NumCopies = fpdlg.Copies
Else
  Msg$ = "Invalid Number of Copies: " + fpdlg.Copies
  Title$ = "Underground Letterhead"
  MsgBox Msg$, Title$, 16
End If
EditGoTo "NameAddress"
CharRight 2
Print "Click Cancel to bypass the Save"
On Error Resume Next
FileSave
If fpdlg.Envelope <> 0 Then
  Dim tce As ToolsCreateEnvelope
  On Error Goto DoneWithEnvelopes
  GetCurValues tce
  Dialog tce
  ToolsCreateEnvelope tce
End If
DoneWithEnvelopes:
REM If you use WOPR, delete the above 8 lines and use this:
REM If fpdlg.Envelope <> 0 Then Enveloper
UserClickedCancel:
End Sub
```

Appendix

F The Easter Egg

Here's the steps to bring up WinWord 6.0's gang screen.

1. Create a new document.
2. Type T3!
3. Select everything and turn it bold.
4. Click Format, then AutoFormat.
5. Click OK, then Accept.
6. Click Help, then About Microsoft Word.
7. Click on the WinWord icon.

T3 was the "secret" internal code name for the WinWord 6.0 project. Note the reference in the gang screen to Arnold S. You've probably seen his T2.

Have fun!

Index

WOPR
Woody's Office POWER Pack™

SPECIAL $10 DISCOUNT FOR
UNDERGROUND GUIDE READERS

Discover why WOPR (pronounced "whopper") has become the number one WinWord add-on. WOPR adds dozens of features that Microsoft missed! You'll use it over and over, every day.

Print envelopes your way, with the bar code where you want it, logos, multiple return addresses, notes, easy font changes, and much more. Take control with an innovative, easy-to-use file manager that helps you copy, move, delete, print, and preview contents before you open, and also organize files by stuffing them into "cubbyholes." Right-click on a misspelled word and BOOM! Stellar Spellar corrects it immediately. Create, organize, maintain, and distribute Toolbar buttons. Use meaningful English-language names for your templates, and stick new files where they belong automatically. Save paper by printing pages on both sides, 2-up, 4-up, thumbnails, and even booklets. Save toner with WOPR's unique toner miser. There's a quick, simple address book, a "restore" feature that keeps track of where you were when you last used WinWord, a clip art scrapbook, a tendon-saving program that looks over your shoulder and tells you when to take a break, and much, much more. WOPR has won many awards and drawn praise from the trade press all over the world. Give it a try. You'll see why.

Created by folks who live, breathe, eat, and sleep WinWord, WOPR advances the state of the art in Windows word processing. *Underground Guide* readers qualify for a $10 discount! Call now, say, "I read Woody's *Underground Guide*," and you'll get ten bucks off WOPR's list price of $49.95 (+$4.50 s/h in the USA). Still undecided? Here's the clincher. We have the best guarantee in the business: if WOPR ever fails to live up to your expectations — doesn't matter what you expected, or why — just send it back to us, tell us how much you paid, and we'll refund your money. Immediately. Period.

Pinecliffe International (Member ASP)
Advanced Support Group
11900 Grant Place
Des Peres, MO 63131

Voice: 800-OK-WINWORD (800-659-4696), 314-965-5630
Fax: 314-966-1833
CompuServe: 70304,3642 or GO WOPR